# BETWEEN TWO HOMELANDS

# BETWEEN TWO HOMELANDS

*Argentine Migration to and from Israel*

ADRIÁN KRUPNIK

THE UNIVERSITY OF ALABAMA PRESS
*Tuscaloosa*

The University of Alabama Press
Tuscaloosa, Alabama 35487-0380
uapress.ua.edu



Typeface: Garamond Premier Pro

Cover image: (*top*) Traditional coffee shop in Buenos Aires, Argentina, istockphoto;
(*bottom*) Old Jaffa, Tel Aviv, Israel, Adobe Stock
Cover design: Lori Lynch

Cataloging-in-Publication data is available from the Library of Congress.
ISBN: 978-0-8173-2171-0 (cloth)
ISBN: 978-0-8173-6103-7 (paper)
E-ISBN: 978-0-8173-9469-1

With love and gratitude to my parents,
Susana Grynman and Mario Krupnik,
who taught me history through comments and anecdotes
as casual as they were profound.

# CONTENTS

List of Illustrations . . . . . . . . . . ix

Acknowledgments . . . . . . . . . . xiii

Introduction . . . . . . . . . . 1

**1.** Jewish Migration: Israel, the Americas, Argentina . . . . . . . . . . 18

**2.** A Clash of Cultures, Economics, and Expectations . . . . . . . . . . 41

**3.** Economic Adversities: The 1966 Israeli Recession and the 1969 Argentine Cordobazo . . . . . . . . . . 62

**4.** Uncertainties and Violence: The Return of Peronism and the Yom Kippur War . . . . . . . . . . 82

**5.** In Times of Argentine State Terrorism . . . . . . . . . . 118

Epilogue . . . . . . . . . . 144

Notes . . . . . . . . . . 159

Bibliography . . . . . . . . . . 187

Index . . . . . . . . . . 199

# LIST OF ILLUSTRATIONS

## Figures

**Figure 1.1.** Number of Jewish migrants to Israel by year, 1948–2016 . . . . . . . . . 23

**Figure 1.2.** Number of Jewish Argentine immigrant arrivals in Israel by year, 1948–1970 . . . . . . . . . . . . . . . . . . . . . . . . . . . . . . . . . . . 35

**Figure 3.1.** Argentine immigrant arrivals in Israel by year, 1963–1970 . . . . . . . . 79

**Figure 5.1.** Number of Argentine migrants to Israel by year, 1970–1983 . . . . . . 118

**Figure E.1.** Number of Argentine migrants to Israel by year, 1980–2005 . . . . . . 145

## Tables

**Table 1.1.** Jewish population in Palestine by year. . . . . . . . . . . . . . . . . . . . . . . 19

**Table 1.2.** Israel's population, national income, and national income per capita by year . . . . . . . . . . . . . . . . . . . . . . . . . . . . . . . . . . 24

**Table 1.3.** Immigrants and emigrants by selected country . . . . . . . . . . . . . . . . 24

**Table 1.4.** Declared and uncovered emigrants from Israel by year and continent of return . . . . . . . . . . . . . . . . . . . . . . . . . . . . . . . . . 26

**Table 1.5.** Total emigrants by year and type . . . . . . . . . . . . . . . . . . . . . . . . . . 27

**Table 1.6.** Number of emigrants from Israel in 1958, ranked by their country of origin before living in Israel (with that same country shown as a destination for a different number of migrants leaving Israel) . . . . . . . . . . 28

**Table 1.7.** Number of emigrants from Israel in 1958, ranked by their country of destination when leaving Israel (with that same country shown as the country of origin for a different number of migrants). . . . . . . . . . . . . 29

**Table 1.8.** Jewish migrants arrived in Canada in 1960 by origin. . . . . . . . . . . . . 32

**Table 1.9.** Occupational distribution of Argentine migrants to Israel, 1954–1967 . . . . . . . . . . . . . . . . . . . . . . . . . . . . . . . . . . . . . 36

**Table 1.10.** Argentine migrants to Israel and returnees, 1948–1964 . . . . . . . . . . 38

**Table 2.1.** Percentage of Israeli and Argentine labor force in 1960 by type of employment and gender . . . . . 43

**Table 2.2.** Arrivals and departures from kibbutzim in 1966 and 1967, by number of families, family members, and singles . . . . . 49

**Table 3.1.** Officially declared family and individual returnees to Argentina aboard the *Jerusalem*, by year of arrival in Israel . . . . . 72

**Table 3.2.** Percentage of emigrants from Israel in 1965 by period of arrival in the country . . . . . 73

**Table 3.3.** Percentage of emigrants from Israel in 1965 by age group . . . . . 74

**Table 3.4.** Israeli citizens who acquired "new immigrant" status and returned to Israel in 1967 and 1968, by country of origin . . . . . 75

**Table 3.5.** Argentine immigrants and returnee citizen arrivals in Israel by year . . . . 76

**Table 3.6.** Returnees in Argentina who registered to remigrate to Israel, by age group . . . . . 80

**Table 4.1.** Percentage of Argentine migrants to Israel in 1963 and 1973 by age group . . . . . 87

**Table 4.2.** Economically inactive Argentine migrants to Israel in 1963 and 1973 by category (not including children under six) . . . . . 88

**Table 4.3.** Percentage of Argentine immigrant arrivals in Israel in 1963 and 1973 by economic status and occupational group . . . . . 89

**Table 4.4.** Liberal professionals and clerical workers among immigrants in 1963 and 1973 expressed in number, percentage of all immigrants (Imm.), and percentage of economically active immigrants (EAI) . . . . . 90

**Table 4.5.** Occupational percentage of Latin American immigrants in their country of origin, one year and three years after arrival in Israel, by age group . . . . . 91

**Table 4.6.** Self-definition (percent) of Latin American immigrant arrivals between 1969 and 1974 by age group . . . . . 92

**Table 4.7.** Migrants to Israel by origin and year of arrival (January–November) . . 102

**Table 4.8.** Number of files opened for Argentine migrants to Israel during the five months after the Yom Kippur War by age group (one file per household) . . . . . 108

**Table 4.9.** Number of files opened for Argentine migrants to Israel during the five months after the Yom Kippur War by type of profession (one file per household) . . . 109

**Table 4.10.** Migrants to Israel from Argentina by month and year . . . 111

**Table 4.11.** Files opened for immigration by month and year . . . 111

**Table 4.12.** Number of migrants to Israel by age group for 1974 . . . 111

**Table 4.13.** Percentage of immigrants by age group for 1973 and 1974 . . . 112

**Table 4.14.** Immigrants by occupation in the first halves of 1973 and 1974 . . . 112

**Table 4.15.** Argentine immigrants in Israel by occupational group and occupation expressed in number, percentage, and percentage of economically active immigrants (EAI), 1963 . . . 114

**Table 4.16.** Number of Argentine immigrant arrivals in Israel in 1973 by occupational category . . . 115

**Table 4.17.** Number and percentage of economically active and inactive Argentine immigrants in 1973 by occupational group, using alternative scenarios (not including children under six) . . . 116–17

**Table 5.1.** Number of petitions submitted by returning citizens by region representing number of people and percentage . . . 124

**Table 5.2.** Percentage of Latin Americans who left Israel by year of arrival, measured after one, two, three, four, and five years . . . 141

**Table E.1.** Immigrants from Argentina by year of arrival: number and percentage of those who left by the third year, by the fifth year, and by 2004 . . . 147

**Table E.2.** Percentage of Argentine migrants to Israel in 2002 by occupation . . . 150

**Table E.3.** Percentage of Argentine migrants to Israel in 2002 by age group. . . . 150

# ACKNOWLEDGMENTS

I thank the reader. Your interest adds a layer of meaning to so many years of work. Is there an exact moment when a book begins to be written? I believe a book begins to be written long before the author even sets out to write. Perhaps the following paragraphs will provide a glimpse into the beautiful personal adventure of which this one is the fruit.

Since the early 2000s, I have been fortunate to have had the generous guidance and expert advice of Dr. Raanan Rein, professor of history at Tel Aviv University. At that time, I was studying sociology at the University of Buenos Aires, and together with several colleagues we had set up a Jewish studies group. I remember being surprised by the attention and prompt response Raanan gave to each of my emails. Today I know that many benefited from the time and energy he dedicates daily to each student who contacts him. Throughout my work he helped me define my line of research, read more than once everything I wrote, and suggested different ways of interpreting documentary sources. The way he improved my performance is a product of his passion for history and his commitment to the role of a true teacher, but it would have been impossible if he were not a great person.

It was always a pleasure to work with Raanan and to visit his office at the Daniel Abraham Center. The door was always open and there was never a shortage of someone to prepare Israeli-style black coffee. His students and collaborators became my colleagues and friends. In the case of several of the Israelis, I watched their families grow as our research progressed. Mahayan Nahary, Lelia Staedler, Hagai Rubinstein, Omri Elmaleh, and Pablo Borenstein shared lunches and all kinds of information with me, enriching my knowledge of Israeli society and helping me sort out those bureaucratic issues that are an immigrant's nightmare. We supported each other with translations of documents and information on how to access certain archives.

The aforementioned center and the TAU School of History provided me with all the necessary resources so that I could devote myself to research for four years. I am grateful to Professors Leo Corry and Aviad Kleinverg, who, from their various management positions, watch over the progress of those of us who joined their community. None of TAU's professors could fulfill their mission without the help of the wonderful and very dedicated staff, among whom I can mention secretaries Eilat Shalev Arato and Sharon Ziv Kafri, and Avi Zarakhovsky, who is responsible for the scholarships for immigrants.

Professor Rosalie Sitman occupies a special place in the years I spent in Tel Aviv. Not only did she give me the opportunity to teach Spanish in the language department under her direction, she also offered me her friendship. Our conversations were some of the best breaks I had in moments of tiredness and frustration. Those shared laughs among South American Israelis confirmed to me that humor is a very serious thing.

During the last part of my work in Tel Aviv, when I was able to dedicate myself more intensely to writing, I had an office in the Rosenberg building, where everything functioned perfectly thanks to the work of Wafa Awad, Guershon Braslavsky, and Rami Tamir. It has been a great pleasure to meet them and appreciate their daily work.

Planning my next steps after Tel Aviv involved challenges that could only be overcome with the support of prestigious academics. In this regard, I am grateful for the generous help provided by Professors Adriana Brodsky, Ruth Bevan Dunner and David Sheinin. Their advice, the information they shared with me, and their tailored letters of recommendation were an indispensable help.

I owe Professor Sina Rauschenbach for hosting me in 2019 as a research fellow at Universität Potsdam as part of the exchange program with Tel Aviv University. My stay at the Institut für Jüdische Studien und Religionswissenschaft allowed me time to write, edit, and meet excellent researchers who are part of its community. I also had the support of the staff of the international office from day one, for which I am especially grateful to Iris Dupont-Nivet, Claudia Roessling and Frauke Stobbe. No less important was the financial support provided by the graduate school of the university, which allowed me to accomplish some of the necessary steps for this publication.

Professor Stefan Rinke has been an excellent support to me in recent years. Since he was my host at a migration workshop he organized in 2018 together with Raanan, he has always been responsive to my queries. As soon as I arrived in Germany, he included me in the wonderful community of researchers he gathers around the Lateinamerika-Institut at the Freie Universität Berlin. He sponsored my stay at the Selma Stern Zentrum in Berlin and at the time of writing provided me with the institutional framework to develop as a researcher. His collaborators Karina Kriegesmann, Preslava Novak, and Claudia Daheim have ensured that I never had to worry about the bureaucratic and administrative issues that a foreign researcher has to deal with. I greatly appreciate their help. The colloquium of researchers that operates under the direction of Professor Rinke allowed me to meet talented people and very good friends, including Vinicius Vivar, Joanna Moszczyńska, and Ximena Venturini.

The Minerva Stiftung has made it possible for me to continue growing as an academic, developing new research, and publishing previous works. I am grateful to this organization for granting me the honor of working to strengthen the cultural exchange between Germany and Israel and I must mention Julia Lechler, who has diligently assisted me from my preapplication consultations to the present. I have also found it very helpful to be part of the Latin American Jewish Studies Association, the Association for Israel Studies, and the Association for Jewish Studies. Their annual congresses and the other activities that they promote have helped me to establish relationships with countless people and expand the horizons of this beautiful profession. Special mention should be made of all those who work every day so that curious people like me can have access to well-preserved archives of all kinds. On behalf of all of them, I especially thank the staff of the Mehlmann Library of the Goldstein-Goren Diaspora Research Center of Tel Aviv University.

At the beginning of the long road that brought me to this book stands the faculty of sociology at the University of Buenos Aires. There I took my first steps in the art of searching for answers, in the framework of a workshop led by Professors Jorge Cernadas and Ana Berletta. There I also met great people with whom discussing is both a pleasure and a challenge. How many readings does a single barbecue with Diego B, Diego Q., Fede, Juan, Fer, Chuchco, and Alber equal? And the time spent with Vicky, Meli, and Mariano? There I met Natalia, who together with Dante and Susan has made me part of their beautiful family and accompanies me in every step I take. It was also there that I met Ezequiel Erdei, with whom I had the pleasure of conducting research in different Jewish communities in Latin America, and it was through the aforementioned professors that I met Emmanuel Kahan, whom I thank for having contributed his views to this work.

In 2007, on the advice of Alejandro Dujovne, then a colleague of the Jewish Studies Group, I applied to the Summer Institute for Israel Studies of the Schusterman Center at Brandeis University and I owe Ilan Troen, Jacobo Kovadloff, and Steven Bayme that fabulous experience of the highest professional level. I was able to take part in it thanks to Diego Freedman, my boss at the American Jewish Joint Distribution Committee, who granted me a paid leave. I am also grateful to him for some good advice. Back in Buenos Aires, I set out to find a way to follow that path and it was my great friend Martin Hadis, whom I met at a congress for young intellectuals organized at the Asociación Mutual Israelita Argentina by Laura Kitzis, who suggested the way to do it. Professor Roberto Russell then introduced me to the program in international studies at the Universidad Torcuato Di Tella, as a result of which I spent a semester at the School of Advanced International Studies of Johns Hopkins University.

I arrived in Israel as an immigrant in 2013, wanting to integrate into the academic system but not having a clear idea of how to do so. I visited Professor Gur Alroey just before he launched a new program in Israel studies, for which he awarded me half a scholarship. The other half I was able to pay for while working as a coordinator of professional immigrants at the Ulpan Etzion in Haifa, the same absorption center where I learned Hebrew.

For every written line, there are a lot of good times with friends and family who have been able to help in a million ways. Exequiel Lakoski inspired me with the desire to go through the experience of becoming Israeli, doing it six months before me. My friends Laura and Matias have granted me a kind of citizenship that no government can offer or revoke. Esteban and the Poponis, Alex, and the Hebrew Lady have helped me to keep laughing in Spanish even if from a distance.

I thank my colleague Mariusz Kalczewiak for all the advice he has given me since I arrived in Germany, especially on how to structure the proposal for this book. Nothing would be possible without the excellent work of Dan Waterman, editor-in-chief of Alabama University Press, who was interested in the sample chapter I sent him by mail and accompanied me throughout the publication process. I am very grateful to the migrants who shared their experiences with me, confiding in me throughout numerous interviews. I hope they can find in these pages a little piece of their own lives.

Finally, I thank my beloved siblings, Carolina, Enrique, and David, for accompanying me every day, wherever I go.

# BETWEEN TWO HOMELANDS

# INTRODUCTION

In 1963 an unprecedented number of Argentines migrated to Israel. Mr. C., his wife, mother, and three children were among them. They arrived at the port of Haifa aboard the *Theodor Herzl* after a three-week voyage and settled in Ramat Gan. Mr. C. and his wife had met in the 1940s in a Zionist group that organized social activities at a synagogue located in Flores, a neighborhood of Buenos Aires. José, the youngest child, was deeply impressed by the voyage, and the theme from the movie *Exodus*, composed by Ernest Gold, which he saw during the trip, remained forever engraved in his memory.[1] Susana, the eldest, was twelve. Contrary to his expectations, Mr. C. was unable in Israel to become the owner of a pharmacy as he had been in Argentina; thus, when their savings began to run out, he felt depressed and useless. Then, Mrs. C., who had been the most enthusiastic of the family members about living in Israel, suggested that they return to Argentina where he could recover and start over again. The family landed in Buenos Aires in October 1965.

The return was difficult for the entire family: while Mr. and Mrs. C. remembered Israel with a mix of love and frustration, the children had to readjust to the Spanish language and join new classes where they had no friends. At the time, Susana was fourteen, and the return migration coincided with the adolescent changes that characterize her age group. Moreover, while in Israel she had enjoyed school and had been among the best students in her class, her academic achievements declined in Argentina. She attended a state school every morning and a Jewish one every afternoon. Although she continued to be an outstanding student in the Jewish institution, where instruction was in Hebrew, she was required to take some state examinations that she had missed in the public school. This experience at the non-Jewish school negatively affected her self-image at a time when she was becoming concerned about the way she looked; she also noticed that she did not share the other girls' culture. "In the 1960s there [in Israel] it was OK to go to the youth movement. Suddenly I arrived in [Buenos Aires] and the girls go out at night, wear nylon stockings . . . there were many differences, they had boyfriends . . . [All] things that were not common at all in Israel in the 1960s in the social circles I was in."[2]

Susana also felt uncomfortable within the Jewish community of Buenos Aires due to the "stigma of being a *yoredet* [(f); descender]," a word used within Zionist circles both in Israel and the Diaspora to refer to those who had left Israel. At the time of our interview, she did not recall any discrimination because of this supposed stigma; however, this was her perception and she considered her return a *kishalon* (failure). Thus, she missed Israel badly and frequently fantasized about returning there. Nonetheless, her mood gradually improved, particularly after she finished secondary school and severed relations with students who knew about her return from Israel. She studied at the Jewish teachers' seminary, the curriculum of which included a graduation trip to Israel, but her parents did not allow her to go because as an Israeli citizen she would have been conscripted into the army. The following year, her Israeli past conspired against her return to Israel a second time. She went to the Jewish Agency for Israel (henceforth, JA) office to explore the possibilities of studying at an Israeli university and was told that she had already received new immigrant benefits. Therefore, she would be considered a "returning citizen." "I argued at the Sochnut [Agency]: 'This is a great injustice. I returned at age fourteen not because I wanted to. I returned because my parents were returning. Could I have stayed alone in Israel? Why do you punish me now by denying me [those] rights?' Finally . . . they gave me the right[s] at a time when it was not yet the rule."[3]

While she was planning her remigration she met Hector, who had already scheduled his departure for Israel. She arrived in Israel in 1970 and they married in 1971. Hector frequently makes fun of her by saying that she "used him" to return to Israel. They lived in Jerusalem and Susana studied psychology. Asked about the "yored stigma," which she had felt as a returnee in Argentina, she said, "I felt that I had redeemed myself." They benefited from a JA housing program and obtained a mortgage. In 1972 Susana became pregnant and in early 1973 the entire C. family left Argentina for Israel a second time. In October of that year, the Yom Kippur War affected them all. Susana and Hector were unsure what to do and needed help from a neighbor to protect the windows with tape. Even more importantly, the war had a lasting impact on Susana. While breastfeeding her baby in the shelter, she decided that she would have no more children, in order to protect her son from conscription: as an only child, he would need his parents' permission to be conscripted to a combat unit.

While Susana continued her academic career, Hector joined the army and learned to work in informatics. After reaching adulthood, their son emigrated from Israel and they began to feel less attached to Jerusalem and its increasingly religious atmosphere. Except for their jobs there was nothing that connected them to Jerusalem, the city where they had lived for almost forty years. Thus, when Hector neared retirement in 2005, he became unhappy due to a change in his working conditions and a desire to return to Argentine awakened in him: "All my life, I felt that I had not closed my chapter with Argentina," he said.[4] In

2007 they decided to spend one year in Argentina, but once in Buenos Aires Hector found a job and wanted to stay. In fact, in 2005 they had bought a house in Argentina that Susana considered a temporary retirement home but he saw as a permanent one. For the second time in her life Susana returned to Argentina even though she wanted to live in Israel. Unlike when she was a child, however, this time it was for the sake of her husband and she was a responsible adult. Nonetheless, her first year in Argentina was hard: "It was a period of loneliness and grief. The only thing that captivated me at the time was that people in Buenos Aires are very warm. The Israeli reaches my soul but, with an Argentine, it is easier to communicate. I would begin a phrase and the other person was able to continue it. People talk everywhere; everyone would tell me their story right after beginning a conversation. [They are] very open people . . . And the trees of Buenos Aires also enchanted me. Because Jerusalem is a very stony city, not very green. Those were the things that, in a way, relieved my great longing a little bit. But it was terrible, terrible."[5]

When she came to terms with living in Buenos Aires, she discovered that her professional background and Hebrew skills were appreciated locally and she began working as a psychologist at Jewish organizations. Moreover, in the new circumstances, Susana made an unexpected professional shift and began to receive private patients, something she had never wished to do in Israel due to her ethical concerns regarding the high cost of psychological care there. People were more used to having therapy in Buenos Aires and it was more accessible. Indeed, the motivation to work with private patients came from non-Jewish women she met at her neighborhood gym. For the first time in her life, she made non-Jewish friends and it was they who referred her first patients to her. At the same time, she began seeing Israeli patients who wanted to be treated in Hebrew. She enjoyed having the opportunity to speak Hebrew with them. As she said jokingly, "I would have been willing to pay them instead of being paid by them because of that joy." On the other hand, treating patients in Spanish was more difficult in the beginning: "Hebrew words used to escape from my mouth . . . then, slowly I resumed [speaking] Spanish, acquiring words I had never used and softening my accent . . . At the time it was very strong. People would ask me, 'where are you from?' immediately after I opened my mouth."

Paradoxically, Susana's new professional path in Argentina gave her the opportunity to treat religious Jews who, due to Israel's strong divide between secular and Orthodox Jews, "would not have contacted me . . . First, they would have checked if I had a mezuzah,[6] I would have had to wear a wig, I would have had to be one of them. And here [in Argentina] . . . they never question anything and open up to me."[7]

As economic and political tensions increased in Argentina, Susana and Hector returned to Israel in 2017. It was the third time that Susana had moved there. They settled in Ashdod, where they "discovered" aspects and groups of Israeli society they had not encountered previously. Susana feels thrilled each time she travels to Jerusalem because her youth, adulthood, and professional beginnings belonged there. It is the place where her son was born and her parents are buried. Nevertheless, she would not like to live there again. She loves Argentina but her nostalgia is connected mainly to one specific area, Recoleta, the Buenos Aires neighborhood where they lived for eight years and where she created her "new professional identity." She continues treating her Argentine patients via Skype. Hector is retired and dedicates his time to study and travel planning. They both miss the cultural life of Buenos Aires and try to visit every summer.

Over a long period, emigration from the country was a sensitive topic for Israeli society even though it was an undeniable phenomenon. The strength of Zionist ideology compelled Israelis to approach emigration from Israel through their own particular lens. Thus, the Hebrew words and ideological terms "aliyah" and "*yerida*," which mean, respectively, "ascent" and "descent," were used to refer to immigration and emigration. These words, which were also charged with religious meaning, were heavily loaded with praise for immigrants and scorn for emigrants. Moreover, at the end of the 1970s, the Zionist ideological approach to emigration still held hegemonic sway, with politicians such as Prime Minister Yitzhak Rabin showing themselves to be especially vitriolic, calling Israeli emigrants "moral lepers," "the fallen among the weaklings," and "the dregs of the earth."[8] That is why Susana experienced deep discomfort during her initial return to Argentina. Nowadays, however, like other Israeli citizens, she and her husband can decide to relocate without being stigmatized.

While the story of Susana and Hector might seem unique, in this book I argue that this is far from true. Indeed, my perspective on migration to and from Israel challenges the Zionist narrative regarding Jewish Argentine immigration to Israel and their connection to the country, which continued even after they left. Moreover, I began my research by focusing on Jewish Argentines who left Israel for Argentina after having spent at least one year as Israeli citizens or residents.[9] Quite early on I noticed that many of them migrated to Israel a second and even a third time. In addition, those who remained in Argentina after emigrating continued to be culturally, socially, and sometimes professionally attached to Israel. Even those who were critical of the Jewish state retained cherished memories and positive emotions associated with their experiences living there.

In this volume, I demonstrate that every peak of Argentine migration to Israel was followed by the return to Argentina of a portion of the migrants. Moreover, within the latter group, an unknown but non-negligible number of people migrated to Israel more than once. I argue that approaching Jewish Argentine immigration to Israel as a cycle that might include return to the country of birth and then back again several times in a person's lifespan allows a better understanding of the migration experience and broadens the perspective on Israel-Diaspora relations. Return migration from Israel should be seen not as an uninteresting byproduct of migration but as an integral and equally fascinating part of the larger phenomenon. Referring to Jewish-European migrants and the United States, historian Jonathan Sarna argues that "almost as much can be learned from those who left . . . as from those who stayed."[10] This book follows Sarna's logic and extends his claim to include those who repeated the migration cycle more than once. In times of fast and affordable transport and communications, migrants can move more than ever before back and forth along a two-way street, allowing them to sustain familial, institutional, religious, economic, and/or political ties with more than one country simultaneously. That is why people who leave modern Israel to relocate to countries where they were born cannot be ignored. Like Susana and Hector, thousands of Jews from all over the world migrated to Israel and have lived thereafter, in one way or another, between two homelands. Furthermore, Israel's departure from an ideological approach to immigration and absorption policies to a pragmatic one has removed many emotional, economic, and legal burdens from the shoulders of citizens and residents who want to leave Israel or choose to settle there a second, or even a third time. Lastly, seeing migration as a two-way street calls attention to the dynamic nature of this process throughout the life of a person. An immigrant might become an emigrant and vice versa, making such characterization dependent on the context.

This volume is dedicated to the Argentine migrants who built their life trajectories—professional path, family dynamics, intellectual and political ideas, ethnic and national affiliations, and notions of manhood and womanhood, among other elements that formed their identities—through migrations to and from Israel. Through their professional activities and everyday life, they have reproduced, transmitted, criticized, and combined Argentine and Israeli culture in the two countries in one way or another. The book also highlights how the return from Israel was, historically, mostly ignored by Jewish and Zionist Argentine organizations, which avoided publicizing an issue that would embarrass the Israeli state. The Israeli government saw Jewish immigration as a priority and the JA worked to promote it no matter the circumstances. Knowing that future migration flows would be influenced by previous ones, both to and from Israel, the authorities perceived news about Argentines leaving Israel as harmful. The book captures the most representative waves of immigration and return: between 1948 and 1978, three decades that offer a rich variety of social contexts and a historical perspective for understanding the phenomenon under study. It analyzes these waves according to the number of migrants involved, their historical significance, and the available documents on them. It also explains how these migrations were seen by Israeli and Jewish Argentine organizations and the role the latter played in Israel's relations with Jewish Argentines. In addition, this study offers the foundations for a discussion about the impact of the Israeli experience on return migrant identities. Specifically, I advance the idea that they developed multilayered identities due to their connections with Argentina and Israel.

Jewish emigration from Israel is not new; even before the creation of the State of Israel, emigration was an observable phenomenon affecting Jewish Palestine.[11] Some four hundred thousand Jews who left Israel since the year 1948 were still living abroad by 1999.[12] Nevertheless, it is only recently that Jewish emigration from Israel has begun to be treated as a legitimate research topic, detached from ideology. In addition, most past research on return migration from Israel has approached the issue from a narrow perspective, either methodologically or geographically, focusing on economic factors and/or referring to North Americans only.[13] More recent works on emigration from Israel have spotlighted Israelis living in the United States.[14] A distinct group of new research perspectives emphasizes the possibility of dual citizenship and the ability to pursue transnational lives in a globalized world.[15] Latin Americans, and Argentines in particular, have not yet been the center of such scholarly research.[16]

At least two additional reasons have contributed to a lack of academic research about Jewish Argentine return migration from Israel. First, Latin American immigrants in general and Argentines in particular have been welcomed by most Israelis, who are attracted to their culture, language, and accents in Hebrew. Moreover, Deby Babis and Luis Roniger observe that Latin Americans have become "invisible" in Israel because, unlike immigrants of other origins, they are perceived as Western, they arrived in a succession of waves rather than in a single massive one, and they have integrated well into every fiber of the social fabric.[17] Their apparent smooth integration is corroborated by the quantitative approach to the labor market pursued by Rebeca Raijman and Ariane Ophir, who have demonstrated that Latin Americans occupy a socioeconomic status similar to that of native-born Israelis, higher than that of immigrants from the former Soviet Union, and relatively lower than that of immigrants from Europe and North America.[18] Second, the historiographic vacuum regarding Jewish Argentine return migration from Israel reflects Argentine circumstances. Argentina has historically presented a positive migration balance; therefore, return migration has attracted limited scholarly interest and is focused mostly on political exiles.[19] Argentine society still perceives itself as *receiving* immigrants; hence, emigrants have attracted little attention.

However, the migration balance and patterns began to change in the 1990s, and even more so following the catastrophic political and economic collapse of 2001. As a result, emigration from Argentina and Argentine returnees are becoming the focus of new academic research, including the research represented in this book.

Furthermore, I see this book as contributing to the field of Jewish history, at the intersection of Israeli and Latin American studies. My objective is to add a broad perspective on Israel-Diaspora relations in general and to provide a case study within the field of migration studies in particular. Through a transnational and nonlinear approach to migration and return migration, this volume joins new historiographic research on migrants whose stories challenged the Zionist narrative about immigration and nation-building.[20]

The present volume has been influenced by two main groups of works. The first group includes research conducted by several members of the Latin American Jewish Studies Association (LAJSA). Their research lines explored previously neglected topics and incorporated new perspectives. Specifically, at the 2007 thirteenth annual meeting of LAJSA, held in Buenos Aires, Raanan Rein and Jeffrey Lesser discussed new perspectives aiming at enriching ethnic studies.[21] Their suggestions have been strongly present throughout my research and in the preparation of this book. In the spirit of Rein and Lesser, I consider the experience of Jewish Argentines to be a lens enabling an understanding of Argentine society and a group comparable with others, such as Italian Argentines, Spanish Argentines, or German Argentines, in that it considers the diasporic *and* national elements of their identities. Moreover, the book describes the gaps between Jewish Argentine and Israeli interests in various circumstances, especially between those of Zionist leaders and officials in charge of immigration to Israel and those of Argentine return migrants. In doing so, the volume offers a broad view of Jewish Argentines and their institutions, highlighting the heterogeneity of the former and the fact that most Jewish Argentines were never affiliated with those organizations. My approach to Jewish Argentine immigration to Israel considers anti-Semitism and Zionism in a balanced manner and within broad social, political, and economic contexts, since Jews have integrated progressively into all spheres of Argentine life.

The second group of works that has influenced this book lies in the research conducted by those exploring the foundations of Jewish Argentine history and charting the demographics of migration. For example, Beatrice Gurwitz's *Argentine Jews in the Age of Revolt* and Emmanuel Kahan's *Memories That Lie a Little: Jewish Experiences during the Argentine Dictatorship* represent two examples of works that explore previously neglected topics while questioning traditional perspectives; they are closely interrelated with the chapters of my book dealing with the 1960s and 1970s.[22] All these contributions would not have been possible, however, without the knowledge base established, in particular, by Haim Avni and Leonardo Senkman. The former's *Argentina and the Jews* was a pioneering work regarding Jewish immigration to Argentina and a key to understanding the origins of their organizations; the latter's *El antisemitismo en la Argentina* was a groundbreaking study regarding anti-Semitism in that country.[23] Within this vein, this book also leans on leading demographer Sergio DellaPergola's findings regarding variations in the numbers of Latin-American migrants to Israel.[24]

Furthermore, global changes in transportation and communication technologies, as well as the increasing number of people with dual citizenship, have produced new academic approaches to immigration. In Israel, these developments have led to a radical change in how Israeli society views immigration to the country and emigration from it. During the first decades of the State of Israel's existence, those leaving the country were the object of passionate criticism because they were seen as abandoning the Zionist cause. A change in the national discourse and the state's approach to emigration from Israel, Israelis abroad, and their return to Israel became evident with new policies during the 1980s aimed at attracting Israelis living abroad.[25] It was during this period, as Yinon Cohen observed, that academic works dedicated to emigration from Israel departed from their focus on the "severity of the problem" and began to study this demographic phenomenon, comparing the case of Israel with that of other countries.[26] Reuben Lamdani's seminal work demonstrated that the emigration rate from Israel, the percentage of Israelis living abroad, and the leaving rates from Israel of new immigrants were no higher than in the cases of other countries.[27] The decreasing weight of the Zionist narrative in Israeli academia made room for new perspectives on migration studies. Gur Alroey's *An Unpromising Land* demonstrated that there was a gap between the Zionist/Israeli national narrative, which emphasized the centrality of ideological motives, on the one hand, and the experiences of most immigrants, on the other.[28] Alroey's approach to Jewish immigration to Palestine influenced my own approach to the Israeli-Argentine question, and, in certain parts of this book I have tried to portray the migrants' experiences with the vividness that he brought to his own descriptions. Furthermore, Sebastian Klor's *Between Exile and Exodus*, dedicated to the study of Argentines who arrived in Israel prior to 1967, has been key to my research.[29] Klor created a database that included information on more than ten thousand immigrants. Emphasizing their socioeconomic characteristics, he questioned the real weight of Zionism as the main driving force behind their immigration. My book is connected directly to the topics raised in Klor's chapter 5, which focuses on the sociodemographics of Jewish Argentines who arrived in Israel during the first half of the 1960s. I quote the evidence he provides in chapter 1 of this book. Klor's work is key again in chapter 4, where I compare his findings regarding 1963 immigrants with my own regarding those who arrived in 1973.

## TERMINOLOGY AND CONCEPTUAL FRAMEWORK

Two principal terms are used in this volume: "Jewish Argentines" and "return migration." The term "Jewish Argentines" emphasizes national identity without denying the diasporic one, as suggested by Jeffrey Lesser and Raanan Rein.[30] However, I do not intend to impose any rigid conceptualization on this study's subjects; instead, I present their voices, offering a variety of definitions about how they relate to Argentina, Israel, and the Jewish component of their identity. In addition, as noted, Jewish organizations in Argentina never represented most Jewish Argentines because most were not affiliated with them. Therefore, I use the term "Jewish Argentines" to refer to the Jewish population in the country, and "Jewish community," the use of which I have tried to reduce to a minimum, to denote Jewish organizations. The terms "Jewish community," or just "the Jews of Argentina," appear frequently in documents and articles produced by Jewish organizations and their leaders, supposedly in relation to all Jewish Argentines. However, such leaders' and organizations' approach to the Jewish population in Argentina is usually biased because it is limited mainly to affiliated Jews, a minority within the country.

No single theory of migration and return can encapsulate the many facets of every single Jewish Argentine returnee from Israel. While economic approaches to return migration once classified migrants as either "successes" or "failures," new transnational perspectives have abandoned this dichotomy. In this book, I conceive of return migration as an integral part of migration, which in turn is considered a cycle going backward and forward,[31] one that might be repeated several times in a person's lifetime. Pursuing a transnational approach, I present the experience of Jewish Argentine migrants in a way that treats their immigration and return as integral components of this cycle rather than as a linear journey.

The term "return migration" often has an ambiguous meaning because scholarly works use it to refer to two entirely different phenomena. It can be found in studies that examine the migration of citizens from one country to another one that is understood as their "original homeland" due to national, ethnic, cultural, or religious ancestry. Thus, return migration is usually linked to or used as a synonym for "diaspora migration" or "ethnic migration."[32] This is the Zionist view of Jewish immigration to Israel because Zionist ideology takes into consideration not the immigrants' nationality according to their place of birth but their biblical origins in the Land of Israel. However, the overwhelming majority of Argentine immigrants, including their parents or grandparents, had never lived in modern Israel, despite their ethnic ties. On the contrary, their return *to* Argentina *from* Israel might well fit into the category of ethnic return migration. Therefore, the term can be particularly confusing in the case of Israel. As used in this volume, it refers to people from a particular country who, after migrating to another country, move back to the first country. Moreover, while this book is about migrants and returnees, the Zionist terms *olim* and *yordim*, derived from aliyah and *yerida*, appear in direct or indirect quotations to better preserve the meaning and tone of the related documents and statements. It should be borne in mind that every migrant is at the same time an "immigrant" and an "emigrant" and that these two conditions are not intrinsic characteristics but contextual ones. I have tried to use the word "migrant" throughout the text, which is neutral regarding the migration direction. However, even though they do not fully reflect the nonlinear perspective on migration, it is impossible to avoid words such as "immigrant," "emigrant," and "returnee." Therefore, the meaning of these words should always be understood in relation to the particular situation described and never as a permanent condition. For instance, a returnee from Israel in Argentina might later become an immigrant in Israel. Lastly, regarding Jewish Argentine immigration to Israel, the adjective "mass" is used here due to the fact that the annual number of migrants has mostly been well above one thousand from the year 1948 until today.

The book examines the returnees' views on their migration and how it was regarded by the State of Israel and Jewish organizations in Argentina. It pays particular attention to the role of Israel and its related agencies in shaping networks in more than one country and defining the rights and duties of immigrants and returnees. At the individual level, it supports the notion that people can develop multiple identities and recognizes that migrants' adaptation to society each time they relocate is not without an emotional cost. In this regard, it offers an introduction to the changing nature of the migrant's ties to Argentina and Israel. Listening to the voices of the migrants in order to become acquainted with their thoughts, feelings, and memories, I felt I truly understood them. According to Alessandro Portelli, "one of the reasons why oral history has been sometimes less than welcome in some circles is that it has disarranged many accepted truths."[33] While Zionism saw a morally weak person in each emigrant and classic economics theory considered a returnee as someone who did not get the expected economic benefit, in-depth interviews discussed here provide a much richer perspective regarding the migrant's relationship with Argentina and Israel.

When interviewing migrants, I paid particular attention to their observations about their Israeli experiences and how they integrated them into their identities at various moments in their lives. In order to address the question of identity definitions and changes resulting from migration experiences, I applied the "identity field" approach to their stories, considering identity to be a changing and complex construct rather than a monolithic one. This methodology acknowledges that "individuals can place themselves in different 'identity points' according to changing circumstances and locations."[34] It also emphasizes that several identity components within the same individual are negotiated depending on the context, with the relative weight of each varying over time and space. Therefore, identity is conceived as a multilayered construct made up of various elements (national, ethnodiasporic, religious, gender, class, professional, and others), like the pieces in a mosaic that may be modified depending on changing circumstances.[35]

While conducting interviews and analyzing documents, I kept in mind John Berry's model, which focuses on identity and culture in the context of migration experiences.[36] The model emphasizes that there is an inherent tension between the immigrant's identity and the new society because the latter challenges the cultural bases of the former. Berry also considers a set of "moderating factors" for such tension, such as age, gender, education, motivations, expectations, language, religion, and personality. The immigrants' encounter with the new society produces changes and strains in their behavior and self-perception; the model offers four categories to describe alternative paths for dealing with them: (1) assimilation—adopting a new culture and relinquishing the old one; (2) separation—the opposite of assimilation; (3) integration—combining the two cultures; and (4) marginalization—finding no comfort in either culture. Finally, it should be noted that the interviews demonstrated to me that migrants are not passive subjects but are in fact active individuals capable of making choices about the specific cultural elements they wish to incorporate or reject from the societies in which they live or lived.

## THE JEWS, ARGENTINA, AND ISRAEL

Most of Argentina's Jewish population arrived between 1870 and 1930; most arrivals were of East European origin, although some came from the Middle East and the Balkans.[37] While the majority settled in urban areas, some took part in the agricultural projects supported by Baron Maurice de Hirsch.[38] During this time period, Argentina maintained an open-door policy toward immigration based on liberal ideas and the colonization project of the founders of the nation. Nevertheless, the traditional elites exhibited authoritarian and xenophobic tendencies, particularly within nationalist and Catholic circles, with their influence peaking during periods of political instability. The most dramatic expression of these tendencies was an anti-Jewish pogrom that occurred in 1919.[39] Nevertheless, Jewish Argentines successfully established their own social, economic, and educational organizations reflecting a broad spectrum of identities and ideologies, from communism to Zionism. They integrated into national life and many reached prominent positions in the economic, artistic, and social spheres.

Jewish integration into the political life of Argentina strengthened in the 1940s and 1960s during the Perón and Frondizi regimes, as both these leaders bolstered Argentine-Israeli relations.[40] Still, when the Mossad kidnapped the Nazi war criminal Adolf Eichmann in 1960, tensions rose between the two governments, and Jewish Argentines became targets of nationalistic attacks. Although the affair was resolved diplomatically within a few weeks, the wave of anti-Semitism lasted for two years. According to supporters of this campaign, Jews loyal to Israel were feigning loyalty to the Argentine state. Two anti-Semitic organizations attacked Jewish students and perpetrated acts of vandalism against buildings owned by Jews. The most aggressive actions included an attack on a fifteen-year-old student, who was seriously wounded by gunfire in 1960, and the kidnapping and swastika tattooing of a university student in 1962.[41] Paradoxically, this wave of anti-Semitism contributed to unifying the organized community and consolidating its identification with the State of Israel.[42] In a context of social, political, and economic deterioration, the number of Jews immigrating to Israel increased fivefold in 1963, reaching a peak of more than four thousand that year. Overall, some three hundred thousand Jews were living in Argentina in the early 1960s; most were unaffiliated with Jewish organizations, the majority of which were dominated by Zionist parties.[43]

Between 1948 and the end of 2018, a total of 69,718 Jewish Argentine immigrants arrived in Israel.[44] Contemporary Argentina's Jewish population numbers 182,000 persons with Jewish ancestry who also self-identify as Jews, the largest Jewish population in Latin America, ranking fifth outside Israel, after the United States, France, Canada, and the UK.[45] This number, however, increases to 240,000 if the definition used by Israel's Law of Return is considered.[46] A population survey conducted in Buenos Aires in 2004 demonstrated that there was a strong link between Jewish Argentines eligible for Israeli citizenship and the State of Israel. Half of them had relatives living in Israel and 30 percent had visited Israel at least once.[47]

## BOOK STRUCTURE

The book draws on a variety of primary sources, including reports, letters, and statistical information written and exchanged by Jewish organizations in Argentina, the Jewish Agency in Israel, and Israeli immigration representatives. In addition, I interviewed more than thirty people in Argentina and Israel who shared with me their testimonies about immigration and return. Some of them also sent me old pictures and personal letters. Their generosity helped me to get in touch with the human aspects of migration to and from Israel. I have tried to reflect the intensity of their personal and even intimate memories in the pages of this book, together with data and historical information relating to the main migration peaks and waves. In doing so, I have been inspired by the idea that sociology is a combination of history and biography.[48] The reader might find contradictions between the testimonies of people who arrived in Israel or left at about the same time, and even contradictions within the testimony of a single person. This is simply because contradictions are an inherent part of human nature and social science has no right to neglect them. Nevertheless, the stories in this book should be regarded in relation to the much less contradictory explaining power of statistics.

The book covers a period of three decades during which, because of their respective regional locations, economic structure, policy choices, and social composition, Argentina and Israel were affected by historical events and global struggles differently. Argentina's incorporation into the international market through the export of primary products, together with the country's domestic-oriented industry, was insufficient for assuring the well-being of its population. As a result, Argentina's social cleavages and political divisions deepened over the years, its democratic system was frequently interrupted by military rule, and cyclical crises marked an economy in decline. Israel, for its part, was involved in several military conflicts with its Arab neighbors and terrorist organizations that, most of the time, seemed to erase its internal divisions. Its economy switched from import substitution industrialization to services and high-tech based on research and development. Therefore, while in 1962 Argentina's GDP per capita was $1,156 and Israel's was $1,095, Israel surpassed Argentina and widened the gap each year after that, so that in 2019 Argentina's per capital GDP was $10,006 compared with Israel's $43,641.[49]

Chapter 1 offers a broad view of Jewish migration trends from the foundation of the State of Israel in 1948 until the mass immigration peak of Jewish Argentines in 1963. It explains that while Jewish immigration was one of the highest values in the eyes of Zionist leaders, the State of Israel, and Israeli society, throughout the country's history people decided to leave, with the Americas as a favored destination in the 1950s, while some Jews chose not to migrate to Israel. Moreover, Argentine emigrants from Israel did not attract any attention at the time because few Argentines were living in Israel. The year 1963 marked a watershed by bringing the first mass wave of Jewish Argentines to the country. Most had been driven to make the move by deteriorating economic conditions in Argentina and expected to continue earning their living as manual workers, shopkeepers, and liberal professionals as they had done in their previous life. In Argentina, they had lacked sufficient savings to thrive during periods of recession or unemployment, difficulties that they would soon face in Israel. Eventually, the return to Argentina of a substantial portion of them would become evident.

Chapters 2 and 3 cover the period until the end of the 1960s, focusing on the clash between the immigrants' cultural background and economic expectations, on the one hand, and the prevailing Zionist ethos and austere reality, on the other. They analyze returnee experiences and the cases of those who moved to Israel a second time. As a starting point, chapter 2 makes a comparison between the Israeli and Argentine cartoon characters Srulik and Mafalda, in order to argue that despite their modest means Argentine immigrants had experienced a process of modernization that shaped their consumer patterns and lifestyles in a way that they could not reproduce in Israel. Therefore, their lives were harder than in Argentina, where at least they were fluent in Spanish and had family and friends. In the context of the 1966 economic recession, the return migration of Argentines was particularly noticeable from Ashdod and Moshav Kochav Michael Sobell. Reporting on this phenomenon, JA representatives and the Israeli press used negative stereotypes to depict Argentines, particularly as the recession also led to a decline in numbers of Argentine immigrants. Despite the growing number of returnees, the Jewish magazine *La Luz* was the only publication that reported on them. Its ongoing criticism of the JA and Israel's absorption of middle-class immigrants demonstrates that not all Jews in Argentina adhered to Israeli policy guidelines.

Chapter 3 analyzes the rapid fluctuations in migration patterns in accordance with changing circumstances in Argentina and Israel. Many immigrants had aspired to open an independent business instead of taking a salaried job and eagerly accepted the credit and loans offered by the JA and other organizations. A lack of controls and coordination led to disproportionate indebtedness and the proliferation of real and exaggerated stories about Argentines leaving Israel without repaying their debts. The departure of the ship *Jerusalem*, which bore Argentine returnees during the worst period of the 1966 Israeli economic recession, serves as a window for examining the negative narrative about them, their response, and the gap between official and unofficial figures. At the time, a new dictatorship, self-defined as the "Argentine Revolution," had begun in Argentina.[50] The regime was characterized by a strong anticommunist stance and the banning of political activities.[51] The university was considered a focal point of communism and students became the main targets of repression.[52] Adalbert Krieger Vasena was appointed minister of the economy; his economic program represented the interests of the upper bourgeoisie, who benefited from the interventionist tools of the state, which abandoned the principles of social welfare.[53] Fears of discriminatory constitutional amendments and the strengthening of anti-Semitic groups became widespread. However, when the president received representatives of DAIA (Delegación de Asociaciones Israelitas Argentinas), he explained that his government's ideas about the "new Argentina" applied to every citizen irrespective of religion or race.[54]

Migration trends changed once Israel experienced a golden period inaugurated by the Six-Day War, but the shift was not immediate. After the war, Israel became an attractive destination for Jews from all over the globe and 211,000 immigrants entered the country between 1968 and 1973. The Ministry for Immigrant Absorption was created at the end of 1968; by then, almost half of the immigrants were coming from the United States and Europe, bringing skills and capital. These Western-educated and urbanized newcomers required an absorption process different from that previously offered to immigrant refugees. The Zionist Congress initiated a reform of the JA and, reflecting the prestige that generals acquired after the war, Uzi Narkis was appointed director general of the agency's Department for Immigrant Absorption.[55] Another innovation was the expansion of the absorption center as a key element in the reception of newcomers. There, the immigrants received Hebrew classes, advice regarding housing and employment, and a program of social and cultural activities. Ideally, a six-month period at one of the centers was intended to function as a "buffer," allowing for a smooth transition to the new Israeli lifestyle.[56]

Argentine immigration to Israel rebounded only in 1969, due to increased economic difficulties and social turmoil symbolized by the Cordobazo, a civil uprising led by workers and students in the city of Córdoba against the military regime. As a result, a portion of those who had returned from Israel left Argentina and moved to Israel a second time. The Cordobazo initiated a period of generalized protests and the military regime was forced to start a transition toward a new democratic government. The number of Jewish Argentines immigrating to Israel, including those who were re-immigrating, continued to rise steadily until the outbreak of the Yom Kippur War in October 1973.

Chapters 4 and 5 focus on how migration and return were affected by three major events: the Yom Kippur War, the third Peronist government in Argentina, and the military regime that came to power in Argentina in 1976. Chapter 4 analyzes the emigrants who left Israel in 1973, when Argentina was experiencing economic expansion in the midst of increasing internal conflict. In May 1973 Héctor José Cámpora, Perón's designated candidate, was elected president of Argentina. Perón had been exiled for almost twenty years and was banned from running in the elections. As a result of a plot within the Peronist movement, Cámpora resigned after forty-nine days and Perón won an overwhelming victory in September.[57] The Cámpora and Perón governments shared an economic program, with José Ber Gelbard as minister of the economy.[58] The program aimed at an expansion of domestic production based on an alliance between unions and national producers, a partnership that represented the core of Peronism. In an attempt to overcome cyclical problems and bottlenecks in Argentina's economy, which were leading to currency shortages and devaluations, Gelbard tried to increase exports.[59] Within a context of economic turmoil, Gelbard's Jewishness often became a target for attacks by his political enemies.[60]

Views on Peronism differed among Jewish leaders in Argentina, Israel, and the United States. The most salient characteristic of migrants at this time was that, unlike previous and later waves examined in this book, their departure from Argentina was not driven by economic decline. They had experienced social mobility and expected to continue on that path. In fact, some of them wanted to purchase property after their arrival in Israel, but the housing shortage there, created by the surge in immigration after 1967, caused serious dissatisfaction. In October 1973 the Yom Kippur War led to a reversal in Israel's economic boom and social euphoria. As a result, the number of Argentine migrants to Israel fell sharply; among those who did come was a large group of youth. Zionist leaders believed that negative news and letters from Israel were dissuading people to stay in Argentina instead of moving to Israel; at the same time, they became concerned about the participation of Jewish youth in Argentine leftist organizations. Moreover, anti-Semitic propaganda in Argentina was increasing; outright anti-Semitism was not new, but it now included threats to Jewish organizations, their leaders, and Jewish businessmen, as well as the bombing of two well-known synagogues in Buenos Aires.[61]

Chapter 5 explores the noticeable presence of returnees in Buenos Aires and Córdoba in 1974. These people left Israel due to distress caused by the war but arrived in a society in which armed conflict between guerillas, paramilitary groups, and the army was becoming commonplace. Perón, who was expected to stabilize the nation, died in July and internal violence continued.[62] The old leader was succeeded by his wife, vice president María Estela Martínez de Perón. But her obscure aide, a former police officer called José Lopez Rega, emerged as the strong man of the government and subsequently there began a period of clandestine state-sponsored repression against the opposition, broadly labeled as leftists. At the time Jewish-Argentine youth presented two opposing tendencies: a small portion migrated to Israel while a larger one joined the Argentine Left. Youth indifference to Zionism raised a premonitory alarm among JA emissaries. Indeed, one of the factors that led to an increase in migration from 1976 was not ideology but rather the state terrorism pursued by the military, which accounted for more than one thousand Jews among its victims. Other factors included the regime's economic program and a chain of anti-Semitic incidents. Meanwhile, the organized Jewish Argentine community underwent a process of transformation, reflecting the decline of Zionist ideology and people's desire to remain in the country. For his part, Israeli prime minister Menachem Begin believed that Jewish Argentines should migrate to Israel as soon as possible and, in 1978, created a special committee to promote that goal and a variety of programs to absorb the immigrants. Jewish Argentine leaders were not convinced but agreed to cooperate. Nevertheless, immigration to Israel waned.

Finally, the epilogue elaborates on the changing numbers and characteristics of Argentine migrations to and from Israel between 1948 and 1978. It describes how return migration has affected Israel's relations with Jewish Argentines and Jewish Argentine organizations and assesses the impact of the Israeli experience on return migrants' identities. This last chapter also highlights the importance of economic motives in leaving Argentina for Israel during the years 1986 to 2006, a time when the circulation of migrants between the two countries became easier. Argentine's unsolved problems are the background to understanding the main peaks in immigration to Israel. At the same time, cheaper and faster transportation and communications, as well as the waning of Zionism as an ideological constraint against emigration and a compass for state policies, have allowed Jewish Argentines to experience the full migration cycle, including return, and to repeat it, without becoming the subject of scorn or experiencing a sense of guilt. Lastly, the epilogue includes suggestions for new research directions, topics, and comparative studies beyond the confines of this book.

# 1

# JEWISH MIGRATION

## Israel, the Americas, Argentina

Jewish immigration stood at the heart of Zionism and the State of Israel from their very beginnings and is fundamental to understanding Argentines' experiences in Israel. Israel is a country created by and for immigrants and the immigration-emigration balance continues to be one of the main indicators used by the political elite and the general public to assess the nation's development. While immigration has been historically celebrated, emigration was and remains a cause for deep concern. Unlike the Israeli perception of arrivals and departures, however, the role played by Argentines in this story did change. During the 1950s, people leaving Israel mainly departed for the Americas and there were no reports of Argentines among them. However, after the first massive wave of Argentines arrived in Israel in 1963, this situation began to change. The Argentine immigrants were mostly salaried workers, small independent businessmen, and young people at the beginning of their professional careers, who lacked the savings to thrive in times of unemployment. Therefore, when the 1966 recession in Israel set in, the vast majority began to struggle, and the first stream of return to Argentina became noticeable.

### ISRAEL: A COUNTRY MADE BY AND FOR IMMIGRANTS

In order to fully understand Jewish Argentine migration experiences within the Israeli historical context, it is necessary to go back in time to the origins of Zionist ideology and Israel. Zionism emerged in Europe as a national movement of the Jewish people in reaction to the progressive weakening of multinational formations, such as the Austrian-Hungarian and Turkish-Ottoman empires in the nineteenth century. During this time period, national groups within these political structures increasingly claimed their right to self-determination and their own nation state.[1] For the Jewish people, the rise of nationalism posed particularly thorny questions, given the fact of the global diaspora with the largest cluster of population concentrated in Europe, far away from the historical homeland. The evolution of Zionism into a political project linked to the Land of Israel as the desired nation-state required massive migration as a condition sine qua non of its success. Zionist thinkers argued that anti-Semitism stemmed from the fact that the Jews were always considered guests in other countries and did not have their own state where they could act as hosts; they expected that the creation of such a state would bring about the end of anti-Semitism.[2] In terms of where this state should be, the main arguments for founding a Jewish state in the Turkish-Ottoman Empire and, subsequently, British Palestine included the Jews' historical roots and their continuous presence there since ancient times. Nevertheless, at the moment of the emergence of the Zionist movement the Jewish population in the territory was quite small (table 1.1).

Ideally, the Zionist project envisioned the relocation of all Jews to Palestine. Such a titanic enterprise required strong ideological motivation, extensive fundraising, and large-scale logistical efforts. Although Zionism as a political project was an indisputable success, leading to a Jewish state in the Land of Israel, immigration to Israel did not always occur in the manner that Zionist leaders had imagined at the outset or in accordance with the narratives they presented of the actual immigration waves. In addition to presenting historical, sociological, and statistical facts, Zionist historiography refers to each of the five waves of immigration that has to date arrived in Jewish Palestine as an aliyah (ascent), each of which has branded into Israel's popular memory in a particular way.[3] A brief characterization of these waves demonstrates the disparity between the national narrative and facts on the ground, a disparity we will later relate to Argentine experiences.

The first wave of immigration took place after the Russian pogroms of 1881–82, when almost thirty-five thousand Eastern European Jews arrived in

**Table 1.1. Jewish Population in Palestine by Year**

| Year | Population |
|---|---|
| 1800 | 7,000 |
| 1890 | 43,000 |
| 1914 | 94,000 |
| 1922 | 84,000 |
| 1931 | 175,000 |
| 1947 | 630,000 |

Source: Sergio DellaPergola, *Population Change and Political Transitions Demography in Israel/Palestine: Trends, Prospects, Policy Implications* (Jerusalem: Hebrew University of Jerusalem, 2001).

Palestine. Half of them left the territory within several years; the majority of those who remained—the idealistic ones—established rural settlements.[4] The second immigration wave began in 1904 and continued until 1914. Against a background of political instability and increasing anti-Semitism in Europe, nearly forty thousand Jews migrated to Palestine, many of them young and inspired by socialist ideals.[5] Again, almost half of the total left Palestine due to the harsh living conditions. Nevertheless, those who remained built the pillars of the Yishuv (the modern Jewish society until the end of the British Mandate), founding Deganya (the first kibbutz), Hashomer (the first self-defense organization), and Tel Aviv (the first modern Jewish city). These immigrants also encouraged the revival of the Hebrew language through literature and newspapers and established political parties and the foundations of workers' organizations.[6] Ignoring the story of those who left Palestine, popular memory and Zionist narratives of these first two waves cultivated the image of agricultural workers who struggled against inclement weather, disease, and Arab and Turkish opposition. However, the majority of Jews who arrived in Palestine from 1881 to 1914 "sought in Palestine what emigrants sought anywhere else": improved living conditions, security, and freedom; further, most would have preferred to live in cities and had arrived in Palestine "almost by chance."[7]

The gap between the prevailing narrative and reality may also be seen in the stories of later arrivals. After the Balfour Declaration, the Zionist movement gained new momentum, sparking the third immigration wave. Its core was the arrival of 650 Jews from Odessa aboard the SS *Ruslan*, which included "intellectuals from among the best of the Russian-Jewish intelligentsia, as well as a group of enthusiastic but penniless young people."[8] Spanning 1919 to 1923, this immigration came to be known as the "pioneering aliyah." According to the Zionist narrative, the pioneers, *chalutzim*, were ideologically driven and ready to make sacrifices to accomplish the creation of the Zionist project. Nonetheless, most of the thirty-seven thousand people in this immigration wave had received no Jewish education; some were motivated by Jewish nationalism and others by the dream of changing the world or creating a new society.[9] For most, the Russian Revolution and the Ukrainian pogroms served as the main driving forces in the decision to migrate.

The fourth wave began in 1924, caused by the closure of the United States to new immigrants, increasing instability in the USSR, and, notably, the rapidly eroding living conditions of the Polish middle class.[10] For the first time in Zionist history, masses of Jews began arriving in Palestine, in a wave that lasted until 1929. Out of more than eighty thousand immigrants who arrived during this period, sixty thousand came in just two years. Characterized as it was by high numbers of middle-class Poles, this immigration wave came to be remembered as the one that brought the middle classes, even though it included a greater number of pioneers than the previous wave had. Moreover, when the Polish Jews arrived in Palestine, only four categories were used to classify immigrants: people of means, workers, religious leaders, and relatives. As a result, a high proportion of these arrivals was categorized as "people of means," even though they were in fact lower middle class and had spent all their money on their tickets to Palestine. Aspiring to an urban lifestyle similar to the one they had in Poland, most went to Tel Aviv, Haifa, and Jerusalem.[11]

Lastly, the fifth wave, in the words of Anita Shapira, "entered Zionist consciousness as the German aliyah," even though most of the immigrants—as their predecessors had—came from Eastern Europe. While this wave, which lasted from 1932 to 1936, brought some fifty thousand German Jews to Palestine, they made up less than one-third of the total number of immigrants.[12] Still, their contribution to Palestine, which at this time experienced a period of prosperity, was outsized enough to explain why this immigration came to be remembered as "German." Arriving in Palestine in the shadow of the rising Nazi threat in Germany, more than one-third of the immigrant Germans were classified as "people of means" and many held university degrees. Their arrival raised the standards of the Hebrew University of Jerusalem, as well as the banking system. The Bauhaus architectural style they imported is still visible in Tel Aviv, and the capital that some of them possessed contributed to the Yishuv's incipient industrialization due to the Transfer Agreement signed in 1933 between Nazi Germany and unofficial Zionist bodies.[13]

Each of the five immigration waves arrived in a specific historical context and left its mark on the Yishuv. All of them took place at times when immigration to Palestine was regulated either by the Ottoman Empire or by the British Mandate. The British Mandate imposed quotas and strict regulations on Jewish immigration to Palestine. In 1939, the British authorities reacted to the Arab revolt by issuing the White Paper, which established further cuts in the number of entry visas issued to Jews.[14] This is why those escaping from Nazism after the rise of Hitler to power—as well as eventual Holocaust survivors—technically entered illegally. This kind of immigration was referred to in Zionist historiography as Aliyah Beth.[15] More than seventy thousand people began their journey somewhere in Europe—typically a Displaced Persons camp—and arrived in Palestine on one of more than one hundred ships that made the crossing during this period.[16] Despite all the restrictions, the Yishuv's development over the thirty years of the British Mandate led to the foundation of the Jewish state, a productive agricultural and industrial economy, Jewish settlements throughout the country, and a population of 650,000 Jews at the time of independence.

In 1948 Israel's Declaration of Independence coincided with the end of the relative economic prosperity enjoyed by the Yishuv during the war. When the British Army left the Middle East, its demand for local products ceased.[17] The decline was felt particularly in citrus production. In addition, the joint Arab armies declared war on the new state in a conflict that exhausted the new country's resources. Israel's first years were characterized by austerity due to the cost of war, as well as the efforts required to absorb the masses of new immigrants, who were now coming as a direct response to the new state's ideological framework. Indeed, the Declaration of Independence referred to the right of Jews to migrate to Israel as the "ingathering of the exiles," and more than 300,000 Jews from Arab countries and 130,000 from European DP camps arrived during the first three years of statehood. Their arrival necessitated the creation of housing (initially solved by the creation of temporary tent camps) and, perhaps more importantly, jobs. A few Jews from Argentina arrived in Israel at that time (including some volunteers during the war and members of Zionist movements), but their total number was negligible.

The Law of Return, so central to Israel's identity as a Jewish state, embodied the realization of the Zionist ethos. It aimed at providing a home for Jews from all over the world if they wanted to live in Israel, on the one hand, and at maintaining Israel as a Jewish state by securing a Jewish majority, on the other. Passed unanimously on July 5, 1950, the anniversary of the death of Theodor Herzl, the law gave all Jews the right to live in Israel and gain Israeli citizenship.[18] In his declaration to the Knesset (the Israeli parliament), Prime Minister David Ben-Gurion declared that the law did not create a new right; rather, it "reaffirmed" a right that the Jews had already held as part of the Jewish people's "historic and unbroken" connection to the Land of Israel. Since then, upon arriving in Israel, Jews receive *oleh* (immigrant; lit., "person who ascends") status and are entitled to full citizen rights. As a result of the law's passage, Israel has been the destination of millions of people, mostly Jews, from all over the world (figure 1.1), with the largest waves of immigrants arriving during the first years of statehood and after the collapse of the Soviet Union. Each mass wave after independence had its own unique characteristics, found the country at a different stage of development, and took place in a different international context. Because of these distinctions, all of them represented new challenges and opportunities for the young Jewish state.

The capacity to absorb immigrants is intrinsically dependent on the given country's economy. During its first years, the Israeli economy relied on loans from commercial banks, the sale of national bonds, and the printing of money. This strategy caused inflation but successfully limited unemployment, which was at 8.1 percent in 1950, considered a good rate given the context.[19] Over the years, Israel acquired knowledge on immigrant absorption, set up new organizations, and increased the budget devoted to that task. Because the Zionist ideal proposed a Jewish state created for the Jews and its continuous strengthening with each successive immigration wave, the ideology also envisioned that the

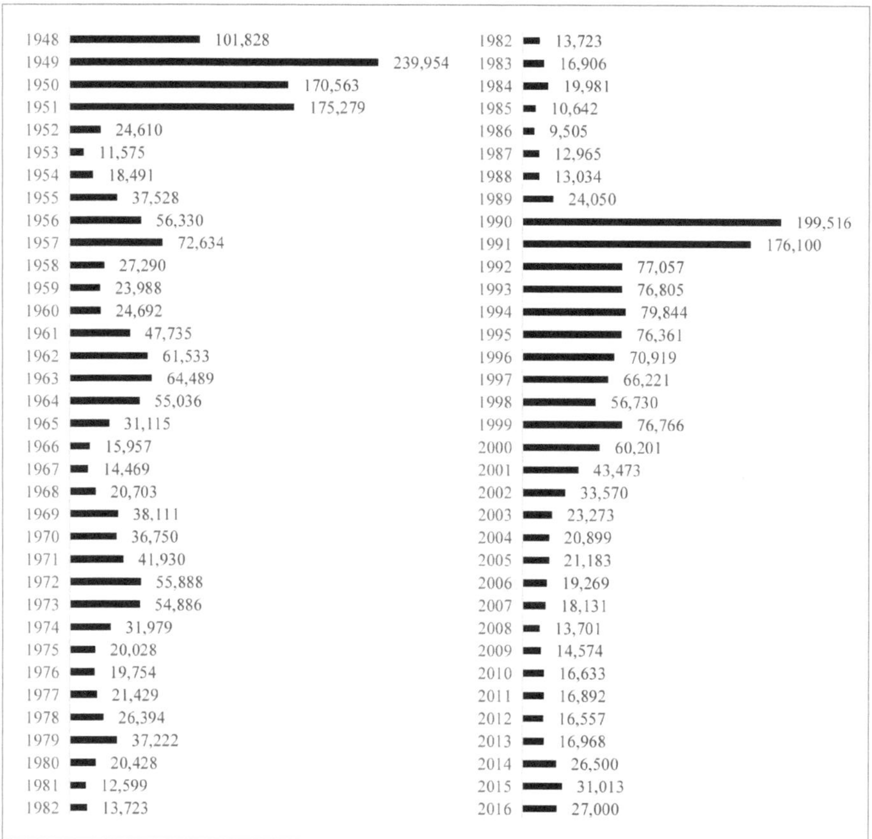


**Figure 1.1** Number of Jewish migrants to Israel by year, 1948–2016. Source: Israeli Central Bureau of Statistics, "Total Immigration to Israel by Select Country by Year," Jewish Virtual Library. Returning Israeli citizens are not included.

wealth of Israel would increase in tandem with the growth of the population (table 1.2).

There is no doubt that Israel's economic development at least partly explains the country's relatively high immigrant retention rate during certain periods. For example, in relation to the size of its population, Israel received more immigrants than Canada, New Zealand, Australia, or West Germany. In addition, the proportion of immigrants that subsequently left Israel was smaller than that from the other countries examined in table 1.3.

Despite the relatively high rate of immigrant retention, all emigration from the country was subjected to social scrutiny, especially during the first decades of statehood. During the pre-state period, emigrants from Jewish Palestine were not judged in moral terms despite their large numbers. Yet, after independence,

### Table 1.2. Israel's Population, National Income, and National Income Per Capita by Year

| Year | Population (Millions) | GDP (in Billions) | GDP Change between dates (Percent) | GDP Per Capita (in US Dollars) | GDP Per capita changes between dates (Percent) |
|---|---|---|---|---|---|
| 1950 | 1.27 | 4.49 | - | 3,546 | - |
| 1960 | 2.19 | 12.90 | 187.3 | 5.896 | 66.3 |
| 1970 | 2.97 | 28.91 | 124.0 | 9,720 | 64.9 |
| 1980 | 3.88 | 48.53 | 67.9 | 12,516 | 28.7 |
| 1990 | 4.66 | 69.50 | 43.2 | 14,916 | 19.2 |
| 2000 | 6.30 | 119.47 | 71.9 | 18,966 | 26.7 |
| 2009 | 7.43 | 152.79 | 27.9 | 20,577 | 8.5 |

Source: Paul Rivlin, *The Israeli Economy from the Foundation of the State through the 21st Century* (New York: Cambridge University Press, 2010), 3.

### Table 1.3. Immigrants and Emigrants by Selected Country

| Country | Period | Immigrants per 1,000 citizens | Emigrants per 1,000 citizens | Emigrants per 100 immigrants |
|---|---|---|---|---|
| Israel | 1948–1979 | 24 | 5 | 20 |
| Canada | 1951–1971 | 8 | 3 | 39 |
| Australia | 1950–1974 | 16 | 7 | 43 |
| New Zealand | 1950–1974 | 14 | 8 | 60 |
| West Germany | 1950–1974 | 11 | 9 | 75 |

Source: Reuben Lamdani, "Emigration from Israel," *Economic Quarterly* 30, no. 116 (1983): 462–78.

the hegemony of Zionist ideology and memories of the hard times that the first Israeli citizens underwent made emigration tantamount to treason.[20] Given that Israel was born as a country created for and by immigrants, even today immigration is nationally celebrated and emigration raises uncomfortable questions—questions that would characterize the Jewish Argentine experience in Israel.

## JEWISH MIGRATION TO THE AMERICAS FROM THE YOUNG ISRAEL'S PERSPECTIVE

During the 1950s Latin America did not feature in the discourse on migration either to or from Israel. The number of Latin Americans in Israel was small and other regions attracted the attention of observers due to their prominent role as emigrant destinations. Between 1948 and 1951, a mere 904 Argentine immigrants arrived in Israel.[21] Even added together with those who came before the creation of the state, their number was not as impressive as that of other groups in the new Israeli society. Still, Argentine contribution to the country was noticed occasionally and commented upon in the Israeli press.[22] For example, at the end of 1952, *Davar*, a respected newspaper founded in 1925 and politically aligned with the Histadrut (General Organization of Workers), reported on a public event attended by political leaders and Argentine ambassador Pablo Manguel; the event celebrated the establishment of Kfar Argentina, an agro-industrial village founded by Argentine immigrants (such a village was not a kibbutz but a private initiative based on shareholders originated in Argentina).[23] The combination of industry and agriculture at the site offered an innovative approach toward immigration, aimed at attracting middle-class immigrants and providing them with living conditions similar to those they had enjoyed in Argentina. Many among the future residents of Kfar Argentina were experienced agriculturalists.[24]

Israeli newspapers featured news and statistics on migration on a daily basis, an ongoing reminder of the importance of the issue to the growing state. These reports offer insights into emigration from Israel during the 1950s and on how Israeli society perceived the departees. In January 1954, the ship *Jerusalem* left Haifa for the United States with 260 passengers on board, including "many *yordim* [plural of *yored*]."[25] An Argentine tourist returning from Israel in a different ship sent a letter to *Davar* describing what he saw. He denounced "yordim who converted to Catholicism" in order to get visas for Latin American countries and suggested that the government publicize their names and make them known to Jewish communities in Latin America in order to thwart any possibility of them working as Hebrew teachers.[26]

If, due to their small numbers, Latin Americans in general did not receive much attention in Israel in the 1950s, Latin America was frequently mentioned in the press because it was one of the main destinations for people leaving Israel. For example, in 1954, *Al HaMishmar* reported on six hundred people who had left the country aboard the *Jerusalem*, two hundred of them as yordim headed for Canada and South America.[27] At the end of 1955, a journalist referred to the large number of Israelis allegedly going on vacations. He believed that they were actually emigrating and mentioned South America among their destinations.[28] At the same time, news coverage of Argentine Jewry was scarce, and what there was focused on general information and Jewish education. For example, a journalist described the Jewish community in Argentina as the closest in style to Eastern European Jewry, noting the population of half a million Jews in the country and the vitality of the Yiddish language. Regarding Hebrew education, he noted that only 20 percent of Jews were enrolled in Jewish schools; the level was "as bad as in the Diaspora in general," awful in the countryside but better in

Buenos Aires.[29] There were also reports of prospective Argentine immigrants to Israel receiving agricultural training in preparation for departure.[30]

While there was no specific mention in the media of Latin Americans leaving Israel during the 1950s, the evidence demonstrates that some Israeli-born Jews and Jews originally from Europe and the Arab world had left the Jewish state to live in Latin America. In 1959 Foreign Minister Golda Meir, interviewed after a visit to Latin America, was asked whether she had met with yordim. Her expression immediately became "serious, she lit a cigarette" and answered, "I did not want to meet them! What would I have to talk about with them? If one of them had something to tell me, I would have listened, but I did not enter into conversations with them. You can write this: If they tried to talk to me, it was to deny that they *yardu* [descended]. 'We will return—they would say—next year, in another two years, but yordim, God forbid!' It surprised me a little that precisely those yordim thought that they deserved a meeting with me . . . [her face softened slightly] . . . At the end of the day, their situation there is poor. The local Jewry cannot stand them and . . . they stood in a corner. I perceived their hidden sense of shame in the very fact that they did not stop shouting, 'We will return!'"[31] The quotation demonstrates that there were certainly more than a handful of Israeli emigrants in Latin American countries. However, their departure did not attract the attention of the press because they represented a small percentage of all those leaving Israel. In fact, the insignificant number of Latin American departees explains the use of a single category, which omitted

**Table 1.4. Declared and Uncovered Emigrants from Israel by Year and Continent of Return**

| | Year of Return | | | | |
|---|---|---|---|---|---|
| **Continent** | **1953** | **1954** | **1955*** | **1956*** | **Total Period** |
| **Americas** | 1,909 | 2,769 | 1,370 | 1,338 | 7,386 |
| USA | 742 | 1,639 | 770 | - | - |
| South America | 447 | 865 | 473 | - | - |
| Canada | 720 | 267 | 127 | - | - |
| **Europe** | 822 | 1,028 | 511 | 356 | 2,717 |
| **Asia** | 886 | 751 | 313 | 119 | 2,069 |
| **Africa** | 947 | 439 | 99 | 172 | 1,657 |
| **Oceania** | 189 | 302 | 308 | 308 | 1,107 |
| **Unknown** | 3642 | 8 | 9 | 3 | 3,662 |
| **Total** | **8395** | **5297** | **3540*** | **3183*** | **20,415** |

Source: "Declared Yordim according to Country of Return," data from October 1, 1956, found in letter from Dov Yosef to Interior Minister Bar Yehuda, January 14, 1959, CZA, S60/334.

*Since 1955 included eleven months and 1956 only four, the total was adjusted. Between 7 and 8 percent were non-Jewish.

**Table 1.5. Total Emigrants by Year and Type**

| Emigrants | Year of Return 1953 | 1954 | 1955 | 1956* | Total Period |
|---|---|---|---|---|---|
| Declared: Official and uncovered | 8,400 | 5,300 | 3,500 | 3,200 | **20,400** |
| Nondeclared: Covert | 4,600 | 2,500 | 3,500 | 5,700 | **16,300** |
| Total | 13,000 | 7,800 | 7,000 | 8,900 | **36,700** |

Source: "Declared Yordim according to Country of Return," data from October 1, 1956, found in letter from Dov Yosef to Interior Minister Bar Yehuda, January 14, 1959, CZA, S60/334.

*Half year

their country of origin, when referring to them in various reports. The question for Israeli society was not about the nationality of those leaving Israel but about their destination, and the main destination for emigrants between 1953 and 1956 was the Americas, with South America ranking second within the region (table 1.4).

That official number, as their reports make clear, was based on the information obtained by the JA's representatives, who questioned the migrants. The questioning was aimed at identifying people leaving Israel under the pretense of a tourist trip. Such people were later referred to as "uncovered" emigrants (*galuiim*). The quoted report did not specify the percentage of such "uncovered" emigrants or the procedure for identifying them (table 1.5). However, the sole mention of a considerable proportion of this kind of migrant, also mentioned as "nondeclared covert emigrants" made it clear that official numbers regarding emigration were much lower than the real figures.

The increase in the number of emigrants from Israel in 1957 may have been a result of the 1956 Suez War. Newspaper articles referring in alarm to a "peak" and a "new record" were collected at the time by JA officials, reflecting their intense scrutiny of emigration.[32] The JA also compiled their own data, according to which 2,424 emigrants left officially through the port of Haifa in 1958.[33] These emigrants are ranked in table 1.6 by country of origin and by country of destination in table 1.7. There are clear variations in the rank that each country or region occupied as a source of immigration to Israel or, conversely, as a destination for emigrants from Israel. Thus, forty-two Latin Americans left Israel in 1958 and Latin America ranked twelfth among the regions of origin of those leaving Israel (table 1.6). Conversely, 161 emigrants from Israel headed for Latin America and the region ranked fifth as a destination for Israeli emigrants (table 1.7). Table 1.7 reflects the reality that (1) during the postwar period,

**Table 1.6. Number of Emigrants from Israel in 1958, Ranked by Their Country of Origin Before Living in Israel (with That Same Country Shown as a Destination for a Different Number of Migrants Leaving Israel)**

| Rank | Country | Origin | Destination |
|---|---|---|---|
| 1 | Poland | 637 | 56 |
| 2 | Romania | 362 | 4 |
| 3 | Arab countries | 236 | 99 |
| 4 | Hungary | 214 | 75 |
| 5 | Czechoslovakia | 188 | 32 |
| 6 | France | 128 | 341 |
| 7 | Egypt | 85 | - |
| 8 | Italy | 76 | 188 |
| 9 | Germany | 66 | 80 |
| 10 | England | 55 | 81 |
| 11 | Bulgaria | 53 | 5 |
| 12 | South America | 42 | 161 |
| 13 | China | 42 | - |
| 14 | United States | 38 | 847 |
| 15 | Austria | 36 | 40 |
| 16 | Belgium | 30 | 30 |
| 17 | Yugoslavia | 26 | 25 |
| 18 | USSR | 25 | 15 |
| 19 | Canada | 25 | 149 |
| 20 | Holland | 19 | 38 |
| 21 | Turkey | 15 | 26 |
| 22 | Iran | 6 | 11 |
| 23 | Australia | 5 | 59 |
| 24 | South Africa | 4 | 16 |
| 25 | India | 4 | 4 |
| 26 | Switzerland | 4 | 6 |
| 27 | Sweden | 2 | 2 |
| 28 | Denmark | 1 | 4 |
| 29 | Burma | - | 2 |
| 30 | Liberia | - | 1 |
| 31 | Ghana | - | 16 |
| 32 | Spain | - | 6 |
| 33 | Norway | - | 3 |
| 34 | Finland | - | 2 |
| **Total** | | **2,424** | **2,424** |

Source: Kalman Levin to Dov Yosef, February 6, 1959, CZA, S60/334.

Table 1.7. Number of Emigrants from Israel in 1958, Ranked by Their Country of Destination When Leaving Israel (with That Same Country Shown as the Country of Origin for a Different Number of Migrants)

| Rank | Country | Destination | Origin |
|---|---|---|---|
| 1 | United States | 847 | 38 |
| 2 | France | 341 | 128 |
| 3 | Italy | 188 | 76 |
| 4 | Canada | 149 | 25 |
| 5 | South America | 161 | 42 |
| 6 | Arab countries | 99 | 236 |
| 7 | England | 81 | 55 |
| 8 | Germany | 80 | 66 |
| 9 | Hungary | 75 | 214 |
| 10 | Australia | 59 | 5 |
| 11 | Poland | 56 | 637 |
| 12 | Austria | 40 | 36 |
| 13 | Holland | 38 | 19 |
| 14 | Czechoslovakia | 32 | 188 |
| 15 | Belgium | 30 | 30 |
| 16 | Turkey | 26 | 15 |
| 17 | Yugoslavia | 25 | 26 |
| 18 | South Africa | 16 | 4 |
| 19 | Ghana | 16 | - |
| 20 | USSR | 15 | 25 |
| 21 | Iran | 11 | 6 |
| 22 | Switzerland | 6 | 4 |
| 23 | Spain | 6 | - |
| 24 | Bulgaria | 5 | 53 |
| 25 | Romania | 4 | 362 |
| 26 | India | 4 | 4 |
| 27 | Denmark | 4 | 1 |
| 28 | Norway | 3 | - |
| 29 | Sweden | 2 | 2 |
| 30 | Burma | 2 | - |
| 31 | Finland | 2 | - |
| 32 | Liberia | 1 | - |
| 33 | China | - | 42 |
| 34 | Egypt | - | 85 |
| **Total** | | **2,424** | **2,424** |

Source: Kalman Levin to Dov Yosef, February 6, 1959, CZA, S60/334.

Latin America represented a region of opportunity for many people who could not enter the United States, Canada, or Europe; (2) many of those leaving Israel were originally from Arab or socialist countries and were re-emigrating to third countries; and (3) the United States, France, Italy, and Canada were the most attractive destinations for the emigrants.

Lastly, these tables highlight the fact that not every person leaving Israel for another country held that country's nationality or origin. Mostly, such detailed information was missed and the category of "returnees" obscured the phenomenon of remigration. For example, the latter often included cases of families or couples formed by people from different countries who met each other in Israel. In such cases, while one partner was returning to Latin America, the other was remigrating. Still, despite inaccuracies, the available data clearly show that in 1958 Latin America was more apparent as a destination for Israeli emigrants than as their land of origin. The unprecedented immigration of Latin Americans that would take place within the next five years and the portion of them that would later leave Israel should be understood against this background.

At the beginning of 1959, Interior Minister Yisrael Bar-Yehuda approved a budget for research on emigration, lamenting that "even in a year of great aliyah, we have to fight against yerida."[34] The research would be conducted by a team from the Hebrew University of Jerusalem under the supervision of Y. Goldin, the director for immigration and planning at the Interior Ministry.[35] The researchers interviewed three hundred "self-declared" emigrants who required official permits to leave the country, from January 15, 1939, to March 15, 1959. Their report was printed in October but due to budgetary restrictions and lack of time the data was not processed fully.[36] It should be emphasized that even the sociologists heading the research used the biased Zionist terms *yerida* and *yordim* in their report.[37] Regarding Latin America, the region was not actually listed as a category within the sample, which included a total of 266 interviewees.[38] Although the report was not intended to be statistically representative, the absence of Latin Americans among interviewees reflected their minor role among the emigrants. In addition, Latin America appeared to be the chosen destination of three people within the sample, while the United States, Canada, and Australia ranked as the top three.[39] In terms of the emigrants themselves, most were Eastern Europeans.[40]

Thus, Latin America was clearly not at the center of discussions on Israeli emigration during the 1950s due to the small number of Latin Americans in Israel and the prominence of other regions as destinations for people leaving the country. Canada, for example, attracted the attention of JA officials, who observed with alarm the number of Israelis relocating there: 543 in 1958; 1,156 in the first half of 1959, and a total of 7,676 between 1945 and 1959.[41] Israeli emigration to Canada was depicted as "acute" by Baruch Duvdevany, director general of the JA's immigration department in Jerusalem, in 1961.[42] There was an ongoing discussion on how to attract these people back to Israel and one document suggested the creation of a "Committee for the Return of the Yored," paradoxically recommending as a first measure avoiding the pejorative term *yored* and replacing it with the one used today, *chozer Yisraeli* (returning Israeli). Moshe Sharett, then-chairman of the JA, agreed with the proposed change. Nonetheless, yored continued to be used in official documents and as part of colloquial language.[43]

Another very negative report on the emigrants appears in a letter sent by a JA emissary named Yehuda Sar, after his encounters aboard the *Zion*, which left Israel in April 1961. Sar was traveling abroad to promote immigration to Israel and he was shocked by the ship's atmosphere—its "poker and dance saloons." In his report to Yehuda Dominitz, JA's secretary for immigration, Sar complained that the *Zion* was "full of yordim." Among them he mentioned an Israeli leaving behind his wife and children to go to Canada; an American who had arrived in Israel "only" to seek a wife; olim families with children who were leaving even though they were settled and employed; and young men who were "great poker players and saloon dancers, very noisy men." Sar lamented that the "atmosphere of revelry" onboard was harmful to potential immigrants. "A trip like this might overwhelm the willingness of Jews who visited the country to settle there. In fact, a tourist told me that he did not recognize the Jews anymore and did not know what was happening on this ship. When he traveled to Israel on the same ship, [people] danced and sang Hebrew songs; danced the hora, etc. . . . With these Jews in the *golah* [Diaspora] my work will not be easy."[44] Sar recommended seeking a "remedy for the sickness" of emigration, using a medical metaphor frequently used at the time. Besides his questionable idea of immigrants dancing the hora and emigrants playing poker, his worries regarding the negative effects of emigration on Israel's immigration goals were based on his personal experience.

In the near future, Argentines leaving Israel would become the focus of similar reports. In the meantime, Canada continued to be the center of JA discussions because it was an attractive destination for Jews from all over the world, especially Israelis. In August 1961 Shlomo Zalman Shragai, head of the JA's immigration department, asked Sharett to pay close attention to the number of Jewish migrants who had arrived in Canada during the previous year (table 1.8).

In addition to Canada, Brazil and Algeria demanded the attention of the JA, for different reasons. In a separate letter, Shragai commented on the number of Jewish migrants to Brazil based on the Brazilian government's figures. For the period 1954 to 1960, Brazil received a total of 10,725 Jewish migrants; of these, 4,566 arrived holding visas issued in Israel.[45] As the possession of a visa from Israel demonstrates, they were not Brazilian but either Israeli-born emigrants or people re-emigrating from Israel. Some were probably Europeans displaced by the war.[46] The case of Algeria was different. Six thousand Jews had migrated to

**Table 1.8. Jewish Migrants Arrived in Canada in 1960 by Origin**

| Origin | Migrants |
|---|---|
| Israel | 1,474 |
| United States | 579 |
| United Kingdom | 283 |
| Europe | 226 |
| Soviet Bloc | 206 |
| Islamic States | 101 |
| Latin America | 91 |
| **Total** | **2,960** |

Source: S. Z. Shragai to M. Sharett, August 1, 1961, CZA S65/187.

Israel and the return rate was estimated at 20 to 25 percent.[47] JA representatives found this hard to believe and insisted on the need to double-check the information.[48] The case demonstrated the challenge that returnees posed in small communities, since their stories could influence the decisions of others. In one case, for example, the majority of a group of thirty families cancelled their plans to immigrate to Israel from Algeria due to "negative propaganda" from returnees. The emissary who reported this story added that the "atmosphere of yerida" and expectations of French reparations as a result of the Vichy government's stripping Algerian Jews of citizenship in 1940 complicated his job.[49]

A wide set of changing circumstances affected migration and return, posing new opportunities and challenges to JA officials in relation to every population they worked with. While Latin Americans in general and Argentine returnees from Israel in particular did not receive attention due to their negligible numbers, after 1963 the situation began to change.

## FIRST MASS JEWISH ARGENTINE MIGRATION TO ISRAEL

Early in the morning of March 5, 1963, the Italian ship *Flaminia* docked in the port of Buenos Aires. More than seven hundred passengers would board via a plank emblazoned with the Hebrew message *Veshavu banim ligvulam* (And the sons will return to their land). The port workers of Puerto Nuevo worked incessantly throughout the day to load hundreds of containers full of furniture, appliances, and clothes. The JA, which for the first time had chartered a ship to bring Latin Americans to Israel, cared about their comfort; each "ample and clean" cabin had spare beds while single men and women had separate areas. At 18:00 hundreds of passengers were to be seen lining the decks, exchanging farewells with their family and friends on the dock. Five thousand people had turned up to say goodbye; many had organized picnics. By 23:30 the crowd had shrunk noticeably and although there were still five containers waiting to be loaded, the ship had to depart; some migrants would have to wait several months before their belongings arrived in Israel. As tugs began to nudge the *Flaminia* away from Argentine soil, the passengers sang Spanish and Hebrew songs, one of which would have had new meaning for them: "Hatikvah" (the hope), the Israeli national anthem.[50]

The former description is based on the only Spanish-language news item related to the departure of the *Flaminia*; the JA and the local Jewish leadership had opted for a low profile regarding the event. Conversely, the Israeli press celebrated, reporting extensively on the ship's voyage, which would end in Israel almost a month later. *Davar* emphasized the middle-class character of the immigrants who, it stated, had been making aliyah since the wave of anti-Semitism that erupted following the Eichmann affair (1960).[51] Just after their arrival, the religiously oriented national newspaper *Hatzofe* declared that the seven hundred immigrants from Latin America, and in particular those from Argentina, were beginning a "mass immigration movement," adding "hundreds of healthy young people, mostly professionals, to the Israeli population." This kind of journey, explained the reporter, had been unimaginable a year or two earlier; however, severe economic distress had since then led to a new aggressive form of anti-Semitism in Latin America, similar to that which had swept Europe before World War II. The immigrants were coming, he said, from places where Zionist pioneering education was important. Balancing ideological and practical aspects, he wrote, "The future of aliyah depends on accurate and convincing information, on the fulfillment of the promises made [to immigrants], and on the depth of Jewish-Zionist education among the new generation."[52]

Three days after the *Flaminia*'s arrival, *Hatzofe* provided a detailed description of the immigrants and their journey. The ship had brought the body of Pinhas Said, a young man murdered in Montevideo in an anti-Semitic attack.[53] The JA's main representatives were present at the ceremony welcoming the "largest group" ever to have arrived in Israel. There were six hundred immigrants from Argentina, sixty-two from Uruguay, and sixty-six from Brazil. The group included mostly young people: 400 were under thirty-five, including 250 members of Zionist movements. Ben Zion Fixler had been in charge of everything during the three-week voyage, including a daily minyan (a quorum of ten Jewish men required for prayer) and Hebrew classes. Chairman of the JA Moshe Sharett, a former prime minister and foreign minister, referred to a "historical event" because, from his point of view, two past and "contrasting immigration streams" from Eastern Europe were being reunited. Decades ago, he explained, various parts of the Jewish population had gone either to Palestine-Israel or to Latin America. The *Flaminia*, according to Sharett, was the symbol of their reunification brought about by the "aliyah of the sons" of those that had migrated to Argentina.[54]

Even a week after the *Flaminia*'s arrival, *Hatzofe* continued to describe the trip, highlighting the happiness of a Friday afternoon on board when Moises Herzcowitz and his wife became parents; the newborn was named Gal (wave). The journalist referred to "carpenters and weavers, shoemakers and tailors, dressmakers, shopkeepers, and national and municipality employees . . . many of whom sold everything in their countries of origin." He also claimed that the *Flaminia* was the topic of conversation in every synagogue, club, and place where Latin American Jews gathered. The JA, together with the Israeli navigation company ZIM, had provided the immigrants with an "Israeli atmosphere," including kosher food, lectures, a synagogue, Hebrew classes, music, and folk dancing. The travelers organized a daily bulletin to share news, amusing stories, and social events on board, such as bar mitzvahs and birthdays. Captain Di Marzzo had already brought ten thousand migrants to Israel and ZIM representative Yaakov Ronen was also on board. However, the key facilitator was Fixler, a veteran of Jewish immigration since its illegal period. According to passengers, "although he was a religious man with a kippah," he managed to gain the esteem of secular immigrants. A number of young people "gave me more than a few problems," Fixler declared. For example, he had to explain that it was not permissible to add cheese to meat ravioli. Similarly, when a storm delayed the arrival in Rio de Janeiro and the ship docked on a Friday afternoon, many wanted to tour the city and Fixler had to explain about the Sabbath restrictions.[55]

While many ships had made this trip, the considerable press coverage set the *Flaminia*'s journey apart, for good reason. The *Flaminia* voyage marked the peak of an immigration wave that brought more than four thousand Argentines to Israel in 1963. JA representatives tended to perceive this group as escaping from anti-Semitism and, as the banner on the ship's gangplank proclaimed, as "returning" to their ancestral homeland rather than immigrating to a young nation state. This ideological conception facilitated the incorporation of immigrants into the Zionist narrative, but history and statistics provide a different story. True, in 1960 the Mossad captured the Nazi war criminal Adolf Eichmann and, although the international affair was resolved diplomatically within a few weeks, a wave of anti-Semitism erupted in Argentina which lasted for two years.[56] In protest against Israel's violation of Argentine sovereignty, anti-Semitic organizations attacked Jewish students and buildings owned by Jews.[57] This wave of anti-Semitism contributed to unifying the organized community and consolidating its identification with the State of Israel.[58] Moreover, all this took place in the context of already existing social, political, and economic deterioration. As a result, the number of Jewish Argentine immigrants arriving in Israel increased fivefold in 1963 (figure 1.2).[59]

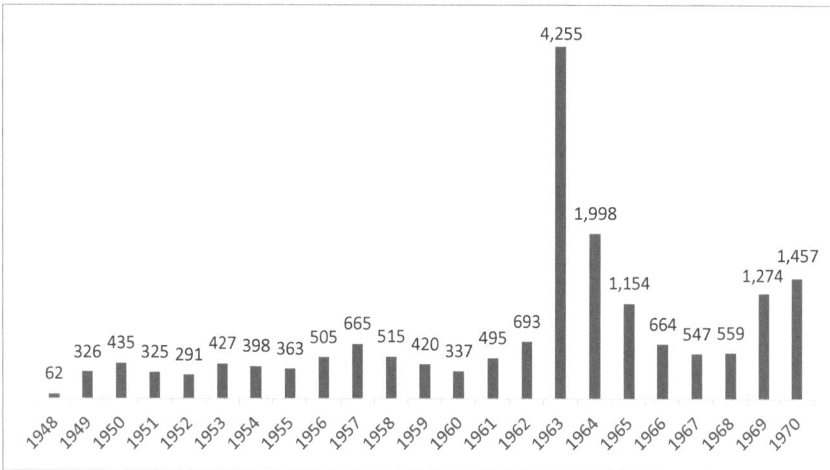


**Figure 1.2** Number of Jewish Argentine immigrant arrivals in Israel by year, 1948–1970. Source: Israeli Central Bureau of Statistics, "Total Immigration to Israel by Select Country by Year, Jewish Virtual Library. Returnee citizens are not included.

Nonetheless, the number of immigrants represented a small proportion of total Jewish Argentines. As noted, there were some three hundred thousand Jews in Argentina in the early 1960s and while most of their organizations were led by Zionists, the vast majority of Jews were unaffiliated.[60] Argentine society had faced an economic recession every three years since 1952. This succession of crises eroded salaried workers' share in the GDP, from 49 percent in 1954 to 40 percent in 1962.[61] While the wave of anti-Semitism suffered by Argentine Jews, combined with Zionist teachings, might have played a role in the increased number of immigrants, the combined effects of economic decline and migrant characteristics suggest that economics was the main driving force.

Historian Sebastian Klor analyzed the sociodemographic and occupational profile of these immigrants and found that what he defined as manual and blue-collar workers represented 25.5 percent of the total. The group included artisans (10.8 percent), unclassified (8.8 percent), skilled craftsmen (4.8 percent), and farmers (1.1 percent), altogether accounting for 47 percent of economically active immigrants (EAI). On the other hand, white-collar workers, including liberal professionals, clerical workers, merchants, and industrialists made up 53 percent of EAI (table 1.9). The breakdown of occupational categories shows that artisans were represented mainly by tailors, needleworkers, carpenters, weavers, engravers, and jewelers. The category of skilled craftsman included mainly technicians of various sorts, such as electricians and mechanics. Among the liberal professionals, the main subcategories were teachers, physicians, bookkeepers, engineers, chemists, biochemists, pharmacists, accountants, architects, psychologists, social workers, journalists, and lawyers.[62]

Notably, Klor observed that most of the professionals were "young and newly embarked on their careers."[63] In addition, when he compared the occupational stratification of the migrants to that of Jewish Argentines in general, he found that while two-thirds of Jewish Argentines at the time were merchants, industrialists, clerical workers, and liberal professionals, their share was smaller among the immigrants.[64] He thus concluded that Jewish Argentine migration reflected an "economic and selective" immigration represented mainly by people from the "lower middle class."[65] Here I will use a wider definition to refer to these immigrants, emphasizing their characteristics in relation to Argentina's economic cycles. In my reading, they comprised people from a variety of occupational categories that were specifically affected by the country's economic fluctuations, especially recessions and currency devaluations. The group included middle- and

**Table 1.9. Occupational Distribution of Argentine Migrants to Israel, 1954–1967**

| | All Immigrants | | | Economically Active |
|---|---|---|---|---|
| **Occupational Category** | **Number** | **Percent** | **Percent by aggregated categories** | **Percent** |
| Artisans | 988 | 10.8 | | |
| Unclassified* | 800 | 8.8 | 25.5 | 47 |
| Skilled craftsmen | 441 | 4.8 | | |
| Farmers | 97 | 1.1 | | |
| Liberal professionals** | 1,211 | 13.2 | | |
| Clerical workers | 737 | 8.0 | 28.1 | 53 |
| Merchants and industrialists | 630 | 6.9 | | |
| | | | | **Total 100** |
| University students | 311 | 3.4 | | |
| Elementary and secondary school pupils | 2,306 | 25.2 | 46.4 | |
| Housewives | 1,597 | 17.4 | | |
| Pensioners | 38 | 0.4 | | |
| **Total** | **9,156** | **100** | **100** | |

Source: Sebastian Klor, *Between Exile and Exodus* (Detroit: Wayne State University Press, 2017), 136. While the table refers to immigrants who came between 1954 and 1967, over one-third arrived in 1963 and more than half between the years 1963 and 1965.

*"Unclassified" includes day laborers and people older than eighteen but still at school.

**"Liberal professions" includes teachers and bookkeepers.

lower-middle-class sectors, such as young professionals, salaried workers, and self-employed artisans, who had no savings to depend on in times of recession and diminishing real wages. Hence, while a journalist quoted in this chapter in reference to the arrival of the *Flaminia* noted that many of the immigrants had sold everything they had, the majority might not have had much to sell in the first place.

The mass arrival of Latin American immigrants added a new community to Israeli society and led in late 1963 to the founding of *Aurora*, a weekly Spanish-language paper. Its pages offer an idea of how economic success was conceived by many of the immigrants and the kind of businesses they could attain. For example, a large family succeeded in opening a shop only five months after the arrival of the first of its members. After the latter worked as an employee for a big chain in order to learn Hebrew and become familiar with the local culture, the family opened a shop in Bat Yam selling a wide range of goods, from candies to furniture.[66] In a special supplement on Beersheba, *Aurora* dedicated a full page to new ventures set up by immigrants from Argentina in the Negev. A factory producing footballs was opened and moved on to manufacturing shoes and other products for export for the Defense Ministry and for a major chain store. The factory's payroll as well as its premises expanded significantly. A plastics factory opened by two Argentines is another example. These entrepreneurs gathered a small amount of capital and launched their company in a tiny room with two employees. By 1964 they had a 210-square-meter plant with twenty-nine workers. Their success was possible due to subsidies from the JA and the Industry Ministry. A furniture factory was also started by immigrants in southern Israel.[67]

Yet, despite entrepreneurial opportunities promoted for immigrants, most would be forced to work for a salary due to their lack of capital, even those who had been owners or self-employed in Argentina. Moreover, they would have to adapt to the Israeli culture and learn the Hebrew language, and would not be able to take part in cultural life as they had in Argentina. Lastly, research on the middle class and self-identification in Argentina found that for wide sectors of the population, "'culture' was highly valued as a manifestation of social status, even more so than money"; lack of access to it would diminish these immigrant's middle-class status in their own eyes.[68] Ultimately, a considerable portion of Argentines would find life in Israel harder than it had been in their country of origin and would experience a sense of downward mobility. Here, expectations collided with reality. Since the early 1960s, they had come to Israel driven by expectations of material prosperity, or at least by the possibility of reversing the process of deterioration that threatened their living conditions in Argentina. For some, Israel's own economic deterioration from 1964 to 1966, together with the cumulative effect of the obstacles they faced in Israel, catalyzed a return to Argentina, which became evident with the onset of the 1966 recession. Return was facilitated by the fact that Argentine nationality law is based both on jus soli (right of the soil) and jus sanguinis (right of blood) and permits dual citizenship; migrants found no legal obstacle to repatriation.

By the end of 1963, *Davar* reported the return of forty-two Latin Americans aboard the *Theodor Herzl*; twenty-five were Argentines.[69] This was not described in a dramatic fashion because the number of returnees for the whole year was similar to that of the previous year (table 1.10). However, the scale of the return became evident in 1964, when their number jumped to 317. Such augmented numbers started to reflect, in a delayed fashion, an unraveling of the mass immigration of previous years. Such figures could not remain unnoticed for long.

At the end of June 1966, the Organization of Latin American Immigrants in Israel (OLEI) held its eighth annual convention in Tel Aviv. The conference proceedings refer to the contrast with the previous conference, which reported an increase in immigration from Latin America in general and Argentina in particular. Now, the return of Latin Americans was being discussed by the Israeli press and the atmosphere was gloomy. Still, while participants believed that the problem was serious, they felt that figures published by the press were inflated, estimating that 11 percent of Latin American had returned since 1948, most having arrived during the period from 1961 to 1965. They believed that the returnees' decision was caused by social and material difficulties, unwillingness to adapt to a new lifestyle, and inappropriate guidance.[70] During the meeting, Abraham Cygel, director of the JA's absorption department, declared that "the Latin Americans have a middle-class mentality but if they lack the means to support it, they have to resign themselves to rolling up their sleeves and lowering their social status."[71]

It is clear that key players within the absorption system understood the gap between the aspirations of many immigrants and their material situation. Nevertheless, appealing to their willingness to "lower their social status" would have sounded ironic to people who had changed countries precisely in order to avoid lowering it. Moreover, Israel's economic difficulties were no doubt experienced more deeply by those immigrants than by the ideologically motivated

**Table 1.10. Argentine Migrants to Israel and Returnees, 1948–1964**

| | 1948-1951 | 1952 | 1955 | 1957 | 1960 | 1961 | 1962 | 1963 | 1964 | Total |
|---|---|---|---|---|---|---|---|---|---|---|
| Immigrants | 1,134 | 239 | 1.146 | 1,065 | 1,157 | 495 | 628 | 4,090 | 1,826 | 11,780 |
| Returnees (declared) | 164 | 49 | 24 | 25 | 31 | 82 | 71 | 87 | 317 | 850 |

Source: M. Haram to A. Pincus, November 25, 1965, CZA S62/351.

ones. There were immigrants employed as industrial workers who had "rolled up their sleeves," as suggested, but their earnings were not enough for a decent standard of living. Even before the beginning of the recession, one such immigrant worker sent a letter to the editor of *Aurora*, titled "No One Can Eat Zionism," supporting a proposed bonus for workers: "Like many other *olim* from Argentina, I am now a modest worker who earns a monthly salary of IL400 and I believe you will not think that I am . . . overstating it or embittered . . . if I say that this is not enough for a family of four . . . the bonus would help me and many other workers in similar conditions . . . no matter how Zionist you are, no one can eat Zionism."[72] The quotation reflects the tensions between material circumstances, which determined the immigrants' everyday life, and Zionist ideology, which those responsible for immigrant absorption tended to see as the actual or desirable motive for immigration to Israel. It also demonstrates the multiplicity of elements integrating the immigrant identity mosaic: the writer was from Argentina, acting as an Israeli citizen, claiming his rights from a class perspective, and questioning the Zionist discourse. Various dimensions of this mosaic could become more or less relevant according to the context and play differing roles in a migrant's decision to stay in Israel or return to Argentina.

In the end, while majority of immigrants from Argentina stayed in Israel, a considerable proportion returned to across the Atlantic. The return migration occurred at a time when groups of pioneers, the poor, and refugees had already integrated into the new nation and Israel's capacity to absorb middle-class arrivals was being widely discussed.[73] According to the Zionist program, immigration to Palestine would follow an order based on social class. Herzl had argued clearly: "The old house is not abandoned before the new one is ready. Only those that are sure to improve their position emigrate. First, the desperate; after them, the poor; next, the prosperous; and, last of all, the wealthy."[74] Therefore, the phenomenon of those leaving Israel—Argentines in particular—was discussed in connection with the Israeli obstacles and challenges to absorbing "middle-class" migrants.

Encouraging Jewish immigration has been an essential goal of the State of Israel since its inception and over the years new organizations, improved expertise, and expanded budgets have been dedicated to that task. In the past, the hegemony of Zionist ideology made emigration tantamount to treason and even today, despite Israel's high immigrant retention rate, immigration continues to be nationally celebrated while emigration raises uncomfortable questions. Until 1963 Latin American emigration from Israel did not receive much attention because there were not many in the country, even though Latin America was a very attractive destination for people of any background leaving Israel. In fact, during the postwar period, it was the best choice for those who could not enter the United States, Canada, or Europe.

In contrast, after 1963, the number of Latin Americans in Israel in general, and Argentines in particular, increased significantly and, therefore their emigration began to be noticeable. The *Flaminia* voyage marked the peak of an immigration wave that brought more than four thousand Argentines to Israel in 1963. JA representatives tended to perceive members of this group as escaping from anti-Semitism and as returning to their ancestral homeland, an ideological conception that facilitated the incorporation of immigrants into the Zionist narrative. Nonetheless, the number of immigrants represented a small proportion of total Jewish Argentines, who were driven mainly by economic circumstances to leave Argentina. Those affected by Argentine recessions and currency devaluations belonged to the middle- and lower-middle-class sectors, such as young professionals, salaried workers, and self-employed artisans without savings to depend on in such times. Therefore, a considerable portion of these new arrivals would find life in Israel harder than it had been at home and would experience a sense of downward mobility. They had expected a certain material prosperity, or at least the possibility of reversing the process of deterioration already suffered in Argentina. As a result of Israel's 1966 economic recession, together with the cumulative effect of the obstacles they faced as newcomers, a considerable number of them returned to Argentina. Their return occurred at a time when Israel's capacity to absorb middle-class arrivals had become a subject of public discussion. The next chapter is dedicated to analyzing their migration experience in relation to their cultural and economic backgrounds, examining the cases of those who settled in a new city or in a moshav, and looking at how the Jewish Argentine biweekly *La Luz* reported on them.

# 2

# A CLASH OF CULTURES, ECONOMICS, AND EXPECTATIONS

Once in Israel, Argentine immigrants faced obstacles to their integration into Israeli society due to differences between the two societies' cultures, consumer patterns, landscapes, and hegemonic values. This chapter discusses these differences through an analysis of two cartoon characters, Srulik and Mafalda. In addition, it describes the experiences of Argentines who settled in the city of Ashdod, where they tried to continue their former occupations, and those of immigrants who settled in Moshav Kochav Michael Sobell, where they struggled to make a living from agriculture. It was from those two places that a return to Argentina became noticeable toward the onset of the 1966 Israeli recession, a matter that went unreported either by Zionist-dominated Jewish Argentine organizations or their affiliated newspapers in Argentina; in fact, the biweekly *La Luz* was the only Jewish publication that covered the issue.

## THE LAND OF SRULIK WELCOMES MAFALDA

Two popular cartoon characters, Srulik and Mafalda, serve to illuminate both the culture clash experienced by Argentines in Israel during the 1960s and the reasons the returnees were depicted as middle class. Srulik was created in 1956 by Hungarian Holocaust survivor Kariel Gardosh, "Dosh," whose work appeared in the daily *Maariv*. Srulik, the diminutive for "Israel," represented the sabra, a young native Israeli who wore a pointy sunhat known as a *tembel* (popular among kibbutz members in the 1930s), biblical sandals, and khaki shorts. A pioneer Zionist and a farmer, during wartime he put on a uniform and carried an Uzi machine gun to defend the State of Israel.[1] In 1958 Srulik became the official icon of Israel's Independence Day celebrations and since then Zionist organizations have used this figure to promote their values in Israeli public schools and Diaspora communities.[2]

The other cartoon character, Mafalda, first appeared in 1964; the image was published in various magazines. She was created by Joaquin Lavado, "Quino," the Argentine son of Spanish immigrants from Andalucía. According to historian Luis Alberto Romero, she became the symbol of the modest middle-class family, which owned a car and could afford two weeks of vacation a year.[3] As mentioned by Elizabeth Montes Garcés, Umberto Eco highlighted Mafalda's oppositionist attitude toward social rules, and Isabella Cosse considered her character in relation to the young generation of the 1960s and the student rebellions against political oppression.[4] Of course, not every Argentine immigrant was like Mafalda and not every Israeli was like Srulik. Nonetheless, the former encapsulates the Argentine culture that shaped these migrants' lifestyles while the latter epitomizes the hegemonic Zionist ethos they encountered in Israel after they arrived. At the same time, the cartoons are cultural productions that need to be understood in relation to differing national histories and economic backgrounds.

In the early 1960s, both Argentina and Israel implemented import substitution industrialization (ISI) programs; however, their social circumstances were very different. In Argentina, ISI provided jobs to vast sectors of the population, which also became consumers of these products in the domestic market, while the agricultural and meat production sectors were competitive enough for export. The expansion of industry meant an increasing need for foreign currency to import technology and supplies. Thus, Argentina grew based on a "stop and go" model, according to which each expansive cycle was followed by bottlenecks, foreign currency shortages, and crises involving devaluation, recession, and inflation.[5] These crises, which arose every three years, eroded the share of salaried workers in the GDP: while in 1954 it was 49 percent, in 1962 it had fallen to 40 percent.[6] Moreover, the incapacity to overcome structural constraints in the economy led to political instability. In 1955 Juan Domingo Perón—who had held the post of president since 1946—and his movement, which had the support of the workers, were outlawed. Perón went into exile, but no other leader or party was able to win over his followers and their unions, which remained loyal to him. Consequently, the political system was unable to resolve social conflict, leading to recurrent interruptions of the democratic process.[7] Argentine citizens, numbering more than twenty million, were divided by sociopolitical cleavages. Industrialization failed either to take hold among the political elites, whose wealth was based on agriculture, or to provide an image powerful enough to compete with social memories of the mythologized "world's granary."[8]

Israel, on the other hand, was a much younger nation; its population was fewer than 2.5 million in 1963, and its internal divisions were negligible compared with the external threats it faced. During the first years, the government implemented austerity and the rationing of goods, known as *tzena*. Moreover, during the 1950s, ISI in Israel was accompanied by foreign exchange shortages, which the government tried to solve by devaluating the Israeli lira, relaxing price controls, and budget cuts.[9] The 1952 Reparations Agreement with Germany temporarily mitigated these problems.[10] Additional cash was obtained through sales of bonds, mainly in the United States. As a result, the economy grew and unemployment remained relatively low, but the cost of living rose in parallel with a flood of imports and a decline in exports. In 1962 the government launched a stabilization program, but the trade deficit grew and difficulties became more acute when German reparations ended in 1964. As of 1965 Israel became increasingly dependent on short-term borrowing, and attempts to steady the economy led to a recession (*mitun*). While the GDP had increased by an average of 10 percent per year from 1950 to 1955, the rate fell to 2 percent in 1966 and 1967. As a consequence, domestic consumption and investment decreased while unemployment tripled during those two years.

Despite the differing contexts, on the surface, the similarities between Israel's and Argentina's economic structures offered certain bases for optimism about the Argentines' economic absorption in Israel. In fact, most of the immigrants stayed. Moreover, beyond slight differences, in 1960 the proportion of employers and employees within the labor force was similar in the two countries in 1960 (table 2.1).

**Table 2.1. Percentage of Israeli and Argentine Labor Force in 1960 by Type of Employment and Gender**

| | Gender | Employee | Self-Employed | Employer | Unpaid Family Member | Kibbutz Members | Other |
|---|---|---|---|---|---|---|---|
| Israel 701,800 | Male (75%) | 69 | 24* | | 2 | 5 | - |
| | Female (25%) | 63 | 6* | | 18 | 13 | - |
| Argentina 7,524,469 | Male (78%) | 67 | 13 | 14 | 3 | - | 3 |
| | Female (22%) | 80 | 11 | 4 | 3 | - | 2 |

Source: *Censo Nacional de Población 1960* (Buenos Aires: Dirección Nacional de Estadísticas y Censos, 1960); Yoram Ben Porath, "Self-Employed and Wage Earners in Israel: Findings from the Census of Population 1972" (research paper, Institute for Economic Research, Jerusalem, 1981).

*Including members of cooperatives. The comparison between the Argentine and Israeli labor forces is not 100 percent accurate, because the Argentine figures include people from a younger age group. Nevertheless, this distortion does not affect the broader picture. In these two cases, there were no distinctions (in the available sources) between the two categories (self-employed and employer), so, the two cells and the quantities are merged. This is why the number is centered between the two headings. In the case of Argentina, the two separated quantities were available, so there are two different columns for them.

However, by 1966, as a result of economic deterioration and doubts about the nation's future, many Israelis were leaving the country. Newspapers were filled with statistics, reports, and even cartoons about those departing. Given this context, there was a new focus on Latin Americans and a change in the approach to their experiences. The observation according to which Latin American immigrants had a middle-class mentality but not the means to support it was recurrent and deserves sociological analysis. However, at the time the emotional and ideological Zionist approach to them was dominant and, therefore, observations tended to be more passionate than sociological. Emigration from Israel was viewed with contempt, and return migration was rarely perceived as an integral part of migration in the public discourse. Stereotypes and simplistic explanations were more abundant than deep consideration of the returnees' economic and cultural backgrounds and the obstacles they faced. In reality, most of the Argentines lacked sufficient savings and suffered the effects of the Israeli recession. And yet, the fact that Argentine industrialization and cultural modernization processes had accustomed them to habits and lifestyles that could not be reproduced in Israel was not taken seriously. Instead, their adaptation problems were taken either as a demonstration of weak ideological commitment and a feeble national character or as a sign that the process of immigration selection was flawed.

By the end of 1965, the press began to speak of a Latin American "wave of yerida." Guidon Abramovich, director of the Histadrut in Argentina, declared to the right-wing nationalist *Herut* newspaper that 25 percent of the migrants from the mentioned country had returned from Israel because they were middle-class people dedicated to commerce and craftsmanship, without Zionist motivation. In his view the JA did not know how to help them. He emphasized that such immigrants were different from those coming from poor countries or professionals from developed economies.[11] *Davar* took a similar stance, explaining that "a portion" of Argentines had arrived "very excited and full of hope" but returned to Argentina "irritated, somber, and discomforted." Most, the reporter said, were from the middle class and had experienced unemployment in Israel. According to an anonymous JA official, the journalist expounded, their self-defined condition of middle class was outdated because they had come without the necessary capital to earn a living. He blamed JA emissaries for its poor selection of immigrants. In the same article, OLEI representative Zeev Kaplan estimated Latin American emigration from Israel at more than 20 percent.[12]

Various observers who covered Argentine "middle-class" emigration indeed referred to the challenges faced by immigrants who sought to be self-employed. However, they failed to recognize the real significance of their habituation to a certain standard of living and tended to explain their absorption problems as a result of their personality. Questioned in the weekly journal *Mabat Hadash* about Latin American returnees, Baruch Duvdevany, director general of the JA's immigration department, said that prior to their arrival these immigrants had heard only what they wanted to hear. His deputy, Haim Zadok, went further, referring to their complaints about their assigned places of residence. They were "problematic people who usually changed their minds on the ship or one minute after arrival," he asserted. The locations had been agreed upon before immigration, he added, but then they spoke with relatives and grumbled that "15 km from the city" was too far.[13] The depiction of prospective immigrants as hearing only what they wanted to hear was the reverse side of the accusation according to which JA emissaries had told the immigrants lies or created a rosy picture. Probably, both had tried to be honest while also believing that certain details could be discussed later. Of course, both sides would have had different ideas about what a "detail" meant and while fifteen kilometers distance from the city was a detail for Zadok, it was not an unimportant issue for most Argentine immigrants, who were used to living in greater urban areas.

Both Israel and Argentina were clearly majority urban in 1960: 74 and 77 percent of their populations living in cities, respectively.[14] Nonetheless, there were great differences in demography, landscape, and urban geography. In 1960 the city of Tel Aviv-Jaffa had 738,000 inhabitants and, not surprisingly, most Argentine immigrants desired to settle there, leading to complaints when this was not possible.[15] At the time, the population of Buenos Aires and its surrounding metropolitan area, where the majority of Jewish Argentines lived, was 6,762,000.[16] Other migrants came from Rosario (669,173), Córdoba (591,563), La Plata (404,129), and Mendoza (330,727).[17] Distances are social constructs and for immigrants from Argentina, where the first subway was inaugurated in 1913, the idea of living fifteen kilometers from the city would have been terrifying. Most were what locals called *bichos de ciudad* (lit., city bugs). Even those who migrated to the Tel Aviv area could not avoid noticing great differences between city life in Argentina and the urban environment in Israel.

In 1849 the Argentine writer Esteban Echeverria termed Buenos Aires "La Reina del Plata" and the expression became popular in 1923 when it was used in the tango titled "Buenos Aires," recorded by Carlos Gardel. From the last decades of the nineteenth century, thanks to booming ties related to the export of agricultural products to Europe, European architecture was imitated by the Argentine elites and still characterizes the capital's downtown area, including palaces and official buildings built in the classical style. The idea of Buenos Aires as a South American Paris infused the identity of Argentine city dwellers, especially those from the capital. The social, albeit not always demographic, prevalence of Argentines of white European origin in the national narrative strengthened this identity. Buenos Aires was considered a world-class metropolis, an idea that still held merit in the 1960s.

Despite economic upheavals, foreign investment in Argentina reached a historic high between 1958 and 1963 and, with the establishment of new companies, various cultural changes took place and consumption levels rose. In large cities vast sectors of the population gained access to new products; supermarkets and commercial enterprises proliferated during the 1960s, along with publications that incorporated English words and promoted products and cultural trends already popular in the United States. The middle class also enjoyed free access to higher education.[18] Interestingly, Buenos Aires became the source of the world's largest community of Freud followers.[19] Proud Argentines believed that Buenos Aires offered a sophistication equal to that of many European cities and, indeed, living standards during this period were much higher than those that would characterize the country in the decades to come.

In Israel prior to the Six-Day War, on the other hand, austerity prevailed and memories of the rationing period were still fresh. Within this context it is worth noting some significant differences between the two countries in terms of consumption patterns and urban and cultural landscapes. While Argentine TV broadcast for the first time in 1951 and private channels began operations in 1960, Israel National TV was inaugurated in 1966 and a second channel was launched only twenty years later. Construction on the residential thirty-one-story Kavanagh building in Buenos Aires, which included a central air-conditioning system, began in 1936; the building was the tallest in South America. In contrast, the Shalom Meir office tower, which was to be the highest in the Middle East at the time of construction, was built in Tel Aviv only in 1965. Local production and distribution of the iconic Coca Cola label began in Argentina in 1942, whereas it arrived in Israel only in 1968. When Israel signed its first contract for the installation of an automobile assembly plant in Ashdod, in 1960, Argentina was already producing cars locally and more than twenty multinational companies had set up plants there.[20] Moreover, Argentine immigrants' tastes and consumption patterns had been shaped by their country's relatively successful industrialization and cultural modernization. Saúl S., who emigrated from Buenos Aires to Haifa in 1965 and studied at the Technion recalled his impressions as follows: "We [students] had a very simple life; we would share an omelet and a half portion of French fries . . . but in the Israel of that time, we were all poor . . . The whole country was poor . . . people's clothing, possessions, their apartments. It was not typical to own a car; we all wore blue dress pants and a white shirt . . . In Argentina, those were good years and people used to live much better."[21]

Disregarding the accuracy of his examples, Saul's impression of the entire country as being poor and his focus on clothing style are revealing. Indeed, Argentine immigrants would often zero in on clothing, even decades later. According to historian Anat Helman, the austerity of the Yishuv, represented by

Srulik's clothes, reflected Zionism and the national ethos, as well as bearing the mark of Soviet ideas. Sophisticated dress, which had become prevalent in Western societies, was considered a form of consumerism, arousing moral criticism.[22] Israeli austerity, in contrast to Argentine prosperity, was also a recurrent motif among prospective returnees, who emphasized Argentina's cultural or economic standards, as detailed in the following letter sent to *Aurora* in 1966: "I did not come to Israel to make money: I worked for fifteen years in [Zionist] movements, disinterestedly, wasting precious time and a precious youth in false and cheap propaganda . . . I have tried everything, in all sorts of jobs. I suffered hunger . . . How should we explain to the gentleman at the JA that we come from a 'developed' country? Soon I will be among the yordim."[23] Noteworthy is the writer's ambiguous relationship to Zionism and contradictory statements regarding his material needs. His letter was probably a reaction to the accusation that Argentine emigrants lacked ideological commitment and were not content with the salaried jobs available.

Emigration from Israel put Zionist organizations and political party members on the defensive, and efforts to deflect blame proliferated.[24] The JA was under attack for the disproportion between the allegedly large number of representatives posted abroad and the small number of immigrants they inspired to come to Israel.[25] Moreover, the principle of unrestricted Jewish immigration began to be questioned, as some called for imposing selection criteria in addition to national belonging. In reaction, JA immigration department head Shragai, who was a religious Zionist, declared that critics who highlighted absorption problems and opposed unrestricted immigration were damaging the "sacred cause" and that the ingathering of "all Jews" included even "the old and the sick."[26] David Ben-Gurion also reiterated that immigration should be treated as Israel's main priority.[27] In the midst of this furor, those responsible for the absorption of Latin Americans continued to argue that emigrants were a minority. Their practical assessments were combined with ideological considerations. For example, OLEI president Moshe Kitron declared that "each yerida" was a "spiritual tragedy" but recognized the logic of those that had arrived last being the first to leave because of unemployment.[28] JA director Aryeh Pincus criticized press coverage of emigration, arguing that journalists had "no idea about the possible destructive effects of this kind of news in Latin America." However, he did not blame the emigrants, believing that the economy and cultural barriers played a critical role in their decision to leave.[29]

As has already been indicated, economic and cultural barriers indeed operated against Argentine acclimatization in Israel, and those who suffered most were probably the former self-employed who wanted to continue working as such. Considering the high proportion of self-employed Argentine immigrants within each of their main occupational groups (discussed in the previous chapter), they were also likely to be prominent among those leaving Israel, they were most likely the majority (recall table 1.9). Indeed, they became the focus of reports on Argentine returnees, which tended to refer to the middle class, to merchants, and/or to petty traders. Conversely, former salaried immigrants who had just enough to pay their bills probably had fewer expectations and, in some cases, did not even have enough funds to pay their tickets back to Argentina.

Even for native-born citizens, self-employment was more challenging than working for a salary. It typically required experience and a certain amount of capital or equipment. Therefore, at least prior to the digital era, it could be attained only later in life. In addition to job-related skills, self-employment required managerial and entrepreneurial knowledge normally acquired while working for someone else during early career stages.[30] Such knowledge was dependent on the social context and, therefore, an Argentine shoemaker, or carpenter, or engineer who expected to work independently had to relearn almost everything in Israel, a process complicated by the language barrier. Surveys of immigrants' command of Hebrew found that two years after their arrival only 42 percent claimed they were able to speak the language fluently, while 33 percent declared they could speak it haltingly.[31] However, younger salaried workers who performed simpler tasks might learn Hebrew and gain labor experience simultaneously. A return migrant who lived in Israel between 1963 and 1965 recalled his father's encounter with the Israeli reality: "It was very difficult for my father who had been a self-made man and had owned a pharmacy in Buenos Aires. He tried everything, but to own a pharmacy in Israel at that time was practically impossible. Everything was administered by the *kupot holim* [health insurance organizations] . . . it was even more difficult for someone without a diploma, as was the case for him. But he tried everything. He opened a bridal beauty salon, he worked in a bakery and made bread deliveries at sunrise, he worked in a butcher's shop later . . . nothing worked and we depleted our savings."[32]

After the family's return to Argentina the father in the story just related opened a new pharmacy. The majority of immigrants were young professionals, salaried workers, and people with their own small businesses and were vulnerable to economic recession and currency devaluation but had experienced relative prosperity and cultural modernization in Argentina. In Israeli emigration reports, they were referred to as middle-class people unprepared to lower their living standards and lacking sufficient Zionist motivation. Their material situation might or might not improve in Argentina after their return, but at least they could speak Spanish, take the subway to enjoy the theater downtown, and stay close to their loved ones. Argentines who decided to leave Israel for their birthplace during the 1960s, and whose experiences are described in the next pages, had more in common with Mafalda than with Srulik.

## URBAN AND AGRICULTURAL CHALLENGES: ASHDOD AND MOSHAV KOCHAV MICHAEL SOBELL

Following the creation of the State of Israel, geographers and professionals from many other disciplines were involved in planning and building the new country.[33] Aiming to achieve the highest results at the national-collective level in the long term, the government applied a policy that required acquiescence at the individual level in the short term. In order to settle the country, the state committed itself to "population dispersal," which meant, in reality, assigning migrants to specific locations within Israel.[34] Most Argentine migrants who arrived in Israel during the peak period of 1963 accepted their allotted destinations without resistance. Almost two-thirds of this group started their life in Israel in kibbutzim and development zones while the remaining third settled in big cities or in the center of the country.[35] However, the immigrants' departure rate from kibbutzim was high, as most went there only for an initial period in order to learn the language. Attracting the attention of policymakers, Zionist leaders, and the press, most of the Argentines who left Israel in 1966 had settled in new development areas. Table 2.2 reflects how the kibbutz served as a short-term first home for immigrants who then departed in large numbers, compared with new arrivals in general.

Many Argentines tried to continue their imported petit bourgeois lifestyle in Ashdod, which was designed by Israel's early urban planners as a "development town." The purpose of such settlements was to provide jobs and housing while also helping to decentralize Israel's industrial capacity, thereby enhancing the country's economic resilience in the event of war. Two limitations soon became evident, however: a low standard of infrastructure and poorly chosen locations.[36] Israel continued working to improve the towns' designs but overlapping

**Table 2.2. Arrivals and Departures from Kibbutzim in 1966 and 1967, by Number of Families, Family Members, and Singles**

| | | All Immigrants | | | | Latin American | | | |
|---|---|---|---|---|---|---|---|---|---|
| Year | Status | Fam. | Fam. mem. | Single | **Total** | Fam. | Fam. mem. | Single | **Total** |
| 1966 | **Arrived** | 84 | 222 | 237 | **459** | 73 | 193 | 97 | **290** |
| | **Left** | 107 | 231 | 107 | **353** | 69 | 231 | 11 | **242** |
| 1967 | **Arrived** | 99 | 267 | 350 | **617** | 76 | 204 | 158 | **362** |
| | **Left** | 66 | 201 | 19 | **220** | 31 | 101 | 6 | **107** |

Source: *20 Years of Aliyah and Absorption* (Tel Aviv: Jewish Agency's Unit for Publications and Demography, 1968), 17, ISA, 3497/9.

administrations also created problems. Specifically, the towns were administered by the Housing Ministry, population targets were set by the Interior Ministry, and immigrants were overseen by the JA, which led to misinformation, competing agendas, and bureaucratic complications.[37]

Ashdod was founded in 1956 and its port, expected to become the gateway for the country's export of agricultural products, began operations in 1965.[38] By the time Argentine immigrants began arriving, the road to Jerusalem was functioning, but the one to Tel Aviv in the north was still in the planning phases, while the link to Beersheba and the Negev in the southeast was only partly built. Originally, the city was planned for ten thousand residents, but there were more than fifteen thousand in 1963 and over thirty thousand by 1966. Ashdod attracted several industries: in 1966, the largest factory employed more than four hundred workers; the Leyland truck assembly plant, two hundred; two diamond-cutting plants, two hundred; and six smaller plants engaged a total of two hundred workers.[39]

Ashdod has been presented in academic works as a case study of social integration in multicultural cities because of the egalitarian neighborhoods it proposed, which were intended to foster cross-cultural awareness and understanding between communities.[40] While the original project envisioned schools and commercial centers as the geographic center for the gathering of the various groups, the successive housing programs created competition between secondary areas. During the 1960s Ashdod's main ethnic split was between Jews from European countries and those from Arab countries. European Jews took over the white-collar share of the job market and Mizrahi Jews, originally from Middle Eastern countries and often referred to pejoratively as "black Jews," concentrated on factories and manual labor.[41] It has been argued that social differences in new towns tend to disappear when the economy is good.[42] The case of Ashdod during the economic recession of 1966 suggests that the opposite is also true: in times of hardship, social cleavages are exacerbated.

In early 1965, *Aurora*, quoting *Haaretz*, reported that Argentine immigrants from Ashdod were leaving Israel.[43] In September, an article on Argentine immigrants appeared in *Haaretz*. Noting that a thousand of them lived in Ashdod, the largest Argentine concentration in Israel, the article claimed that the role anti-Semitism in Argentina played in their immigration had been "exaggerated."[44] Moreover, many middle- and lower-middle-class immigrants complained they had been misled by JA emissaries and had arrived with expectations of owning a business. The loans provided by the JA were insufficient and, because of the surge of immigration during the previous years, housing and rent costs had escalated. Among the prospective Argentine returnees the journalist interviewed were a former accounting director who worked as an unskilled laborer in a factory until he got fed up; a former independent building contractor who refused to work as a construction worker and depleted his savings within six months; and twenty families who lost everything they had brought with them when the *Atzmaut* ran aground and their containers were flooded. The article continued, "It is difficult for them to adapt to Israel. They do not know how to push, beg, and plead and stand on their own. Life in Argentina was easy and here they feel helpless and hopeless. Despite Ashdod's dynamic development, the lack of employment is felt in town . . . The small trader from Argentina does not want to work because in Israel he has to toil in an industrial plant. He wants to perform the same job he did there and he can't."[45]

Interestingly, the *Haaretz* journalist believed Argentine immigration was motivated by a rational choice based on economic expectations rather than Zionism or anti-Semitism. At the same time, her characterization of the returnees enjoying an "easy life" in Argentina and being incapable of "standing on their own" reflected the dominant Zionist notion of the new Israeli Jew as being stronger than the Diaspora Jew. Be that as it may, by the end of 1965, unemployment was not the only motive for discontent among Argentines in Ashdod; they also organized public protests against "inadequate living conditions" due to the lack of paved streets and a plague of rats in the Vav neighborhood.

Excessive bureaucracy and a lack of information repeatedly surfaced as the main topic of immigrants' complaints. Pinchas Shamir, a JA envoy to Chile and Uruguay, pointed out that Latin Americans were not used to the vast net of regulations and the need for permits to open a business in Israel. In their countries, he said, there was less order but also less bureaucracy.[46] Seeking to deflect blame, JA representatives in the city believed that the problem was due to carelessness in the selection of immigrants. In their view, there were two groups: people inculcated with Zionism, and those who lacked "a bit of idealism" and were prone to return to their country of origin "in the face of initial obstacles."[47] Those responsible for immigrant absorption in Israel tended to blame the rate of return on the migrants and those in charge of their recruitment in Argentina. The JA director for Western immigration, Reuven Golan, lamented the lack of "chalutzim spirit" among immigrants who were unprepared to invest three years in adaptation and expected the state to provide them with a home, a business, and a lifestyle similar to the one they had enjoyed prior to immigrating.[48]

In early 1966 Argentine emigration from Ashdod appeared as a headline in *Aurora*. Teodoro Ducach, a journalist whose coverage of emigration from Israel made him an unpopular figure within Zionist circles, compared the returnees from Israel with the Italians who returned from Argentina in the previous century, arguing that in both cases no one cared about them.[49] He criticized OLEI and the JA, which reported that 18 percent of Argentine immigrants had returned. Ducach described how Ashdod had been presented to Latin American communities during an exhibition that toured the continent in 1963: "The pictures of wide, beautiful avenues and the modern buildings of Ashdod made a deep impression. The JA emissaries enthusiastically registered thousands of candidates without any selection. The whole truth about Ashdod was not told. No one mentioned whether [it] was suited to the absorption of [people] without a profession or to those lacking the minimum capital to open a workshop or a small factory."[50] By September, several articles had appeared about Latin American emigration from Israel in general, and Argentines from Ashdod, in particular. Many versions circulated about their numbers, and immigrant absorption workers were reluctant to accept the figures given in the press reports but were unable to provide any themselves. Shragai, the JA's immigration department head, wrote to Cygel, director of the absorption department, "I was told that during the last week the prime minister met with Ashdod's city council and was informed that from January 1, 1966, to September 1, 1966, yordim from Ashdod included 422 families, meaning over 1,500 people. I do not believe that these figures are accurate."[51]

Cygel's reply arrived two months later. In it, he differentiated between self-declared emigrants and temporary departees. However, he recognized that many in the second group were "not going to return due to the prevailing job-related situation."[52] According to his estimation, at least nine hundred people originally from Europe, Latin America, Morocco, and Tunisia had emigrated from Ashdod. Indeed, the impact of the economic recession on Ashdod's immigrant population was public knowledge by 1966. At the beginning of that year, the city's port workers had organized a prolonged strike.[53] Ashdod and other development towns experienced violent clashes during the May 1 celebrations, when the police repressed worker demonstrations in support of those fired from the Leyland plant, which had implemented a massive redundancy plan.[54] The scene of mounted police quelling workers was already familiar to Argentines. However, the sight of banners with the inscription "Work for Olim" was new.[55]

Argentine emigration from Israel due to unemployment did not surprise those who believed that the immigrants had been driven to Israel by the Argentine recession. Ducach noted sarcastically that after the middle class became bankrupt, "they turned into Zionists, people who had never before considered Aliyah, remembered the Jewish state, and gripped it like a lifeboat." The emissaries' propaganda had done its part.[56]

While the majority of those who returned to Argentina did so because they failed in their attempts to continue their independent occupations, this was not the only cause of return. Kochav Michael Sobell (Kochav), a moshav located between Ashkelon and Kiryat Gat, was populated entirely by Argentines in 1963 after the Brazilian ship *Princess Leopoldina* brought 514 immigrants from Latin America. They were welcomed by JA representatives Yehuda Dominitz and Ben Zion Fixler. Thirty-six Argentine families had arrived to settle the abandoned moshav.[57] On a moshav, a type of settlement conceived by former kibbutz members who rejected the excessive intimacy of the communal environment, each family owns their own parcel of land.[58] Here, collective production and administration do not undermine the preeminent role of the family unit and individual freedom.

The Argentine group at Kochav was composed of young professionals and educated people without agricultural experience who had begun organizing their immigration in 1962. Another ten families arrived in December. They were taken straight from the port to Kiryat Gat, where they undertook a one-month agricultural training program that included instructive visits around the country.[59] Once on the moshav, each family received a fifty-four-square-meter house with two bedrooms and a living room. The collective compound included a renovated cultural center donated by Michael Sobell, a British Zionist whose name was given to the new settlement. At the beginning, the settlers worked for a salary paid by the JA, which also provided tractors, horses, and training. Forty people labored producing jute bags while the others engaged in agriculture and raising livestock. Additionally, nine Argentines invested in the project and a co-operative of equal shareholders was created.

Dov Feldman arrived with the first group, at the age of twelve. He had taken part in a movement that, under the name Ikar HaOved (peasant worker), met in Argentina to study Hebrew prior to their immigration. Most of the group consisted of families with two or three children but there were also five single people. Dov never forgot the experience aboard the *Princess Leopoldina*, including its luxurious salons, the fun atmosphere created by youth groups, and the ports of call during its three-week voyage. His parents had worked as photographers in Buenos Aires. In an interview for this book, Dov recalled his first impressions and provided an idea of the hard work that Argentines were willing to do while also conserving some of their habitual living standards: "The houses were not yet ready when we arrived; [those from the previous moshav] were being renovated. The men helped to clean the terrain in the last stage of construction and had established one condition for coming to the moshav: bathrooms inside the homes."[60]

Indeed, many kibbutzim and immigrant settlements shared outside bathrooms. The establishment of the new Argentine moshav was part of the Kiryat Gat regional plan of 1954. The fertile region between Tel Aviv and Beersheba was envisioned as integrating rural and urban settlements. A net of villages, each comprising between eighty and one hundred families, would surround a "rural service center," whose function would be the provision of schools, youth centers, health services, shopping areas, and markets. Kiryat Gat was created as the regional urban center for all rural service centers and was expected to provide industry, administration, and services.[61] Kochav was part of this project and two years after their arrival, as was agreed, the Argentines became full members, at which point each family received thirteen dunams (about nine hundred square meters) of land. However, they soon discovered that agricultural production from the land was not enough to cover their needs and many continued working for a salary.

In 1965 the Israeli press mentioned Kochav only in regard to an amusing anecdote. Lacking a ballot box for its board elections, the members used the national mailbox. They had to wait until the next day to do the counting because only the postman had a key to open it.[62] However, the next press reference in mid-1966 was not at all amusing. An article reported that "many" families from Kochav had decided to return to Argentina in August and another eight families planned to follow them in December. Raanan Weitz, director of the JA's settlement department, declared that he was aware of only perhaps four such families; he lamented their decision, adding that the issue was not a simple one. "It is difficult to move from an easy life in Argentina, with cheap services and where there is no need to work hard, to a life in Israel, even with the special and comfortable conditions that the Department for Settlement created at Moshav Kochav. This emigration will not affect the rest of the residents who know why they came to Israel and have considered the issue in the long term."[63]

Weitz's mention of an "easy life" in Argentina reflected a common belief at the time; such a perspective on the reasons for the Argentine decision to return propped up Zionist values and their image of the ideal Israeli as the new Jew ready to work hard and make sacrifices, a model not attainable by all prospective immigrants. In the Argentine province of Córdoba, the news about Kochav prompted the JA emissary there to ask for additional information about what had happened to cause the families to leave Israel.[64] The answer he received was as follows: "It is known that they received good absorption conditions, were not socially isolated, and their economic situation had been consolidated . . . So it seems that the main reasons for their emigration were their poor physical shape for agricultural and physical work and their desire to return to the 'pot of meat.'"[65]

The JA representative's stigmatization of Argentine immigrants contrasted strongly to the virtues of those who persisted in working for the Zionist enterprise. Moreover, the use of the biblical expression "pot of meat," referring to Jews who preferred to be slaves in Egypt as long as they were given food, lent this argument stronger ideological support.[66] Without blaming the migrants, *Aurora* also referred to the emigration from Kochav, while in Buenos Aires the Argentine biweekly *La Luz* reproduced the information originally provided by *Haaretz*.[67] In March 1967 the moshav factory at Kochav was in a critical situation, and *Maariv*, in a full-page feature, claimed that fourteen families had returned to Argentina. According to the reporter, this demonstrated that the agricultural sector and the kibbutzim were also "suffering yerida" due to the recession. Here, too, the secretary of the moshav repeated the common notion about the returnees: “The yordim returned to Argentina due to homesickness and the search for a pot of meat.”[68]

His declaration combined the narratives of both sides. He referred to the homesickness of his fellow Argentines without elaborating; no doubt he understood their feelings himself. However, his reference to the “pot of meat” incorporated the hegemonic view: the moshav secretary was an Argentine immigrant, but he was also becoming a Zionist Israeli. A deeper explanation of how the moshav members viewed those who left is provided by Dov who, as a teenager experienced the change of country, language, and culture as an adventure but was also very conscious of the hard work of his parents and how difficult it was for two photographers to adapt to their new jobs. Discussing the returnees, he said, “There were six or seven families that got scared before the war and left. Many were [our] relatives, they left family here [at the moshav], so they were understood . . . There were problems, not everyone adapted, it was difficult.”[69]

While Dov’s narration demonstrates empathy for moshav members who decided to leave, his memories merged two different groups of returnees into a single story. In fact, all the emigrations mentioned here in reference to this moshav occurred during the economic recession of 1966, but Dov’s reference to members “scared before the war” relates to a different event. Five moshav heads of households sent their families to Argentina in 1967 before the Six-Day War, claiming that they were going back only for a visit. They themselves served in the military during the conflict but then left their homes, carrying everything that they could take, including JA property. They used a stolen stamp from the moshav to buy items with falsified checks and obtain credit from a bank. Then, they traveled as stowaways on a cargo vessel from Ashdod and were detained in Barcelona for traveling illegally.[70]

Nevertheless, despite the press coverage and the attention given to the Kochav Argentines’ experiences in Israel, those who left were a minority. In 1970 Kochav was presented as an “example of a successful aliyah” and another twenty-five families were recruited in Argentina. Altogether seventy-seven Argentine families settled in Kochav; their industry had proved successful, and the opening of a new polypropylene factory was on course.[71] The moshav had consolidated its economic progress and even opened its own kindergarten.[72] An article about its history celebrated its “thorns becoming flowers,” as Kochav’s blooms represented an important share of total Israeli flower exports from 1969. Difficult times had passed and those who left were not forgotten. “Many members of the first group . . . abandoned Israel; they could not overcome the first blows, the first mistakes, and the first illusions quickly discarded. They abandoned the moshav in a bitter moment for those that remained, knocking against an iron block . . . a group of Argentines that may not speak fluent Hebrew but succeeded like the first chalutzim from the 1900s.”[73]

The returnees became part of the narrative that constituted the identity of those who remained in Israel. For some to be pioneers, others need to be left behind. By 1971 absorption in moshavim was presented as a successful option, with Kochav as a model.[74]

## A DISSONANT VOICE IN BUENOS AIRES: THE BIWEEKLY *LA LUZ*

In Argentina, a unique source reported on return migration from Israel: the magazine *La Luz*. In fact, *La Luz* had been reporting on Argentine returnees from Israel for several decades; the publication's director had a personal connection to the issue. *La Luz* was a biweekly, twenty-four-page magazine founded in 1931 by David Elnecavé, who was born in Turkey and claimed to have rabbinical roots in Toledo. The name of the magazine referred to Genesis 1:3, "Let there be light," and its purpose was to promote "Jewish values, Zionism and a critical view of Jewish institutions."[75]

The founder's son, Nissim, became the director of *La Luz* in 1955. He had migrated to Palestine from Turkey with his wife, Bruria, and lived on Kibbutz Mesilot. According to Bruria's memoir, which describes the rusticity of kibbutz accommodation and infrastructure, she did not adapt well to living conditions there.[76] Consequently, in 1938 the couple joined the rest of the family in Argentina. Nissim Elnecavé's first article from Buenos Aires stated, "I was in Palestine, not as a tourist . . . No! I was one of those many settlers that are building the new homeland."[77] He also worked as the Latin American correspondent for the British *Jewish Chronicle*, became president of the federation of Sephardic organizations, and was among the founders of *Nueva Sion*, Hashomer Hatzair's newspaper.[78] Under his direction, *La Luz* began to criticize the JA regarding Argentine immigration even before the departure of the *Flaminia* in 1963; the magazine would continue to do so for years to come. Elnecavé recurrently put forward the arguments that Israel was not ready to absorb middle-class immigrants; that the JA did not have a strategic plan to deal with them; that its emissaries were mere propagandists; and that Jewish Argentine leaders acquiesced to the Israeli emissaries, disregarding their community's interests.

*La Luz*'s reporting stood in stark contrast to that of the other Spanish-language Jewish Argentine publications, which followed the Zionist editorial line of refusing to cover the issue of return migration. Elnecavé's stance led to his involvement in several controversies. For example, before the departure of the *Flaminia*, Elnecavé argued that the JA had neglected the "permanent interests of Argentine Judaism" by chartering the ship instead of using a regular liner. In his view, the JA was trying to create an atmosphere of "Argentine exodus," evoking images of ships that brought refugees and Holocaust survivors to Palestine. Such a goal, he argued, was dangerous because it could create "panic" in the Jewish community. Elnecavé asserted that the JA was using methods employed with immigrants from Algeria, without acknowledging that Argentine immigrants were different. Further, he complained about the "secrecy" regarding Jewish Argentine migration figures.[79] Indeed, prior to the Six-Day War, Zionist-dominated Jewish Argentine organizations did not publish figures and maintained a very low profile regarding the emigration issue.

In another article, Elnecavé referred to "incompetence" in organizing middle-class immigration and praised the "Union of Immigrants from Britain in Israel" for their complaints about it. He referred to "taboos" imposed on the Jewish community of Argentina regarding discussion about immigration to Israel. When it came to the *Flaminia*, he added, there had been opposition to the use of "catastrophic" symbolism within Argentine Zionist circles. Nonetheless, in the end the local leadership agreed to follow the Israeli line.[80] Within this context, Elnecavé denounced "constant pressure by local Jewish institutions" to silence the spread of news about immigration figures and returnees.[81] Not surprisingly, the magazine aroused enmity within Zionist organizations. When Yitzhak Kurland, director of the JA's economics department for Israel and the Diaspora, visited Argentina and held a press conference in Buenos Aires, *La Luz* covered the event, while making clear that its reporters had not been invited and denouncing the "boycott."[82] In an open letter to Emilio Gutkin, president of the Zionist Organization of Argentina (ZOA), Elnecavé argued that *La Luz* reported on Jewish immigration to Israel as part of its commitment to issues of public interest.[83]

Two weeks after the open letter to Gutkin, the magazine noted that during his visit to Argentina, JA chairman Moshe Sharett, a former Israeli prime minister and foreign minister, had received a cable from the *Jewish Chronicle* asking him to mediate in the "conflict" between the local branch of the Zionist organization and *La Luz*. Elnecavé explained that the "boycott" and the "economic sanctions" against his publication resulted from news printed in the magazine that the organization disliked. Thanks to Sharett's intervention, he added, *La Luz* had agreed to end the dispute as long as it would "not harm its right to free speech."[84] This mediation could have been one of the reasons that from that moment to October 1964 the magazine criticized Zionist actions only twice and even then the journalist focused on JA emissaries in Buenos Aires rather than on Israel's immigration policy. The other reason could have been the fact that no other episode like the departure of the *Flaminia* took place. It is also evident that Elnecavé used his connections in the *Jewish Chronicle* to make his case and that there was a certain degree of vanity in his exposing the "conflict."

In the period between the conflict's settlement and October 1964, Elnecavé then wrote that "local Zionist authorities" were "monopolized" by JA emissaries whose number and salaries in Argentina were "fantastic" even though they were unprepared to do their job. He considered their methods to be inappropriate and lacking in understanding of Argentine lifestyles.[85] In another article, he claimed that several years earlier, a stream of emissaries had arrived in the Argentine community, wasting financial resources due to their overlapping activities and undefined goals. In addition, in his view the emissaries repeated antiquated messages without inspiring the masses, expounding "mere routine" and "propagandistic vociferation unable to convince anyone." Asserting that the emissaries were just bureaucrats lacking credibility, Elnecavé demanded that local leaders muster up the courage to reject some of them.[86]

Apart from the mentioned critiques, the first explicit reference in *La Luz* to Argentine emigration from Israel appeared in August 1965 when the magazine mentioned "rumors about many returnees." In November Elnecavé claimed the return rate could reach 60 percent of those that had arrived in Israel since 1963.[87] A week previously, he had published a similar claim in the British publication the *Jewish Chronicle*, but without sources to support it. He wrote, "The feeling now prevails here that the Agency lacks the experience and know-how to deal with middle-class immigrants from the West."[88] Elnecavé's article in the British press and his inclusion of the Argentine case within the wider categories of "Western" and "middle class" generated an international reaction. A week after it appeared, Shragai sent an annotated copy to Schneier Levenberg, a JA representative in London, in which he rejected the figures and described Elnecavé as someone who "appears in newspapers writing against Zionism and the State of Israel."[89] In a letter to another colleague in Israel, Shragai wrote, "At the last board meeting, articles of journalist Elnecavé, from the newspaper *La Luz* [actually a magazine], published in the *Jewish Chronicle* . . . were discussed. [They] are not the first. This newspaper [*La Luz*] frequently publishes articles against the Zionist Organization. On the other hand, I heard that your unit provides financial support to this newspaper. If this is correct, I do not think this support is appropriate."[90]

Recalling that Elnecavé had previously denounced a boycott against him, Shragai's messages suggest that Jewish organizations, both in Israel and Argentina, had in fact avoided advertising in *La Luz* or cooperating with it due to its criticism.[91] The article in the *Jewish Chronicle* prompted Gutkin to send a letter to the British newspaper. "Sir," he wrote, "in your November 5th issue there was an incorrect report about Argentine immigrants leaving Israel . . . We believe that the information you gave is untimely and certainly inappropriate." The letter was published by the newspaper, together with a comment by its editor William Frankel. The latter considered Gutkin to be "mistaken" and believed "it would be foolish" to overlook the problems encountered by many of the immigrants.[92] Later, Elnecavé admitted the inaccuracy of his figures, claiming that the "taboo" against emigration and a lack of information had forced him to rely on "rumors."[93]

Intensifying its criticism, in 1966 *La Luz* published a total of twenty-four articles on absorption problems and return migration from Israel, thirteen of which referred directly to Latin American return migration. In addition, two caricatures mocked the JA and the balance of Israeli immigration-emigration. The information regarding return migration from Israel was extracted partly from the Israeli press but also elaborated by *La Luz*'s own correspondents. For example, the magazine's reporters described ships departing from Haifa, discussions at OLEI conventions, and stowaways escaping from Ashdod. Such reports were well-known to the Israeli public but did not circulate abundantly in the Argentine press or within Jewish Argentine organizations. Therefore, the focus on Argentine returnees in editorials and articles written by *La Luz* correspondents, and the fact that the rest of the Jewish Argentine press in Spanish remained silent about the issue, made *La Luz* a special case. In addition, the polemical character of its editor, his willingness to exaggerate occasionally, and his own experience in Palestine before the creation of the State of Israel contributed to turning *La Luz* into a prominent source of criticism of the JA. A polemicist had found a controversial topic that allowed him to become a notable player on the Jewish international political scene. Claiming the high value of aliyah but criticizing its practical application in relation to the local Jewish community and Israel itself, Nissim Elnecavé adopted a very particular position within the constellation of Jewish Argentine public discourse. At the same time, the magazine published announcements about the arrival of new immigrants in Israel, celebrated the aliyah of Sephardic Zionist groups, and received advertising from the Israeli company ZIM. During this period, the magazine also held public debates with other Jewish Argentine newspapers and organizations.

In February 1966 Raya Yaglom, director of the Women's International Zionist Organization (WIZO), translated into English an article published in *La Luz* titled "Latin Americans Are Leaving Israel" and sent it to Shragai.[94] She added the following comment: "*La Luz* . . . has a wide readership. Articles like this can cause serious harm to aliyah and Zionist affairs in general."[95] Concerned, Shragai circulated the message among his colleagues.[96] Further along these lines, *La Luz* interviewed Nicolas Goldberg, a former Zionist leader who was planning to return to Argentina to launch a campaign about the "real situation" in Israel. It also reported on the southern city of Ashdod, where unemployment was high and Argentine immigrants were "disappointed about their aliyah and humiliated socially."[97] In addition, Elnecavé criticized use of the term *yored* because of its moral implications; he also lambasted the policy of territorial dispersion applied to Latin American immigrants, relaying accounts of "aggressive scenes" on board the ships due to immigrants' reluctance to accept their assigned destinations.[98]

The magazine also quoted Duvdevany, director general of the JA's immigration department, who labeled Elnecavé an "anti-Zionist."[99] Elnecavé responded to Duvdevany by arguing that the "anti-Zionist" label was the answer of official Zionist representatives to those whose opinions differed from their own.[100] Throughout 1967 *La Luz* published a total of nine critical articles, five of which were related directly to return migration and were published before the Six-Day War. Following the war, the magazine continued its criticism of the JA by claiming that everything done regarding middle-class immigration had been "mere improvisation;" in the same article, the correspondent in Israel described JA employees as lazy.[101] In October Elnecavé sent a letter to Shragai arguing that middle-class aliyah was being handled badly, on the basis of "standards for refugees." "I am . . . asking here your emissaries to tell me what your actual program for middle-class aliyah is," he wrote. "Literally, no one is able to answer . . . Did you seriously think that people are ready to leave their homes, parents, friends, economic status, only because Israel needs aliyah? . . . where are the proper arguments without mere propaganda?[102]

Elnecavé's understanding of the Israeli reality, his professional correspondents there, and his position as Latin American correspondent for the *Jewish Chronicle* allowed him to become an outspoken element on the Jewish international scene. There is no doubt that the term *yored* would have had personal resonance with him due to the three years he spent in Palestine. Although that experience in undeveloped 1930s Jewish Palestine remained embedded in his memory and might have influenced his opinion of 1960s Israel, it did provide him with the basis to criticize Israel and its policies. Still, most of his magazine's information regarding the return from Israel was not substantially different from that of the Israeli press. In general, Elnecavé's most extreme criticism regarding immigration could be interpreted as a reaction to Zionist negation of the Diaspora. Over the years, the editor of *La Luz* argued that the Jewish Diaspora and Israel's interests were not always identical, and although he defined himself as a "Zionist from the cradle," he had decided to live in Argentina.[103] He did so assuming a Jewish Argentine identity that entitled him to free speech. The fact that the magazine was based financially on the contributions of its readers and advertisers indicates that there was an audience willing to receive such a perspective. Its consistent focus on the returnees, and the fact that the rest of the Jewish Argentine press in Spanish remained silent on the issue, made *La Luz* a conspicuous and unique voice.

As can be seen, cultural and economic differences between Argentina and Israel produced a gap between migrants' expectations and reality. This discrepancy became noticeable after their unprecedented mass arrival in 1963 and would reach its zenith in 1966 during the Israeli recession. The next chapter focuses on how economic hardships made debt a relevant factor that would push the migrants away from Israel. It recreates a return trip on board a ship crowded with Argentines and analyzes how a portion of them moved to Israel a second time toward and after 1969, when the Israeli economy was skyrocketing and Argentina was experiencing another of its cyclical downturns.

# 3

# ECONOMIC ADVERSITIES

## The 1966 Israeli Recession and the 1969 Argentine Cordobazo

Because most Argentine immigrants did not have considerable savings, some of them, especially those who wanted to open a business, incurred excessive debts, which they feared they would be unable to repay. As a result, stories—both accurate and exaggerated—circulated of Argentines leaving Israel without paying their arrears. For this reason, JA officials supervising the departure of ships from Israel to Latin America tried to unmask people who were pretending to go on holiday but were in fact leaving the country. This chapter provides further insight into how emigration was perceived by Israeli society and experienced by its protagonists, offering a discussion of the departure of the *Jerusalem* as a vivid example of the ways in which Argentines in Israel confronted their failure to succeed in their new country. We will follow the returnees to Argentina only to discover that, in a cruel twist, history turned the tables on those who had tried to escape the Israeli recession. After the Six-Day War, a golden period began in Israel while Argentina experienced a new period of economic, political, and social upheaval. Armed now with firsthand experience of both countries, some of the returnees in Argentina decided to relocate again to Israel.

### "TO PAY OR NOT TO PAY": INDEBTED MIGRANTS AND STOWAWAY STORIES

On December 5, 1965, the front pages of Buenos Aires newspapers covered the impressive success of NASA's Gemini VII mission, whose crew spent almost fourteen days in orbit; Charles de Gaulle's chances in France's presidential elections; and the football matches played over the weekend, during which fans celebrated the victory of Boca Juniors against Chacarita, 1–0. Summer had almost arrived and, like any other Sunday in the capital city of Argentina, *porteños* were enjoying a well-needed rest. Many had overslept and, while still in bed, heard the church bells breaking the tranquility of their residential neighborhoods.

Later, many would share traditional Italian pasta with their families or enjoy a variety of meats at a day-long asado (barbeque), which would end with maté and *facturas* (pastries). While the day did not stand out as unusual for most Argentines, one family, in particular, would remember it well. A sick man and his family waited for their only daughter to arrive from Israel.

In Israel, the day had begun six hours earlier. Sunday was the first working day of the week, and winter was coming. Marta Toronchik had received the ticket sent by her family and boarded a ship in Haifa in the hope of visiting her ailing father. She was twenty-one years old and had migrated to Israel aboard the *Theodor Herzl* in 1960. She had studied Hebrew in Kibbutz Mesilot, lived in Kibbutz Ruchama, completed her army service, and lived in Tel Aviv. To her surprise, while waiting for the ship to depart on that Sunday morning, she was ordered to disembark by border police because of a court order sent in response to a JA representative's request. The authorities claimed that Marta was planning to emigrate without honoring her commitments to the JA. Indeed, like many other immigrants assisted by the JA, the day she arrived in Israel she had signed a document assuming the cost of the ticket from Argentina as a debt to be repaid. The debt amounted to $185 (IL555) and in order to be allowed to leave she was required to repay it in full. Although the order was rescinded a couple of days later, it was a very uncomfortable episode, with Marta's lawyer questioning the validity of her signature on the original document because she was under the age of eighteen when she signed it.

Although Marta's case was reported by Jewish magazines in Argentina and Brazil, it was not at all typical.[1] Young Marta appeared to be a victim of the overreaction of a system which, having noticed the consequences of a lax policy of enforcing debt collection, was trying to strengthen its control, resulting in an innocent person paying for the sins of others. As previous chapters have shown, after mass Argentine immigration peaked in 1963, Israeli immigration and absorption professionals came to notice the phenomenon of return migration; with awareness came an effort to observe and measure the return rate in order to find ways to curb it. Debt emerged as an important instrument in this regard.

The Commission to Stop the Yerida of Latin American Olim, created as a temporary interdepartmental body dedicated to examining particular cases, mostly debt-related, held its first meeting as early as January 1964. David Ziman, representing the JA's absorption department, submitted a proposal that located the problem in the immigrants' expectations and the absorption system's weaknesses. On the one hand, immigrants wanted to own a business but, lacking the necessary capital, had tried to set up shop based exclusively on loans. On the other hand, a large number of uncoordinated entities were providing credit without a serious investigation into immigrants' abilities to repay it. Ziman believed that immigrants should "give up" their desire to own an independent business and find either a salaried job or a position as a small artisan, without "troubling themselves and others" with excessive loans. In addition, the state and the JA should prioritize the regulation of future loans and not focus solely on migrants who were planning to leave the country. Ziman's recommendations were accepted by his colleagues, with Mr. Fains, OLEI's representative to the commission, adding that many immigrants were in debt not only on their own behalf but as third-party guarantors for other people's loans.[2]

The commission agreed on a JA-OLEI joint effort to gather information about problematic cases and interview people to discuss possible solutions.[3] Nevertheless, it is not clear how systematically the commission pursued its goals.[4] There were difficulties coordinating the commission, and disagreements about its structure and scope.[5] In early 1966 discussions about the need for better coordination still continued.[6] Two years after the creation of the commission, legal aspects related to unpaid debts were not even clear to those who were in charge of the problem. For example, Moshe Kitron, OLEI's president, wrote to JA director Aryeh Pincus asking about the responsibilities of those who signed as guarantors for a passage paid by the JA to a third person.[7] Finally, the commission's composition as an ad hoc body, which suffered from frequent membership changes, made it difficult to turn decisions into coherent policies.[8]

Within this context, the problem of debt-ridden immigrants became a public affair of dramatic proportions, combining true stories and sensationalism. Spanning the years 1965 and 1966, in an atmosphere of severe economic deterioration, reports of the illegal emigration of people as stowaways proliferated in the press and attracted the attention of JA representatives. Historian Tom Segev noted that the case of two immigrants from Argentina who fled Israel in 1966 as stowaways led to a series of articles expressing understanding of the difficulties that Latin American immigrants faced in Israel and "indirectly in their decision to leave": "'One of the key factors leading to desperation among these immigrants is an almost daily trampling [in Israel] of the dignity and pride they felt in their countries of origin,' wrote *Haaretz*. Other papers adopted a similarly self-accusatory tone. 'We do not accept immigrants living among us,' concluded *Maariv*, and *Yedioth Ahronoth* attributed emigration to the contrast between the ideal world the immigrants had hoped to find in Israel and the reality they discovered."[9]

These arguments did not address the key issue of the stowaway phenomenon: if Israel was a democratic state, why would a person need to leave illegally? The answer lies in the debts that immigrants had acquired with the JA and, in extreme cases, the lack of funds to purchase a return ticket to Argentina. On August 20, 1965, Shragai sent a letter to the chief of police, Benchor Shitrit, asking for a response to an article in *Haaretz* the day before that reported on "large illegal emigration" of immigrants from Argentina. According to the article, indebted immigrants had managed to arrange their escape in a bizarre manner, which was nevertheless credible enough for Shragai to request the following: "I would . . . appreciate it if you could assign someone to investigate . . . fishing boats off the coast of Ashdod that smuggle olim from the country."[10] The chief of police responded, nearly two months later, "There is no truth in the news about the escape of yordim on fishing boats. Just imagine the risks the captain would take in accepting escaped travelers onto his ship mid-sea in the eyes of his crew and passengers."[11]

Considering the length of time Shitrit took to respond to Shragai's inquiry, it appears that he undertook an investigation of the issue. Whether urban myth or reality, the boat escapes were noted in *Aurora* and appeared again in the news eight months later when a *Hayom* journalist wrote about Latin American emigration, giving ample space to the issue of debt.[12] For example, a young woman who had borrowed money to rent her apartment compared the JA's loans to a "bear hug." Others argued that when they took out loans disproportional to their income they had been told that their signature was a mere formality that would not impede them from leaving the country. According to the article, a group of young immigrants had concocted an "original" way to avoid their debts. Their plan was to rent a dilapidated boat and navigate "secretly" to Cyprus. One of them declared, "We have no other alternative, even though we do not like to evade our debts. There is no other way to pay back the Jewish Agency for the fantastic tales that they told us in Argentina and with which they brought us here."[13]

This kind of justification came from young people who were undoubtedly immature and unprepared to take on responsibility for the loans they received. In addition, if their idea was to flee in secret, their comments in newspapers made their escape look fantastical. Nevertheless, their strange story represented an extreme manifestation of a problem that affected many among the immigrants and worried those in charge of absorption. A week later, in June 1966, Cygel admitted that debt had been the reason for the emigration of thirty-nine Latin American families. These families had gotten into trouble by restructuring and extending their payments over time.[14] In August the Argentine ship *Río Quequen* docked in the port of Ashdod; special measures were taken regarding its security because, according to *Haaretz*, "it seems that escaping as stowaways is the way to emigrate [*laredet*] from the country among olim from Argentina who accumulated debts with the Jewish Agency and private entities and did not repay [them] . . . many olim from Latin America cannot raise the money, some . . . even lost what they brought."[15]

Also in August, *Aurora* reproduced details from *Haaretz* about the "escape" of two Argentine immigrants from Ashdod, a prospective student and an unemployed painter, who had arrived two years earlier. The OLEI representative in the city, Leon Shatz, argued that it was "an isolated case" and criticized the JA's "excessive assistance," which, in his view, had created "parasites." His colleague A. Sofer questioned the quality of Latin American immigration to Ashdod and suggested that "harmful elements" should be allowed to leave without even repaying their debts because they created a "poisonous" atmosphere and in any event were going to escape.[16]

According to *Aurora*, the proliferation of illegal emigration among Latin American immigrants was connected directly to debt and unemployment, socioeconomic problems affecting in particular those that had arrived in 1963 and 1964.[17] In Buenos Aires, *La Luz* reported on the escapes, adding details about a failed attempt in which a person was imprisoned for three months after being caught by the crew of the ship where he was hidden.[18] Indeed, the existence of various reports of teenagers and even children discovered as stowaways mid-sea indicates that it was possible to board a ship without a ticket or without clearing customs procedures.[19] On the other hand, whether myth or reality, stories about stowaways had reached Argentines even before the hard times of 1966. According to Mario L., whom I interviewed in Jerusalem in 2017, "I was in Israel in 1963. I came to the leadership school [*machon lemadrichim*]. I remember that we were in the cafeteria aboard the ship returning to Argentina, having lunch and talking, and there were people that were not part of our group. There was a guy and one of us [was talking] about the people that were leaving aboard ships as stowaways . . . And this guy, sitting with us at the same table said, 'You're telling *me*? How do you think I'm traveling?' Then he added: 'There are [life] boats covered with canvas and you hide there at night . . . during the day, no one asks . . .' He was a stowaway."[20]

Still, even if stowaway stories were not new, debt was a real issue among immigrants and for the organizations that worked for their absorption in Israel. For example, OLEI had to send subpoenas to more than twenty families residing in the Tel Aviv neighborhood of Ezra Ubitzaron who were not making their payments for the IL500 loans they (as had many other immigrants) had received from the organization. An *Aurora* reporter emphasized the sad irony: OLEI was working as a mediator in the disputes over debt that the JA had with more than fifty families. The reporter also commented on three families from Ezra Ubitzaron that had left the country "illegally," providing the householders' names (such disclosures often occurred during this period). One of them had planned a holiday in Cyprus but, once there, continued on to Argentina. Another sent his family to Argentina by regular commercial transport and later traveled himself as a stowaway on a merchant ship.[21] The debt process was depicted by an immigrant who complained about the JA in a letter to *Aurora*: "Since my arrival, everything has been failure and deception because of the Jewish Agency . . . I went to the JA to demand assistance in relation to a job. Instead, they offered me a loan of IL300. Naively I took it but I had to find three guarantors . . . The days went by and I returned to complain and again they offered me IL500 and I had to find four guarantors. Today, I can hardly find a way to repay part of my debt . . . I am ordered to pay a debt which I guaranteed [to repay] and even the police have taken up the issue."[22]

The letter's author implied that he had been forced by the JA to take the loans. Possibly, Zionist rhetoric and the resources offered to immigrants created, for some, an excessive sense of entitlement or passivity regarding their own destiny, a perception resulting from the organization's treatment of their absorption. The provision of loans by different bodies under conditions that a bank would never have allowed and the well-intentioned decision to give "maximum support for the payment of loans" turned out to be problematic: harmful for those who accumulated large debts and detrimental to the organizations' own funds and prestige.[23]

To be fair, the organizations doling out loans did seek equitable solutions: each debtor's case was analyzed to determine the reasons for the interruption of payments. In special circumstances, the individual was allowed to leave the country and required to repay the load from abroad. Yet this leniency had its own pitfalls: as reports from the JA unit for debt collection suggest, resolution required the migrants' cooperation, which was not always forthcoming. The permissibility of the system is reflected in the case of a pair of sisters who evaded their $1,160 debt for almost two years, until the JA gave up pursuing repayment. Specifically, "their passage to Argentina was paid by the JA . . . Both sisters have no money and live on a subsidy received from AMIA [Asociación Mutual Israelita Argentina] . . . The father and one sister of the girls, both very wealthy people, who definitely refuse to take charge of the debt, also stated, 'we do not want to hear about them.' Regarding the sisters . . . [their] mental stability is doubtful. They have an irritable nature and have been the cause of scandals both in Argentina and in Israel, including at the Argentine embassy in Tel Aviv . . . This case is practically without any chance of solution. There is no one to contact and we do not even have documents to legally demand reimbursement of the debt."[24] If people whose mental health was in doubt had received loans, the system, evidently, had been far too lenient.

The aspirations of many migrants to own a business combined with the absorption system's credit policy created the context for the formation of large debts. The minority who left the country without honoring them reflected the broader challenge of the problem. Moreover, such escapes or illegal emigration call attention to a cultural aspect of the issue. The Hebrew language has no expression for the action of leaving a place or person with bills unpaid. On the other hand, there are several Spanish terms widely used in Latin American societies for the same phenomenon. In Argentina, the expression *paga dios* (God pays) is used for those who blithely leave a bar or restaurant without paying; its ubiquity suggests that the debt-fleeing Argentines were merely engaging in behavior that was acceptable "back home" but was scandalous in Israel.[25] Be that as it may, the articles and rumors about escapees may have negatively affected the image of the large wave of Argentine arrivals from 1963 and certainly contributed to the negative stereotypes that circulated against the background of the 1966 economic recession and emigration wave, as those who left the country in general—and Argentines supposedly used to an easy life in particular—were looked down upon. Debt did not occur in a vacuum; additional problems and frustrations reinforced one another and while those leaving without repaying their debts were a minority, they were an extreme manifestation of the gap between the immigrants' economic situation and their expectations, and the Israeli reality.

## A STREAM OF RETURNEES ACROSS THE OCEAN: ON BOARD THE *JERUSALEM*

On September 1, 1966, the ZIM liner *Jerusalem* departed from Haifa to South America, its final destination being Buenos Aires. The *Jerusalem* was a luxurious floating hotel capable of serving 550 passengers. Paradoxically, by the mid-1960s, this kind of ship had become the cheapest option for those who could not afford the cost of a long-distance flight. When the *Jerusalem* departed from Haifa, the majority of its passengers were going to South America. Most were not on board for pleasure, even though they had left under the pretense of taking a vacation. As was usual by now, even before the ship's departure, a prolonged and heated discussion, documented in the press and in JA internal correspondence, took place relating to the number of Latin American emigrants. They were returning to their country of origin, leaving behind an experience involving mixed feelings and largely untold stories.

In mid-June, an article exposing the absorption difficulties of Argentines who had tried to adapt to Israel had been published in the short-lived, right-wing Israeli newspaper *Hayom*.[26] It focused on returnee stories, as well as their complaints about the absorption system and its employees. Claiming that four hundred people had bought tickets to return on the *Jerusalem*, the article emphasized that young people and even former Zionist leaders were among the returnees.[27] This kind of press item was bad news for the JA officials in charge of immigration and absorption, who were naturally sensitive to what they deemed "inaccurate information." In a letter labeled "urgent" and sent a day prior to the *Jerusalem*'s departure, the secretary of the JA's immigration department in Jerusalem, Yehuda Dominitz, informed the department's head Shragai that the number of "yordim" was far smaller than the alleged four hundred. According to him, in addition to Latin American tourists on board, there were also

Europeans and Israelis taking a vacation.[28] However, he provided no specific figures. On August 31 *Maariv* devoted a long article to the issue, estimating that there were two hundred returnees and adding that almost the same number had returned to Argentina two months previously on the same ship.[29] Quoting an "official JA total" of only "51 returnees," the report noted that most of those leaving had complained about the JA's economics department. Still, according to *Maariv*, many of the *Jerusalem*'s passengers had declared that their only goal in Argentina was to liquidate their business there and promised to return to Israel sometime in the future.

The evidence indicates that at least two JA representatives came on board the ship before it raised anchor—A. Lebanony, from the economics department in Haifa, and Uzi Bitan, who was acting as spokesperson for the organization. They were there to observe the situation and ascertain the status of migrants leaving the country. While some of the passengers had officially declared their return to Argentina, the majority had not. In some cases, people were trying to depart without being noticed in order to evade outstanding debts. Many others did not have anything to declare because they had paid for their own tickets to Israel and had not taken out any loans. Therefore, the officials' task depended on their ability to scrutinize and evaluate the luggage that the travelers were taking with them. The next day, when the ship was already far from Israel, Lebanony sent a report to the economics department in Tel Aviv. He had tried in vain, he wrote, to talk to the returnees: although they spoke Hebrew, they refused to answer his questions. He described them as "embarrassed and disheartened" and referred to his experience as "very unpleasant." "Most of the human material [*homer ha-enoshi*] were over fifty-five-years-old. Their external appearance proves that they did not come to Israel after deep consideration or any selection . . . I saw a high percentage of handicapped and sick people. Unfortunately, [there was] a substantial percentage of children and youth."[30]

Lebanony's description of the returnees was compatible with his personal and organizational interests. In fact, if it were true that these individuals' return could be explained by their age, health, and the failure of the admissions process, criticism should be directed toward the JA's immigration department in Argentina. As a representative of the absorption unit in Israel, Lebanony believed his branch of the organization to be blameless in this situation. However, he contradicted himself in the same quotation regarding the age of the travelers by mentioning a "substantial" percentage of young people. Moreover, toward the end of his report, Lebanony warned that many of the Latin Americans who bade farewell to their departing friends and relatives at the port could themselves "become yordim" if their treatment was not "faster and more effective."[31] Notably, his report did not mention the Israeli recession. Meanwhile, the press continued to provide its own estimations and interpretations to the public.

On September 2, the official Histadrut newspaper *Davar*, identified with the ruling Labor party Mapai, echoed the official narrative in the title of a short article, "50 Yordim among 350 Travelers to South America." The article noted that one hundred of those departing were journeying in order to use their right to go abroad without paying taxes, an entitlement that would expire at the end of their third year in Israel.[32] The next day, *Aurora* described the *Jerusalem*'s departure. It quoted the official number but referred to "approximately 200 yordim," recognizing the inaccuracy of the estimate due to the fact that most of these individuals "made efforts to hide their intentions." The reporter who covered the departure and interviewed people on board emphasized the wide discrepancy between official statistics and actual numbers of returnees.[33]

It took the *Jerusalem* three weeks to cross the Mediterranean Sea and the Atlantic Ocean before arriving at the Río de la Plata. In the Uruguayan port of Montevideo, Abraham Gozik, a JA official, was organizing the boarding of new immigrants with one-way tickets to Israel. The two groups, immigrants and returnees, no doubt crossed paths in the corridors, common rooms, and portside.[34] They probably even conversed, as people in one group met acquaintances in the other, as was the case of Gozik, who noted in his correspondence that he had met JA colleagues aboard the *Jerusalem*.[35] Gozik was also handed a typewritten "Open Letter from the Yordim Traveling aboard the *Jerusalem* to the People of Israel," printed out in Hebrew and Spanish and distributed by the returnees.[36]

The letter, dated September 20, the day of arrival in Argentina, had two things in common with the Zionist narrative about returnees. First, the authors called themselves "yordim," using the pejorative epithet. Second, the notion of "failure" permeated the text, which also abounded with references to painful feelings and harsh criticism of JA professionals. Claiming they were "obliged" to leave the country due to their economic circumstances, the returnees emphasized their love for Israel and gratitude for the opportunity to return to their countries of origin, an option not enjoyed by those who arrived "from concentration camps." They described themselves and their experience as follows:

> None of us are happy about returning to our countries of origin . . . professionals, intellectuals, artist and workers, but most painful is the [case of] young people who, driven by a patriotic spirit, went to Israel to serve in the army and after much effort to . . . settle in the country were unable to do so due to the complete lack of jobs . . . We repeat that the main factor forcing us to make yerida is the complete lack of jobs and, in some cases, an [inability to adapt] to customs very different from our own . . . There are also former kibbutzniks [kibbutz members] among us who, due to a lack of preparation, were unable to adjust to such a disciplined life; they tried to settle in cities and towns but [as in our case] were unable to survive . . .

> We are committed to fighting against the bad administration of the Jewish Agency, to defeat it, and to return to Israel to stay because Israel is not only the homeland of the leaders but of all those who had the honor to have been born Jewish.[37]

The last part of the letter reflects the underlying tensions between the ethnic and national elements of the returnees' identities, as well as highlighting their supposed desire to return to Israel. But now they were arriving in Argentina, and there was Ducach, ready to portray their experience for *La Luz*. He described a "hesitant" JA representative who was attempting to identify passengers and families pretending to be traveling for pleasure or business but carrying too much luggage, including furniture, draperies, and kitchenware.[38]

From Montevideo onward, two other JA officials were observing the returnees on board: Abraham Bar-Kahan and a colleague of his, referred to as David. Both were emissaries based in Argentina and had traveled to Montevideo in order to sail with the ship to Buenos Aires. To his colleagues in Buenos Aires, Bar-Kahan declared that he was "disturbed" by "the shocking images" of "nice children who are returning to assimilation." Their parents, he considered, were unfortunately using the recession in the Israeli economy as a pretext for leaving.[39] Three days later, Bar-Kahan sent his report to Israel, stating that the two emissaries had returned "broken" by the image of children speaking native Hebrew and receiving answers in Spanish from their parents.[40] He estimated the total number of returnees to be "between 68 and 83."[41] This figure, while conservative, was higher than the one voiced by JA officials at the time of the *Jerusalem*'s departure. The difference might have resulted from additional information, as well as the fact that once in Argentina people were less interested in hiding their real intentions. It is interesting to note Bar-Kahn's view of children as potential Israelis, his negative perception of assimilation in the Diaspora, and his idea about the recession in Israel as merely a pretext. He closed his report emphasizing his sadness as well as his compassion. "Whom am I working for? [*Le mi ani amel?*] How much effort did our *shlichim* [emissaries] invest in these families and in particular you in Israel? What came out of it all? Where are they returning to and what will their future hold?"[42]

A month after the *Jerusalem*'s departure, Abraham Cygel sent a letter to the Absorption and Immigration Committee providing a list of 147 persons returning to Argentina (97), Brazil (21), and Uruguay (29).[43] The list, he explained, included 145 returnees who had declared officially that they were leaving, plus two cases of uncovered returnees who were incorporated in the list due to the suspicious nature of their luggage. Thus, the list consisted of "self-declared" returnees, a number that, as previously mentioned, was smaller than the actual figure. Moreover, the inclusion of just two "uncovered" returnees seems to have been useful as a means to recognize the gap between the actual and official number of returnees while still concealing its real dimensions.

Moreover, the document offers information that contradicted the idea that most of the returnees were older than fifty-five, as the JA official had claimed after his inspection in the port of Haifa. In fact, the average age of householders was thirty-nine. The returnees had spent an average of four years in Israel, meaning they had arrived by the end of 1962; the majority had spent fewer than three years there (table 3.1).

Cygel's list detailed the number of family members at the time of their arrival in Israel and when they left. Numerical variations demonstrate that the return represented separation, enlargement, or a combination of the two for different families. Some families were leaving with a baby that had been born in Israel. Some people had arrived in Israel alone and returned to Argentina with a new family. In many cases, the variations reflected the migrants' strategies for dealing with their logistical challenges. Sometimes, the father left first in order to find a house or a job or, conversely, he stayed behind to sell property. In other cases, the return marked a rupture: either between couples or due to the decision of a son or daughter to stay in Israel. For example, José C. was a small boy when he left Israel by sea in 1966. His testimony is an example of the emigrants' strategies and reflects the impact the return had on the family. José remembers the preparations for leaving Israel and the trip without his father, who had traveled first

**Table 3.1. Officially Declared Family and Individual Returnees to Argentina aboard the *Jerusalem*, by Year of Arrival in Israel**

| Year of Arrival | No. of Families | No. of Individuals | Years in Israel |
|---|---|---|---|
| 1951 | 1 | 1 | 15 |
| 1957 | 1 | 1 | 9 |
| 1958 | 1 | 4 | 8 |
| 1959 | 1 | 1 | 7 |
| 1960 | 1 | 4 | 6 |
| 1962 | 4 | 9 | 4 |
| 1963 | 7 | 20 | 3 |
| 1964 | 7 | 24 | 2 |
| 1965 | 8 | 19 | 1 |
| 1966 | 2 | 9 | Less than 1 |
| Missed | 1 | 5 | - |
| **Total** | **34** | **97** | - |

Source: A. Cygel to Absorption and Immigration Committee, September 27, 1966, CZA, S62/316.

to secure a home in Argentina: "Once the apartment was sold we felt like . . . refugees. I mean, we were selling the stuff and . . . 'where do we go?' . . . My mom was under a lot of pressure. A woman who was not used to working suddenly had to be the head of the household with three children."[44]

Due to sensitivity surrounding the issue of emigration, most official statistics were secret. This was the case of a report titled *Facts about the Yerida*, issued a year and a half after the departure of the *Jerusalem* by the director of the JA immigration and absorption department's unit for publications and demography.[45] Due to methodological issues, it reported only for the year 1965. Even so, it forecast that the figures for 1966 were going to be worse. Surprisingly, in light of the preceding discussion, the report contradicted what commonsense would have suggested: new immigrants were not the majority among those leaving the country. In fact, half of the emigrants had arrived before 1947 and more than a third (36.4 percent) had been born in Israel (table 3.2).[46] Hence, in addition to their particularities as immigrants, it would be misleading to study the return migration of Argentines from Israel without also considering general conditions in the country and the broader trend of emigration that was taking place among groups of various backgrounds, not just Latin Americans.

Moreover, "only" 10 percent of total emigrants were over fifty (table 3.3). This fact prompted the author of the report to consider the possible consequences for Israel: "This is undoubtedly a . . . critical problem, in light of the current security, political, and economic needs of the country."[47] If young Israelis were leaving the country, why should it have been different for new Argentine immigrants who were facing all sorts of additional obstacles?

**Table 3.2. Percentage of Emigrants from Israel in 1965 by Period of Arrival in the Country**

| Arrival Year in Israel | Percent of 1965 Emigrants by Arrival Years |
|---|---|
| Born in Palestine / Israel | 36.4 |
| Until 1947 | 13.5 |
| ***Subtotal**** | ***49.9*** |
| | |
| 1948**–1954 | 19.6 |
| 1955–1960 | 9.7 |
| 1961–1965 | 20.8 |
| ***Subtotal**** | ***50.1*** |
| **Total** | **100** |

Source: A. Koblovitz, *Facts about Yerida*. Jerusalem, 1968, CZA, S61/10200, 3.
*Subtotal equals the percent of 1965 emigrants by grouped arrival periods.
**Including May 15, so the report considered that the percent of veterans was even higher.

**Table 3.3. Percentage of Emigrants from Israel in 1965 by Age Group**

| Age Group | Percentage of Emigrants |
|---|---|
| Under 40 | 70 |
| 40–50 | 20 |
| Above 50 | 10 |
| **Total** | **100** |

Source: A. Koblovitz, *Facts about Yerida.* Jerusalem, 1968, CZA, S61/10200.

The document also confirmed something rarely if ever mentioned in public and formal discussions of the issue: the vast majority of people leaving made no official statements when they left the country. According to the report, "most of the yordim" claimed that business, study, medical treatment, or visiting relatives was their reason for traveling. If, as it seems, the majority concealed their return, the actual number of returnees would have been at least double the official figures. This discrepancy bubbled under the surface of newspaper reporting of the situation. The return aboard the *Jerusalem* described in this section was just one of many similar voyages. About a year earlier, *Haaretz* had announced that "more than 200 emigrants left for South America aboard the *Jerusalem*."[48] As already noted, when reporting on the departure of September 1, 1966, *Aurora* recalled that some two hundred returnees had undertaken the same trip three months previously.[49] In February 1967 *La Luz* noted that "around 100" returnees had left Israel aboard the *Theodor Herzl*.[50] Even after the Six-Day War, when anxiety gave way to enthusiasm, an urgent telegram sent from top JA representatives visiting Buenos Aires to their colleagues in Israel contained the following message: "According to information sent to us, 200 olim are about to return to Argentina on the next ZIM ship. Please check whether this is correct and whether it is still possible to prevent this yerida. This fact could destroy all the actions and programs that we made to encourage aliyah."[51]

## TURNING THE TABLES: IMMIGRATING TO ISRAEL A SECOND TIME

The Six-Day War of June 1967 radically transformed Israel's regional and international stance and its self-image as a society. Following its military victory, Israel began to experience an unprecedented economic boom. The recession of 1966, which caused an increase in emigration from the country, receded into memory as a bad dream. On the other side of the Atlantic Ocean, Argentina was experiencing a very different trend. The year 1966 marked the onset of a dictatorship that pursued an ambitious agenda of economic reforms that quickly failed. The repression of all political and cultural activity that the military elite disliked and its adherence to conservative Catholic values turned society into a pressure cooker ready to explode.[52] In 1969 economic policies in conflict with popular interests, coupled with generalized discontent, led to the eruption of social protests throughout the country. The main symbol of that period, the Cordobazo, was a violent insurrection activated by workers and students in the industrial city of Córdoba, which overwhelmed the police and required military intervention.[53] Within this context, many thought that the revolution was imminent and guerrilla groups began operating.

For many who left Israel during the years of economic straits and recession, their decision may have appeared unwise after June 1967, in particular, those who returned to Argentina. Therefore, the return of some of them to Israel was not surprising. In fact, remigration to Israel was not new. For instance, in 1955, newspapers reported on 103 applications for reentry submitted over a period of three months, some from Latin American countries.[54] However, the number of people with Israeli citizenship who returned to Israel increased notably after the 1967 war, regardless of their country of origin (table 3.4). The surge was exponential for the United States, France, Germany, and Britain. In contrast, Argentina experienced only moderate growth.

It should be emphasized that table 3.4 includes only citizens who acquired the status of "new immigrant" and its associated benefits. The actual number of returnees was probably higher because people might have gone back even

**Table 3.4. Israeli Citizens Who Acquired "New Immigrant" Status and Returned to Israel in 1967 and 1968, by Country of Origin**

| | 1967 | 1968 | Total |
|---|---|---|---|
| **Americas** | **187** | **782** | **969** |
| United States | 46 | 414 | 460 |
| Brazil | 33 | 110 | 145 |
| Argentina | 67 | 72 | 139 |
| Canada | 14 | 101 | 115 |
| | | | |
| **Western Europe** | **102** | **846** | **948** |
| France | 57 | 470 | 527 |
| Germany | 21 | 121 | 142 |
| Britain | 8 | 118 | 126 |
| Austria | 10 | 24 | 34 |
| **Totals** | **393** | **1,964** | **2,357** |

Source: *21 Years of Aliyah and Absorption* (Tel Aviv, 1969), 9, ISA, 3497/9.

without any formal application for "new immigrant" status. The ambiguity regarding these citizens is reflected in the terminology used in *Facts about the Yerida* and in many other documents. Israeli citizens who returned to Israel were referred to either by their legal status *toshavim chozrim* (returning residents) or by the colloquial, pejorative term coined by Zionist ideologists, *yordim chozrim* (returnee descenders). In addition to bureaucratic reasons, which affected returning Israelis in general, historical circumstances explain why the number of returnees from Argentina did not increase as sharply as it did for Western democracies.

During difficult times in Israel, many citizens chose developed Western economies as a destination in their search for opportunities. Hence, many people now returning from those countries had been born in Israel. In contrast, the return of Israeli citizens from Argentina was based exclusively on Argentine-born individuals who decided to migrate to Israel a second time, and their number was high in relation to the total number of Argentines who migrated to Israel in 1967 and 1968. Table 3.5 shows the sizable proportion of people who migrated to Israel from Argentina a second time: 12.5 percent of the total.

The proportion of returnee Argentines to Israel who had Israeli citizenship due to their previous immigration may be fully appreciated when considered in light of several historical factors that brought Argentine migration rates to Israel to a minimum in 1967 and 1968. Argentine immigration, which to recall peaked in 1963, was composed mainly of people who were affected by the negative consequences of the countries' cyclical economy; by a certain point in time, those prone to migration due to such vulnerability had already left Argentina. Moreover, when the 1966 Israeli recession created adverse conditions for immigrants in the country, the return to Argentina of many people who could not integrate into Israeli society was noticed by Jewish Argentines. Hence, when the post-Six-Day War period inaugurated an era of economic progress in Israel, news about the recession and the stories of returnees still reverberated among new immigrants, as some of their comments demonstrate. Upon arriving aboard

**Table 3.5. Argentine Immigrants and Returnee Citizen Arrivals in Israel by Year**

| Year | Immigrants* | Returnee Citizens (Second-time immigrants) |
|---|---|---|
| 1967 | 547 | 67 |
| 1968 | 559 | 72 |
| **Total** | **1,106** | **139** |

Source: Israel Central Bureau of Statistics, *21 Years of Aliyah and Absorption* (Tel Aviv: 1969), 9, ISA, 3497/9.
*Not including returnee citizens and immigrants under the age of eighteen.

the *Theodor Herzl*, in January 1967, Usher Strauss, a farmer from Rivera headed for a kibbutz, believed the recession would not affect his plans.[55] Abraham Wull, a former luggage maker, was optimistic about his ability to prosper thanks to the modest amount of capital he had brought, while Raúl Stein, a mechanic and photographer commented on the returnees' criticism of Israel: "Those who decided to return have to talk badly about the country. I do not believe, however, that after three months or even one year, someone can be adequately informed."[56]

The testimonies of those who were not deterred by the Israeli recession demonstrate that its harsh consequences for new Argentine immigrants were known and might have convinced many others to stay in Argentina. This fact was obvious to JA emissaries in Buenos Aires. One month after the establishment of an anti-communist military dictatorship under Juan Carlos Onganía (self-styled the Revolución Argentina), the emissaries gathered at one of their weekly meetings to discuss the damage to Israel's image caused by returnees' opinions and related newspaper articles in the Israeli press; they also complained about the JA's distribution of the newspaper *Aurora*. In their view, the newspaper was anti-Israel. They also mentioned that Israelis themselves were advising people not to move to Israel. Abraham Bar-Khan, a JA emissary in Buenos Aires, lamented that the press and the general public focused only on the negative side. In his opinion, the 10 percent "yerida" of Latin Americans was a small number.[57]

One day after the emissaries' meeting, the military government carried out what Argentine history calls La Noche de los Bastones Largos (the night of the long batons).[58] Making use of new technology—including cameras, transparent plastic clear shields, and long batons—the police fiercely dislodged staff and students from the University of Buenos Aires who were protesting in defense of academic autonomy. In the crackdown's aftermath, hundreds of professors, scientists, and researchers were dismissed and exiled. This expulsion led to JA emissaries exploring possibilities for these people in Israel. Their inquiry, sent in a letter to their superiors in Israel, depicted the situation as follows: "Within the Jewish community, there are many that until one month ago worked as prestigious lecturers and researchers in various departments. The wave of dismissals punished some 1,500 people who were left jobless; 600 are Jewish (almost 50 percent). Many are receiving offers from universities in North and South America. A non-negligible number of them are approaching the Sochnut [JA] and are interested in knowing more about the situation in Israel in the fields of their expertise."[59]

Bar-Khan, the letter's signatory, considered it necessary to work quickly before "other countries succeed in absorbing this excellent material." He emphasized that during the past years, Argentine experts had risen to world-class levels and many were Jewish.[60] Indeed, expectations about an increase in immigration to Israel had been reported since the beginning of the dictatorship. Bar-Khan, who had worked in the country in 1961 and 1962, reported that even though Argentines were used to military intervention, Onganía's regime exhibited new characteristics. The radical Right, he wrote, was in control and had connections with the anti-Semitic Tacuara group.[61] The economic program and inflation were affecting the population while new financial regulations had "liquidated" the cooperative system of credit in which Jews had been key players. The cooperatives, he added, were important both for the middle class, whose members obtained better interest on their savings, and for Jewish community institutions based on these enterprises. The crisis affected the Jewish educational system in particular, with all schools facing financial difficulties and many nearing bankruptcy.[62] As a result, Bar-Khan anticipated a migration wave similar to that of 1963 but with a salient difference. "There is no doubt that the situation here will cause an emigration wave, in particular among our Jewish brethren," he wrote. "The main difference between the situation that prevailed in 1962–63 and that of today is that [while] then the Jews saw Israel as a place of shelter . . . the situation in Israel and the yerida [were] enough to sabotage our work; the community here are watching it through a magnifying glass in light of reports in Israeli publications, which the local news[papers] reprint."[63]

At the end of his message, Bar-Khan explained that, due to the adverse circumstances, the JA office in Buenos Aires was also supporting a small number of Argentines who were returning to Israel to settle down a second time, something he described as unusual treatment. Even so, he reiterated the need to fight against the "plague of yerida," reflecting the then-prevalent Zionist ideological approach to immigration.[64] People willing to move to Israel a second time were usually ignored or asked difficult questions, aggravating the discomfort they already felt at being considered yordim. The emissary's message also demonstrates that the lack of standardized procedures gave JA officials the power to decide who deserved to be assisted and who did not. This situation ended decades later, when Israel adopted a more pragmatic and professional approach to its immigration and absorption policies. But during the 1960s and 1970s those who had returned to Argentina and wanted to remigrate to Israel had to undergo what amounted to an interrogation process, which likened them to traitors or crime suspects. Moreover, while the emissary's assessment of the political and economic context was accurate, the regime's repressive policies and political orientation did not trigger the surge in immigration that he expected. This would change as the detrimental effects of the Onganía regime's economic plan on the middle class would exacerbate after 1969, at which point the Jewish press in Argentina would report on "Jewish poverty" and the increased need for welfare assistance.

The Cordobazo protest occurred in May 1969. One year later Gregorio Fainguersch, president of AMIA, and Moshe Korin, a Jewish educator, drew attention to the problem of Jewish schools, which many parents were struggling to afford. Jewish education in Argentine, they warned, would soon be out of reach for all but the wealthiest families.[65] Jaime Szwarc, AMIA director of social solidarity, noted that the number of people requesting assistance to "survive" had increased sharply. He described those seeking help as the unemployed or people with inadequate salaries. While he was used to seeing older people without pensions or family networks asking for help, he noted that the bulk of increased requests came from members of the "middle class"—former producers and businessmen who were now bankrupt, or those who had lost their savings with the bankruptcy of cooperatives and construction companies.[66]

According to Szwarc's description, most of those requiring assistance were not affiliated with Jewish organizations and represented only a small portion of all those in need. Most people, he said, were ashamed to ask for help. The increase in poverty was also observed by the Asociación de Comedores Populares Israelitas en Argentina (association of popular Israelite cafeterias in Argentina, ACPIA), whose mission was to serve free meals in their establishments. Previously, they had mainly served the elderly, widows, and the mentally ill. According to ACPIA's spokesman Manuel Sznaider, the association was now serving young people, workers, and members of the impoverished middle class. Referring to their feelings of shame, he described seeing a former Zionist leader at a cafeteria, who left once he became aware he had been recognized.[67]

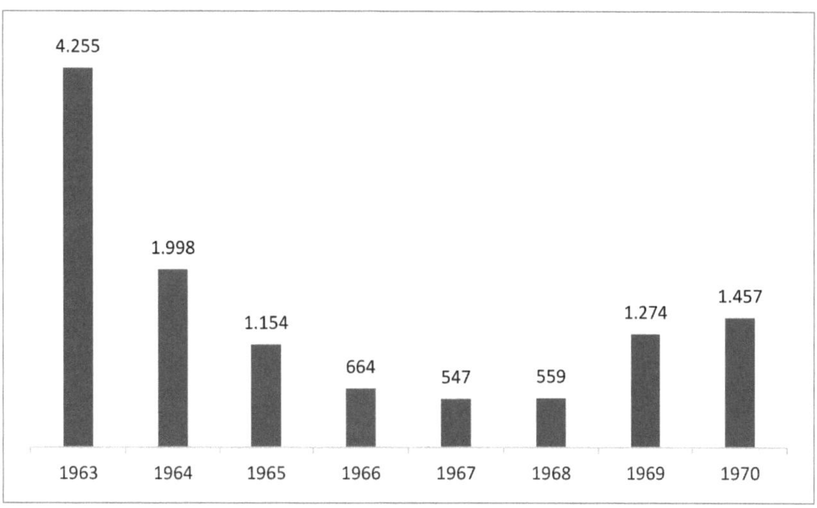


**Figure 3.1** Argentine immigrant arrivals in Israel by year, 1963–1970. Source: Israeli Central Bureau of Statistics, "Total Immigration to Israel by Select Country by Year," Jewish Virtual Library. Returnee citizens are not included.

It was these economic circumstances that finally conspired to provoke a rise of Jewish (re)immigration to Israel, overcoming the reluctance of a population long used to living with military regimes (figure 3.1). The number of those remigrating rose persistently at this juncture; having had first-hand experience in Israel as immigrants, they were in a position that allowed them to compare the two countries, and to choose reentry. In early 1970 a request was made by the JA in Buenos Aires to their superiors in Israel to speed up the discussion about their rights.[68] By June sixty-six people were asking for JA support to move to Israel a second time.[69] They included forty adults (fourteen couples and twelve single people) and twenty-six children. The group was composed predominantly of young people, as shown in table 3.6.

The list of professions of twenty-five householders and lone travelers speaks volumes: six employees, four merchants, two agricultural workers, two students, one pedicurist, one painter, one textile cutter, one waiter, one hairdresser, one telephone operator, one secretary, one unskilled laborer, one carpenter, one weaver, and one engineer. Considering the economically active and leaving aside the engineer whose age is unknown, as well as the two students, the returnees' profiles were consistent with those of individuals who had arrived in Israel in 1963 and returned around the year 1966: people who suffered from Argentina's economic fluctuations, especially recessions and currency devaluations, such as young professionals, salaried workers, and small business owners, without any savings to support them in times of an economic slump. The repetition of the migration cycle demonstrates the vulnerability of their situation in both countries. Five among the total would receive mortgages to buy property in Israel and one family would get a loan to pay for the trip. The other individuals' rights and obligations were considered on a case-by-case basis.[70]

**Table 3.6. Returnees in Argentina Who Registered to Remigrate to Israel, by Age Group**

| Age Group | Cases |
|---|---|
| 0–10 | 16 |
| 11–20 | 12 |
| 21–30 | 16 |
| 31–40 | 14 |
| 41–50 | 7 |
| 51–60 | – |
| 61–70 | 1 |
| **Total** | **66** |

Source: Y. Harel to S. Schmit, June 8, 1970, TLC, 220172.

Since the sixty-six cases were registered during the first half of 1970, the total for the year might have amounted to some 120 Argentines who remigrated to Israel. This estimate is consistent with the number of such migrants for the years 1972 and 1973, which accounted for 102 and 118 arrivals, respectively.[71] The number of two-time immigrants attracted the attention of officials in charge and, in October 1970 a "comprehensive study" on returning migrants from Argentina holding Israeli citizenship was being considered.[72] Moreover, consultations about their immigrant rights and customs tax exemptions for appliances, furniture, and cars continued.[73] Since the JA had no fixed criteria and the government lacked a specific policy, each case was determined following a discussion, resulting in an immigration experience marked by misunderstandings, arbitrary decisions, and bureaucratic problems, whereby certain benefits might be granted and others withheld.

The Israeli economic recession had caused the return of migrants to Argentina around the year 1966, as reflected in the reconstruction of the voyage of the *Jerusalem*. At the same time, JA emissaries in Argentina expected an immigration wave similar to that of 1963 due to the right-wing characteristics of Argentine military rule, its connections with anti-Semitic groups, and the aggressive repression of liberties. However, their hopes were belied. An increase in Jewish Argentine immigration to Israel began only in 1969 as a result of the regime's economic failure, which generated widespread protests, such as the Cordobazo. Economic decline was severe and there were even reports of Jewish poverty. Simultaneously, Israel was experiencing an economic boom which followed the Six-Day War. The tables had been turned and a considerable number of Jewish Argentines migrated to Israel a second time. As the saying goes: "The first time it was a mistake . . . the second time it was a choice."

# 4

# UNCERTAINTIES AND VIOLENCE

## The Return of Peronism and the Yom Kippur War

The year 1973 marked a historical turning point for both Argentina and Israel. In Argentina, exiled Juan Domingo Perón returned to Argentina and took office once again. In an environment of alarming political violence and economic instability, the Argentines voted for Perón, with the expectation that he would restore order and guide the nation to prosperity. In Israel, the country suffered a surprise attack by an Arab coalition on the holy day of Yom Kippur. In both cases, the consequences proved dire: in Israel, the Yom Kippur War put a sudden end to the economic book and self-confidence the Six-Day War had inaugurated, while in Argentina, Perón was unable to restore either national peace or sustainable economic growth.

Until the military conflict, Jewish Argentine immigration to Israel had been rising steadily, peaking in 1973. Further, the 1973 arrivals exhibited unique characteristics in terms of economic and social capital. In contrast to earlier and later immigration peaks, this time the immigrants did not leave Argentine due to pressing economic need and they did not lack savings. However, once in Israel, they encountered housing shortages in Israel that became the source of individual and collective protests. Finally, the Yom Kippur War caused distress to all sectors of Israeli society and to immigrants in particular. Immigration decreased sharply and there was a noticeable stream of Jewish Argentine return migration, which, however, coexisted with a surprising phenomenon of Jewish Argentine students leaving for Israel.

### IMMIGRANTS WITH A DIFFERENCE: THIS TIME IT IS NOT ABOUT THE ECONOMY

The 1973 immigrants are an interesting group to analyze because they encapsulate several historical processes in a unique manner. In fact, unlike earlier and later immigrations discussed in this book, Argentine immigration to Israel in

1973 was accompanied not by reports of Jewish poverty or unemployment but rather by news of the short-term recovery of the national economy in Argentina.[1] Moreover, like most Argentines, Jewish Argentines depended on the domestic market and their economic situation had improved: the economy, while conserving its structural deficiencies, had been reacting positively to the program implemented in 1970, which increased public investment and recovered the buying power of salaried workers.[2] The Peronist governments of Hector Cámpora and Juan Domingo Perón consolidated that path by protecting domestic industry and its labor constituency. Quoting economists Pablo Gerchunoff and Juan José Llach, historian Luis Alberto Romero has pointed out that despite violent conflicts and economic upheavals, the Argentine economy performed adequately from 1963 until 1975, and industrial production grew steadily.[3]

The particular juncture of 1973 allows consideration of the interplay of economic forces and political elements, the main set of push-and-pull factors that drove Argentine Jews to Israel that year. In order to analyze the pool of 2,506 migrants who arrived in 1973, it is helpful to compare them with the 3,767 migrants of a decade earlier. The data for conducting this comparison was elaborated by historian Sebastian Klor and by Kalman Grossman, who worked as a Buenos Aires–based JA emissary in charge of immigration in 1973.[4] The two groups of immigrants present clear differences in terms of four variables: timing, age, education, and occupation. The evidence suggests that the role played by the economy in the 1973 migration to Israel was related mainly to the immigrants' future expectations rather than to their current requirements. Moreover, while push factors operating in Argentina that year were a necessary condition for immigration to Israel, they were not sufficient. Israel needed to offer prospects of economic prosperity and security in order to be an attractive destination.

Unlike the immigrants of 1963, who arrived in Israel at a time of economic recession in Argentina, the immigrants of 1973 left the country during a period of economic expansion, before the cycle returned to recession and devaluation. Thus, their decision was not triggered by massive unemployment or bankruptcy, and those who had assets were able to keep them or to sell them at a decent price. Nevertheless, the situation was difficult to assess at that time. In Argentina, Perón and his movement had elicited controversy since the first Peronist government of the 1940s; contradictory responses to Perón would morph into enduring political alignments and social cleavages that lasted throughout the years of Perón's exile. In addition, the rise of the New Left in the international arena and the revolutionary winds of Third Worldism, which affected Latin America, added new questions about Peronism throughout the 1960s and 1970s. The primary one concerned the role it would have in a revolutionary context: was Peronism a movement destined to implement deep reforms in Argentina? If so, how far would these go? Or, conversely, was Peronism the best political alternative for stabilizing Argentine society and offering a democratic alternative to a leftist revolution?

For Zionist and Jewish leaders, the debate about Perón and the return of his movement to power included a discussion of possible threats to Jewish Argentine citizens. However, Jewish Argentine leaders and their counterparts in Israel and other countries had very different points of view. In Israel, Zionist leaders tended to emphasize that since the whole of Latin America was on the brink of revolution or civil war, Latin American Jews should migrate to Israel. For example, as early as December 1971, JA chairman Aryeh Pincus declared that Latin American Jews were "sitting on a volcano" and should come to Israel "voluntarily, before being forced to leave as refugees." In light of Pincus's declarations, the *Jewish Chronicle* asked its correspondents in Latin America to offer their own assessments. From Buenos Aires, Nissim Elnecavé argued that the JA's main goal was to promote immigration to Israel, but it was "hard to imagine a catastrophe striking Latin American Jewry."[5] Later, but still before Perón's electoral victory, Elnecavé highlighted Perón's friendly attitude toward the Jews and Israel and reasoned that Zionist leaders' forecasts of an increase in emigration as a result of anti-Semitic threats in Argentina were erroneous. Rather, he anticipated that the Peronist government would pursue economic reforms that would conflict with the interests of the wealthy sectors. "In essence, the immediate situation of the Jewish community is that of all Argentines and depends upon whether or not stability can be restored to the country," he wrote. "There are no serious menaces to them as Jews per se. However, it cannot be ruled out that more stringent economic measures will have their effect on the upper middle class in which many Jews can be found, although such measures have no deliberate anti-Semitic intent."[6]

The conflict between Elnecavé and the JA continued in the *Jewish Chronicle*, where JA representative Schneier Levenberg argued that Latin American communities were in a state of emergency and were facing a "revolutionary situation due to the great disparity between rich and poor." Elnecavé responded that the JA was exaggerating the anti-Semitic threat in Argentina because of its interest in immigration to Israel. He also presented a segmented description of Jewish Argentines: some felt they were facing an emergency and were leaving for Israel; a number were going to other countries; and another, "non-negligible," group "identified with the ultra-Left." Therefore, Elnecavé contended, "The outlook of visitors or observers from abroad regarding Argentina is in one way or another alarmist, particularly if Israel or aliyah is the main concern and the theory advanced [is] that the Diaspora has no future and should be liquidated—a view propounded by all Israeli emissaries in Argentina . . . My own evaluation is devoid of wishful Zionist or Israeli thinking that lends itself to propaganda and distorts the situation."[7]

Elnecavé was not the only one who presented a nuanced analysis of Peronism, the Argentine context, and its implications for Jewish Argentine immigration to Israel. In fact, JA representatives in Argentina also perceived the complexities and contradictory aspects of social trends affecting Argentine society. For example, JA emissary Yitzhak Harel wrote comprehensive reports from Buenos Aires; prior to the accession of the Peronist government, he noted that, because of their role in the country's occupational structure and their professional profiles, Jewish Argentines were experiencing a turbulent atmosphere and were worried about their future. Emphasizing the economic aspects of the problem, he wrote that many predicted Perón's return would not be good for the Jews.[8] Nevertheless, Harel also considered that the Jewish public had hopes of a return to democracy.[9] His analysis of parliamentary elections in Argentina showed that Jewish Argentine aspirations did not coincide with the Israeli perspective. Harel believed that the election result was not "bright" for Israel because of cooperation between the Peronists and the Arab League. Moreover, Peronism was feared by certain Jewish sectors, not because of real or perceived anti-Semitism but due to the possibility of leftist economic measures. "According to various analyses, it is not expected to be an official policy directed against the Jews, though they may be hurt as part of the middle class in the event of an economic policy that affects the middle class," Harel wrote. "However, there is an atmosphere of concern and many worries among local Jewry, which we can see based on inquiries asking us for information and the kinds of questions addressed to the emissaries at home meetings and lectures."[10]

While mixed in terms of its assessment of Jewish Argentine prospects in Argentina, this analysis emphasized the potential of increased immigration to Israel and the political risks to Israel of Peronist approaches to the Arab League. For their part, Jewish Argentine political representatives arrived at a very different conclusion about the third Peronist government. After Cámpora's electoral triumph, Nehemias Resnizky, general secretary of DAIA, believed that the vast majority of voters favored "change," supporting various parties that campaigned against underdevelopment, misery, oppression, dependence, monopolies, and international companies. The envisioned "change," he said, "[would not be] detrimental to vital and sectoral interests of the Jewish community . . . Those who have followed the economic development of our community, and considering the previous and current expansion, can speak of a dismantling of the textile and metal industry where there was a strong Jewish presence, bankruptcy of the cooperative system, and the absence of Jews in the landowning sectors and multinational companies. The deterioration of the Argentine economy has also led to . . . the deterioration of sectors of the Jewish economy . . . The vast majority of the Jewish community has interests that coincide with those of the vast popular sectors."[11]

Clearly, Resnizky's analysis of the Peronist victory emphasized the economic dimension of the movement and its beneficial policies for Jewish Argentines. Although DAIA defined itself as politically nonaligned, Resnizky's declarations communicated a new approach to Peronism. The general secretary added that although they faced significant challenges, the Peronist movement represented the best option for Argentina's masses due to its ties to the masses. Moreover, Resnizky believed that it would be a mistake to act against Peronism as DAIA had done in 1946.[12] While not ignoring the existence of anti-Semitism in Argentina, he did not blame Peronism for it. In fact, according to DAIA leaders, the sources of anti-Semitism could be found in the three "internationals": the Nazis/Fascists, the Communists, and the Arab League. Resnizky also presented his political views to Jewish leaders at the World Jewish Congress (WJC) in Jerusalem. After returning from that meeting, he explained to board members that the situation of Latin American Jews was misunderstood in Israeli and US circles. They did not see that the Jewish community in Argentina would benefit from progressive economic reforms and not from the status quo. "They [the US and Israel] regard this place as a huge source of anti-Semitism," he noted. "This is a typical approach and they do not see the reality, the problem. They do not notice that Latin American revolutionary processes are captivating, fascinating because they create ideology, good or bad; they fuel ideology and enthrall our youth. In some meetings we made them aware of this. For example, they did not understand that there are Peronist Jews."[13]

Resnizky saw a challenge for Jewish Argentines in maintaining the connection with Israel while being part of the Third World and its transformations.[14] In this he disagreed with Zionist leaders from outside Argentina, who believed that Jewish Argentines were at risk from the Peronist return and would hasten to migrate to Israel. The Israeli press, too, was far from unanimous about Argentina's political prospects, presenting a wide spectrum of opinions about Perón's return to Argentina and his third government. The interpretations ranged from pessimistic to optimistic, although all the newspapers recognized Perón's charismatic personality and agreed that, given the chaotic circumstances, he was probably the only person who could stabilize the nation.[15] The extent to which there were real possibilities of a revolutionary transformation in Argentina is a topic that still fuels intense academic and public discussions. However, there is no doubt that by the time of Perón's return to the country many Argentines believed in the possibility of revolution, or at least deep social reform. In the end, while some in Argentina, including large numbers of Jewish Argentines, were enthusiastic about Peronism, others felt precisely the opposite.

Moreover, Israel's present and future economic orientation was equally unknown to potential Argentine immigrants; hence, a lecture delivered to them by

JA emissary Kalman Grossman was titled "Israel's Socioeconomic Perspective: Is Israel Moving toward a Neocapitalist Society, toward a Socialist One, or toward a Combination of Both?"[16] Unlike in Israel, however, in Argentina questions about the future were connected also to the increased activity of armed guerrillas and paramilitary groups. Thus, political violence was a powerful push factor for prospective immigrants, as Grossman stated clearly: "The 'Jewish public' is worried due to the unstable political and economic situation and, lately, due to the characteristics of the kidnappings (a significant number of victims are Jews) . . . [These worries] are also expressed in an increase in numbers of inquiries . . . regarding information about possibilities in Israel."[17]

It is worth noting that Grossman mentioned economic and political instability as an Argentine problem, but did not reference poverty or unemployment. Political violence, Grossman believed, might cause an increase in immigration to Israel.[18] In fact, he said, there was already a sharp rise in numbers of candidates for immigration in the cities of Córdoba and Rosario, two of the urban centers where political violence was focused at the time. Nonetheless, his reports also demonstrate that Jewish Argentines were well integrated in Argentina and its political struggles, even to the point of tragedy. After Perón's electoral victory, there were two significant assassinations, namely of the union leader and Perón ally José Rucci, and of a young "Peronist leader, a Jew named [Enrique] Grynberg," wrote Grossman.[19]

In terms of the second variable, age, the 1973 pool of immigrants included a substantially smaller proportion of people under the age of eighteen than the 1963 contingent and a larger one of people older than fifty-one (table 4.1). Therefore, it was a population that was more advanced in their business and professional lives, with fewer elementary and secondary school pupils to support (table 4.2), compared with the immigrants of 1963, who had been strongly family-based and were at the beginning of their careers.

**Table 4.1. Percentage of Argentine Migrants to Israel in 1963 and 1973 by Age Group**

| Age Cohort | 1963 | 1973 |
|---|---|---|
| 0–17 | 35.3 | 28.51 |
| 18–35 | 35 | 35.46 |
| 36–50 | 18.24 | 17.89 |
| 51 + | 11.46 | 18.14 |
| **Total** | **100** | **100** |

Source: K. Grossman to U. Narkis, March 19, 1974, TLC, 220756; Sebastian Klor, *Between Exile and Exodus* (Detroit: Wayne State University Press, 2017), 135–36; Klor, "Database 10,487" (unpublished, provided to author by Sebastian Klor).

**Table 4.2. Economically Inactive Argentine Migrants to Israel in 1963 and 1973 by Category (Not Including Children under Six)**

| | 1963 | | 1973 | |
|---|---|---|---|---|
| Category | Number | Percent of all Immigrants | Number | Percent of all Immigrants |
| Elementary and secondary school pupils | 1,165 | 30.92 | 467 | 20.65 |
| University students | 59 | 1.58 | 307 | 13.58 |
| Housewives and widows without profession | 752 | 19.98 | 461 | 20.39 |
| Retired | 14 | 0.38 | 86 | 3.80 |
| **Total** | **1,990** | **52.86** | **1,321** | **58.42** |

Source: K. Grossman to U. Narkis, March 19, 1974, TLC, 220756; Sebastian Klor, *Between Exile and Exodus* (Detroit: Wayne State University Press, 2017), 135–36; Klor, "Database 10,487" (unpublished, provided to author by Sebastian Klor).

Thirdly, out of the immigrant totals, the proportion of university students jumped from 1.58 percent in 1963 to 13.58 percent in 1973 (table 4.2). This remarkable eightfold leap took place while the share of immigrants between the ages of eighteen and thirty-five remained stable. Thus, clearly, the increase in the number of university students was not produced by changes in the age pyramid. Three main factors explain why a greater proportion of Argentine immigrants had higher education in 1973 than ten years previously:

(a) Despite the introduction of temporary admission examinations during the military governments, public universities in Argentina were free and unrestricted. Higher education in Argentina was never as exclusive as in North America and public institutions did not require a tuition fee. The middle and lower-middle classes were heavily represented within the huge student body.

(b) Jews had demonstrated historically their effective use of higher education as a means of social integration and mobility wherever they were given access, a privilege they enjoyed in Argentina.[20]

(c) During the third Peronist government, the universities became the focus of political struggles that were taking place in the country. In May 1973, education minister Rodolfo Puiggrós declared that "national liberation" required putting the university at the service of the people.[21]

From then on, until 1974, there were recurrent mobilizations and *tomas* (seizures) of buildings by students to demonstrate their support for the new authorities' goal of creating a "national and popular university," and clashes took place between the right- and left-wing Peronist student organizations.[22] The newly appointed academic authorities referred to a "revolutionary" time and to their related goals, using the slogans and expressions dominant within the Peronist left wing, such as *patria socialista* (socialist homeland) and "cultural revolution."[23] The political activities that interrupted regular classes and the politicization that permeated the universities were potent push factors for those who prioritized their careers. In addition, student struggles may have been a warning of higher levels of violence to come in the near future. Thus, Jewish Argentine students were attracted by the benefits and study programs Israel offered to young immigrants as never before. Their increased weight in the pool of immigrants altered the relation between the economically active and the inactive, decreasing the share of economically active individuals in comparison to 1963 (table 4.3). Unfortunately, no information is available enabling a distinction between students who migrated with their families and those who came alone. However, their increased weight within the pool of immigrants and reports about them, referred to in the third section of this chapter, demonstrate that young university students symbolized the Jewish Argentine immigration of 1973.

Finally, in regard to occupations and, specifically, the economically active population of immigrants, the aggregate proportion of artisans, skilled craftsman, unclassified employees, and farmers (which I call Group A) decreased, while the aggregated proportion of liberal professionals, clerical workers, merchants, and industrialists (Group B) increased (table 4.3). While each of the

**Table 4.3. Percentage of Argentine Immigrant Arrivals in Israel in 1963 and 1973 by Economic Status and Occupational Group**

<table>
<tr><th></th><th colspan="2">Economic Status</th><th colspan="2">Type of Occupation</th></tr>
<tr><th></th><th>Inactive (C)</th><th>Active (A and B)</th><th>Group A (Artisans, skilled craftsman, unclassified employees, and farmers)</th><th>Group B (Liberal professionals, clerical workers, merchants, and industrialists)</th></tr>
<tr><td>1954–1967</td><td>46.4</td><td>53.6</td><td>47</td><td>53</td></tr>
<tr><td>1963</td><td>52.86</td><td>47.14</td><td>47.22</td><td>52.88</td></tr>
<tr><td>1973 Scenario 1</td><td rowspan="2">58.42</td><td rowspan="2">41.58</td><td>37,93</td><td>62,07</td></tr>
<tr><td>1973 Scenario 2</td><td>26.99</td><td>73.01</td></tr>
</table>

Source: K. Grossman to U. Narkis, March 19, 1974, TLC, 220756; Sebastian Klor, "Database 10,487" (unpublished, provided to author by Sebastian Klor); Klor, *Between Exile and Exodus* (Detroit: Wayne State University Press, 2017), 136.

two groups represented almost half of the entire population of economically active immigrants in 1963, in 1973 Group B made up more than 60 to 70 percent. In other words, the share of householders categorized as blue-collar workers by Klor in 1963 diminished in 1973 and the share of those considered white-collar workers expanded. The variance was estimated based on two alternative scenarios, a methodology required in order to overcome the obstacles posed by the use of different labels in the categorization of immigrants in 1963 and 1973. Due to these discrepancies, it is not possible to provide accurate numbers. Nonetheless, the tendencies are sufficiently clear in both scenarios. Moreover, the estimated variation in favor of Group B is a conservative one and the increase might have been even larger.[24]

In addition to changes in the proportion of the two main groups of occupations, there were changes within each group. Tailors, textile workers, and carpenters, which were the main subcategories in 1963, became less represented compared to the large variety of technicians concentrated mainly in the construction, metal, and electronic industries in 1973.[25] Moreover, within Group B, there was an observable increase in the proportion of people in commerce and the liberal professions. Meanwhile, considering the proportions within the entire economically active population, the clerical workers remained almost unchanged, while liberal professionals augmented their representation (table 4.4).

Lastly, the increase in the proportion of liberal professionals does not fully reflect the actual increase in the number of university graduates. The graduates were dispersed among several occupational categories. For example, there were accountants and economists with university degrees among those labeled clerical workers, merchants, and industrialists. In the case of engineers and architects, they fall under the category of academic professionals in the list compiled

**Table 4.4. Liberal Professionals and Clerical Workers among Immigrants in 1963 and 1973 Expressed in Number, Percentage of All Immigrants (Imm.), and Percentage of Economically Active Immigrants (EAI)**

| | **1963** (1,850 EAI) | | | **1973** (941 EAI) | | |
|---|---|---|---|---|---|---|
| **Profession** | Number | Percent of all imm. | Percent of EAI | Number | Percent of all imm. | Percent of EAI |
| Liberal professionals | 342 | 9.07 | 19.24 | 223 | 9.85 | 23.69 |
| Clerical workers | 367 | 9.74 | 20.65 | 185 | 8.17 | 19.65 |
| **Total** | **1,009** | **18.81** | **39.89** | **408** | **18.02** | **43.35** |

Source: K. Grossman to U. Narkis, March 19, 1974, TLC, 220756; Sebastian Klor, "Database 10,487" (unpublished, provided to author by Sebastian Klor).

by Grossman (table 4.5), in contradiction with other documents that mention them among the immigrants during that period. Therefore, they must have been included in other categories, such as technicians.[26]

Moreover, the immigrants of 1973 left Argentina during a period of economic expansion, before the cyclical recession and devaluation. In fact, considering their experience of previous economic cycles, many of the immigrants may have anticipated the next downward turn. They were a population with years of experience in their businesses and professional lives and had fewer elementary and secondary school pupils to support than in 1963. The proportion of university students was almost eight times higher than ten years previously. There is insufficient documentation to determine whether the described differences between the pool of immigrants of 1973 and those of 1963 reflected changes affecting Jewish Argentines in general or were a function of the process of self-selection of immigrants. However, such changes and self-selection are not mutually exclusive, and the immigrants' characteristics might have reflected both. In any event one thing is certain: the Argentines who arrived in Israel in 1973 were better equipped with cultural and economic capital compared with their counterparts of ten years previously. They had experienced a trend of social mobility in Argentina and undoubtedly expected to continue advancing in Israel. Israel, for its part, was better prepared to offer improved jobs and long-term careers than it had been a decade earlier.

While prosperity had been cyclically interrupted in Argentina, it seemed

**Table 4.5. Occupational Percentage of Latin American Immigrants in Their Country of Origin, One Year and Three Years after Arrival in Israel, by Age Group**

| | In Latin America | | | 1 Year in Israel | | | 3 Years in Israel | | |
|---|---|---|---|---|---|---|---|---|---|
| **Occupation** | **18–29** | **30–54** | **Total** | **18–29** | **30–54** | **Total** | **18–29** | **30–54** | **Total** |
| Scientific and academic | 23.4 | 18.9 | **18** | 31.7 | 20.9 | **23.9** | 33.6 | 23.5 | **25.3** |
| Professional and technical | 27.3 | 10.1 | **15** | 15 | 6.1 | **9.1** | 19 | 7.2 | **10.3** |
| Managerial and clerical | 25 | 30.3 | **27.3** | (9.2) | 17.4 | **14.9** | 20 | 22.5 | **21.4** |
| Industry, transport, and building | (3.2) | 12.6 | **11.7** | 20.5 | 37 | **30.8** | 13.3 | 26.8 | **24.4** |
| Other | 21.1 | 28.1 | **28** | 23.6 | 18.6 | **21.3** | 14.1 | 20 | **18.6** |
| **Total** | **100** | **100** | **100** | **100** | **100** | **100** | **100** | **100** | **100** |

Source: *Immigrants from Latin America One Year and Three Years after Immigration, Arrived between 1969 and 1974*, Special Series N. 652 (Jerusalem: Central Bureau of Statistics, 1981), 39.

possible in Israel during the interwar period of 1967–73. Argentines who arrived at that time took advantage of this context. Although the available surveys refer to Latin Americans (LA), the majority of these were Argentines. Among economically active LA immigrants, 90 percent were already working one year after arrival and all of them tended to move on to better jobs. The number of those employed in scientific and academic endeavors increased in the Israeli job market during the first year of arrival and continued to grow, meaning that people working in these fields had more opportunities than in their country of origin. They also benefited the most from immigration in professional terms when compared with immigrants in other economic sectors. The language barrier most affected people who had worked in professional, technical, managerial, and clerical jobs before arriving in Israel, and they had to take jobs below their skill level for several years. This other occupational path explains the growth in the number of immigrants found in industry, transport, and building (table 4.5).

The Jews who departed Argentina for Israel in 1973 left behind a situation of

**Table 4.6. Self-Definition (Percent) of Latin American Immigrant Arrivals between 1969 and 1974 by Age Group**

| Self-Definition | 1 Year in Israel | | | | 3 Years in Israel | | | |
|---|---|---|---|---|---|---|---|---|
| | 18-29 | 30-54 | 55-70 | Average | 18-29 | 30-54 | 55-70 | Average |
| Totally Israeli | 10.2 | 20.1 | 30.6 | **18.6** | 13.2 | 33 | 47.5 | **29.4** |
| Israeli and some belonging to country of origin | 20 | 22.3 | 15 | **20** | 26.2 | 20.2 | 14.5 | **21** |
| Equally Israeli and belonging to country of origin | 23.6 | 29.9 | 28.3 | **27.1** | 32.9 | 16.3 | 13.2 | **21.3** |
| Belonging to country of origin and a little to Israel | 26 | 14.9 | 6 | **17.2** | 11.6 | 10.5 | (5) | **9.7** |
| Belonging to country of origin only | 8.3 | 8.6 | 5.3 | **7.9** | (4.6) | 9.5 | (6.5) | **7.2** |
| Belonging neither to Israel nor to country of origin | 11.9 | 4.2 | 14.8 | **9.2** | 11.5 | 10.5 | 23.3 | **11.4** |
| **Total** | | | | **100** | | | | **100** |

Source: *Immigrants from Latin America One Year and Three Years after Immigration, Arrived between 1969 and 1974*, Special Series N. 652 (Jerusalem: Central Bureau of Statistics, 1981), 42.

increasing political violence, while Israel offered them favorable societal conditions. They were not in economic need, a factor that met their long-term considerations and lifestyle aspirations. Their incorporation into the Israeli job market was smooth, as table 4.5 shows; in particular, the component of university graduates and professionals within this migration group succeeded in finding positions. Even more importantly, most of them declared they had acclimatized satisfactorily in Israel (table 4.6). Notwithstanding age group differences, identification with Israel tended to grow with the passing of time.

The Argentines arrived while Israel was still experiencing an economy that had begun flourishing after the Six-Day War. Israeli society was becoming internally more stratified and differentiated, as occurs in most capitalist countries undergoing economic development.[27] While this path proved optimal for immigrants holding the right economic and cultural capital, it may have caused disillusionment among those who didn't. In fact, there were also people who arrived with a distorted or idealized image of the country as that of a kibbutz, whose representativeness of Israeli society was often overestimated by Jewish Argentine organizations. The following story is eloquent in this regard. Oscar C. was one case of radical disappointment. He submitted a complaint to the JA, expressing his wish to leave Israel just four months after his arrival; his chief complaint was having to pay for a dentist to treat his wife. "As time goes by, we are losing our Jewish faith because we think 'is this Israel?' . . . I believed that poor people [like me] could also find peace in Israel and arriving with energy to work was enough," he wrote. "But now I am convinced that Israel only needs tourists and very wealthy immigrants, that those lacking money are of no interest and, because of that, you don't care about their health."[28]

Oscar C. arrived at the end of 1970 and was part of the more vulnerable sectors of the Argentine economy that had suffered from the economic program before the return of Peronism; he left the country during a general economic crisis affecting, among others, Jewish institutions. In contrast, the 1973 immigrants were unique in that they left Argentina at a time of economic expansion and arrived in Israel when the country seemed able to offer them long-term socioeconomic mobility as well as political stability. In fact, almost half of them bought a house three years after their landing in Israel.[29] Such an acquisition was possible, in part, because a substantial portion of them owned property in Argentina, as reports on the difficulties of selling it demonstrate.[30] These migrants arrived in Israel with the necessary capital to obtain a mortgage after they had sold their Argentine homes or had accumulated savings that had not been depleted because they left Argentina before the recessive stage of the economic cycle. However, in spite of the good rate in home acquisition, there were real obstacles and causes for stress. Most of the immigrants had to deal with different obstacles in their efforts to acquire a home.

## THE PROBLEMS OF SUCCESS: HOME OWNERSHIP EXPECTATIONS AND HOUSING SHORTAGES

Abraham K. migrated to Israel with his wife and two daughters in 1972. In Argentina, he had been a Zionist activist for thirty-two years. In Israel, he had plans to produce and sell plastic bags. Shortly after arrival, he learned that his business would be profitable only in the cities of Ramat Gan or Holon. He wanted to reside in one of those places, but after seven months in the Kiryat Yam absorption center, he was offered only one apartment in an unsuitable area. He wrote a letter to Abraham Argov, director of the JA's Tnuat Aliyah (immigration movement), the organization within which Abraham K. had been active in Argentina. He explained that because he did not have a proper home, one daughter was living in the Hebrew University's dorms in Jerusalem, the other was in a moshav, and his wife was forever scolding him about the fact that his lifelong Zionist activism had been worthless.

> 220 days after my arrival in our blessed land, I am still at the starting point, and with problems that, as an activist of many years, astonish me . . . I did not know the curse "I hope you make aliyah and arrive without proteksia."[31] Now I know, but it is hard to swallow . . . The woman in charge of housing says that . . . we will have to wait . . . My wife has begun to talk about returning . . . this is a cause of anguish for me and my daughters, who received a Jewish and Zionist education . . . If you are in a position to rescue me from this pit of anguish, which I do not think I deserve as an old and dedicated activist, throw me a lifesaver and I will continue believing in what I always felt, to be Jewish in my land [emphasis in original] and not in a foreign one.[32]

Implying the possibility of return to Argentina, he alleged that it was his wife's idea while at the same time emphasizing their daughters' and his own Zionist and Jewish background. In addition, his explicit reference to the word *proteksia* infers that, as a veteran activist, he expected such privilege. In fact, he had heard about people who had received apartments in a certain building that would have suited his needs and wanted Argov to help him get one there. Thus, the letter combined a rational request regarding a personal problem with ideological extortion: the former activist wanted assistance with a personal issue in order to continue believing in the Zionist program.

Still, the letter reflects the housing shortage that Israel experienced at the beginning of the 1970s when, following the Six-Day War, immigration escalated, creating a bottleneck in the construction sector. The state offered housing benefits to immigrants, and Zionist organizations promoted them in Diaspora communities. In 1969 Tnuat Aliyah's bulletin, one that Abraham K. himself might have distributed, referred to immigrant opportunities to attain housing in Israel as follows: "Every oleh shall enjoy the right to receive a house to rent [and] have the option to purchase it over a period of three years following signature of the rental contract. If the oleh decides to use the right to pass from rental to acquisition . . . the accumulated rent will be taken into account (if the acquisition takes place within the first year) . . . The buyer will have the right to obtain a mortgage with affordable conditions."[33]

The information provided by the bulletin was accurate and many immigrants enjoyed the benefits of such affordable programs. Indeed, studies demonstrate that the 1970s were the best time to buy property in Israel.[34] As of 1964, the programs were also promoted by *Aurora* to its Spanish-speaking readers, who were introduced to Amidar, the organization in charge of the building and administration of homes for immigrants. At the time, it was possible to buy a house in a development area with a down payment of 10 to 20 percent and a thirty-year mortgage with a low interest rate.[35] However, the overwhelming number of immigrants created a shortage of available units and the consequences for the absorption system became evident at the beginning of the 1970s. It was not an entirely new problem, but the immigrants' socioeconomic background and expectations had risen since the "euphoria" that had followed the Six-Day War, meaning that demands for solution would be vociferous.[36]

Two months after sending Argov his first letter, Abraham K. sent another missive. His mood had swung from distress to happiness. Before receiving Argov's answer to his first letter and, due to "overwhelming pressure" at home, he had contacted Jenny Grynberg, an OLEI representative, who secured a meeting for him at the JA office in Haifa. There he "confronted" the housing officials and explained that it was unacceptable to be waiting eight months for a house, "even worse knowing that . . . I preached from the rooftops . . . that everyone who comes will have his apartment and job [settled] during the time of the *ulpan* [intensive Hebrew-language study program]."[37] A month after that meeting he was offered an apartment in Holon, as he had wanted. Moreover, he was already cooperating with OLEI by "clarifying" to other immigrants about how they should adjust their expectations. He was also advising workers at the absorption center because "they lacked the necessary sensibility" to understand the immigrants. It is interesting how fast this individual, who had talked about returning to Argentina, became an enthusiastic volunteer once his own housing problem was solved. His second letter also demonstrates how immigrants who were unaware of the full picture underlying their problems tended to attribute them to the bureaucrats they encountered. Closing his letter, Abraham K. expressed his desire to make up "the time that someone made me waste miserably, not to mention the health that it cost us meaninglessly and the money that slipped through our fingers."[38]

Beyond the particularities, Abraham K.'s case demonstrates that housing difficulties created emotional and economic obstacles for new immigrants. It also shows how for Zionist activists, continuing their work in Israel served as a strategy for adaptation to their new homeland. A basic activity in that regard was overseeing correspondence at the absorption center.[39] This provided immigrants with an opportunity to create networks in their new home country. However, their capacity to solve problems through contacts should not be overestimated. In the case of Abraham K., it is unclear to what degree his connections made a difference. Moreover, most Diaspora Zionist organizations were not even known to the average Israeli or bureaucrat. Their contact with Israel was limited mostly to requests for informative materials in Spanish.[40]

While Abraham K.'s case was not unusual, a few similar stories gained publicity. On July 10, 1973, *Aurora* commented on "increasing bitterness" affecting Latin American immigrants and hinted that "something was going on" at the absorption center in Netanya.[41] A week later *Maariv* sent a reporter who interviewed several people at the center. According to Jenny Grynberg, there was a yerida of Latin Americans and, while greater in number than the year before, the cases in Netanya were not the most severe. Two of the three immigrants who talked to *Maariv* about their problems referred to housing. Mr. P. and his family had been in Israel for forty-five days and his wife already wanted to leave. They were initially allocated a seventy-five-square meter house in Raanana, but the move-in date was delayed repeatedly. When they finally entered the house, they discovered that it was only fifty-eight-square meters and the bureaucratic complaint procedure required Mr. P. to travel several times to different cities. When they received another house in Lod, it turned out that the person who could authorize the move was abroad. Samuel W.'s family had a similar story, which had caused them eleven months "of anguish" by the time of the interview. When the reporter spoke to them, they were about to negotiate a home for rent with an option to buy in Holon. Complaining that in one office he was told, "if you do not like it, just go," Samuel declared that his wife had sent very negative letters to their Argentine relatives.[42]

The likelihood of public and collective immigrant protests increased because they were all living together in absorption centers. The control of these institutions had always been in the hands of the JA, though the Education and Absorption Ministries, social workers, and local authorities were also involved. A variety of centers existed during the 1970s. Some looked like suburban complexes and others functioned like hotels. The centralized administration in each center, and the direct and frequent contact between authorities and immigrants, on the one hand, and among the immigrants, on the other, created side effects that would not have arisen in a welfare system based on the universal allocation of resources. First, administration officials were free to apply their own criteria and preferences regarding an immigrant's access to certain benefits. Second, the ingathering of immigrants tended to exacerbate tensions between the various groups among them, as well as between the immigrants and the absorption authorities.[43]

The possibility of discretionary decisions made at the centers due to the authorities' preferences for certain kinds of immigrants represented a problem in itself which, combined with other elements, contributed to an immigrant's confusion and potential dissatisfaction. The State of Israel regularly adjusted the absorption benefits offered according to a set of variables that remained unknown to immigrants. For example, a person considered a refugee or who came from a country in deep economic distress could receive subsidies not offered to an immigrant arriving from a Western democracy. Private donations made to the JA, too, could create short-term programs that were offered to a limited number of immigrant groups. Those who did not receive such benefits could feel discriminated against. As a result, a number of protests were observed by researchers, ranging from personal negotiations with the authorities through organized collective bargaining, strikes, and demonstrations, to bribery and violence.[44]

In August 1973, just three months before the Yom Kippur War, the front-page headline of *Aurora* read, "Forty Families of Latin American Olim Threaten to Leave Israel." Most were professionals and had completed the five-month Hebrew-language program at Ulpan Ben Yehuda in Netanya. The group denounced "discrimination against Latin Americans" as the cause of their protest.[45] In the following edition, *Aurora* published a letter signed by twelve men from the group who described their situation as follows: twenty-two families had been residing at the absorption center since March 1, 1973; they were not refugees; they were ideologically motivated; they did not believe in "the use of yerida" as a threat; their arrival in Israel meant human and economic sacrifices; they defined themselves as professionals who incurred no costs on the State of Israel and were willing to pay for everything they were receiving; and they praised the immigration process and the Hebrew program. For all that, they declared, "Suddenly we have fallen into a desperate vacuum created by a disastrous bureaucracy and the inefficiency of the Absorption Ministry."[46]

According to the letter, all the men had jobs but had to spend several hours commuting between their home and their workplace. Their complaints were addressed by a commission that was supposed to deal with such cases once a month. At the end of the process, the petitioners were usually offered a single option of a home on the upper floor in a building without an elevator and far from their jobs, or a residence inadequate for their family size. In the meantime, immigrants from other countries who were studying Hebrew with them had received the kind of homes they had wanted even without having a job or having asked for such homes. They felt that they had fallen victim to a "farce" because they were being pressed to accept the only option offered to them in order to abide by the deadline to leave the absorption center, and to avoid having to continue paying for storing containers at the port. They wanted to meet with the commission's director in person, circumventing the nonpersonal procedure, and remind him that the homes would be paid for.

Most of the signatories were Argentines. While mentioning their ideology, they also emphasized their value as professionals educated in other countries and whose training had incurred no cost to the State of Israel. At the same time, their sole mention of the word "yerida" suggests their willingness to negotiate. One week later, *Aurora* published a response sent by a reader, an immigrant from Argentina who had arrived in Israel in 1969. Ironically addressing "poor" and "refugee" immigrants in Netanya, he recommended that they solve their housing problem by taking a look at the pages of any newspaper and buying a home on the private market, which was full of apartments to rent or buy. "What [do they] think?" he asked. "Homes for free? In Argentina or in any other country, are apartments given as a gift or sold at half price in affordable installments?"[47]

In addition to problems caused by the housing shortage, cultural aspects of the immigrants' protest should be examined, too. Argentines had learned the lesson that "a baby is breastfed only after it cries" (an idiom that means roughly the same thing as the American saying "the squeaky wheel gets the grease"—the loudest complainant is the one who gets helped first). This term is included in the lyrics of their most popular tango "Cambalache," a slang term that literally refers to a junkshop but is used to describe a varied, disparate, and disorganized assortment of things. "Cambalache" means a sort of chaos—the illogical mixture and lack of authority or order which, according to the tango, is the salient characteristic of the twentieth century. The image of the baby "crying" taught every Argentine that one must speak up in order to have one's concerns addressed. Argentine immigrants to Israel in the 1970s, especially those who had studied at public universities, were used to gatherings and collective complaints to promote their interests. Moreover, generation after generation of immigrants in Israel, of all backgrounds, had been taught by their predecessors that they should complain in order to get things done. Indeed, complaining is part of the Israeli culture while a person who does not complain is considered a *fraier* (sucker). Unsurprisingly, the housing shortage offered fertile ground for protests, which were further fueled by corruption scandals related to the administration of immigrant apartments. For example, besides the immigrants' complaints, *Aurora* reported that an Amidar administrator had been sentenced to three years in prison for allocating ten houses in exchange for bribes.[48] Such acts of corruption demonstrate the discretion that regulated systems allowed to bureaucrats and were probably not unique. In 1977, accused of corruption and overwhelmed by an investigation, Housing Minister Abraham Ofer committed suicide. Still, even while corruption played a contributing role, the logistical troubles that immigrants denounced were real and had structural bases.

An Absorption Ministry report explained three main problems related to immigrant housing during this period. First, two frequently contradictory goals were being pursued by the state: population dispersal and immigrant satisfaction. As a palliative to the shortage of apartments in the center of the country, where many immigrants asked to be settled, the ministry provided temporary rental apartments from 1973 to 1975 and assured the beneficiaries that permanent housing would be made available in the same area. By the time the report was published, due to the "slow down and almost complete shortage of buildings in the center," the ministry was having severe difficulties in fulfilling such promises. "We know from experience that it is futile to send unwilling immigrants to areas where the social fabric is weak and employment opportunities are limited. They simply leave," the report noted. "In the long run, such a policy will only cause a further decline in immigration rates."[49]

Second, the lack of variety in residence size affected large families, the elderly, and single individuals, while the standardization of buildings frustrated Western immigrants with higher expectations. And third, construction delays generated a waiting list of thousands of immigrants. Attempts to alleviate the problem by granting permission for immigrant home acquisitions on the private market did not produce satisfactory results. The enlarged subsidized mortgages were insufficient due to high prices, in particular for immigrants lacking additional funds.[50]

The housing problems elaborated in the report were not new; rather, they had acquired higher quantitative proportions and were defined by social variables different from those prevailing in the previous decade. In order to appreciate the distinctions, it is useful to consider an exchange of letters in 1963 between an angry immigrant, who wanted to work as an interior decorator, and the JA emissary who had advised him in Buenos Aires. "You unwisely advised us that I would easily find a job in Beersheba . . . How irresponsible!!!!!," wrote the complainant. "No one has the right to play like that with the destiny of others . . . we made vain attempts to find a job . . . and here begins the second part of our odyssey, as a consequence of your lie . . . It is not possible to get a house, to stay in Tel Aviv or in the surrounding areas. In the meantime, we live in a fourth category room, paid out of our own pocket."[51]

In his response, the JA emissary David Horowitz reminded the immigrant that by the time of his registration for immigration in Buenos Aires in February 1963, he was unemployed and had expressed willingness to work in "any kind of job."[52] We can speculate that immigrants who left their country of origin in times of unemployment, which was the case for many Argentines who arrived in Israel in 1963, were ready to make sacrifices; however, they felt differently once they were in Israel. Conversely, Argentines arriving in Israel in 1973 had the opportunity to access housing benefits but some of them complained if the building did not have an elevator. Such dissatisfaction reflected their improved circumstances compared with those met by their predecessors ten years earlier.

Despite the protests, Argentine immigrant absorption in Israel was satisfactory in relation to housing when considered statistically, and slightly higher than it was for the average immigrant. A study conducted by the Absorption Ministry in 1974 that surveyed people arriving in the country in 1971 and 1973 found that during their first year in Israel, 66 percent of Latin Americans had a permanent address, and 95 percent had one by the third year. Eighteen percent owned a house during their first year and 47 percent owned one by their third year in Israel. More importantly, during the first year, 89 percent were "absolutely" or "quite" satisfied with their housing; this proportion decreased to 79 percent by the third year.[53] The decline in satisfaction might have reflected higher aspirations as well as new problems of adaptation. The survey did not distinguish between national groups within the category of Latin Americans, but Argentines were the majority and certainly influenced the statistical tendency. Among such problems was the undoubtedly pressing need to acquire fluency in Hebrew, which, as one Argentine immigrant said jokingly, was not an easy task. While others who studied Hebrew at the same place and time were protesting about their housing situation, Moshe V. sent a letter of thanks to a JA representative. Moshe, who attended Ulpan Ben Yehuda in Netanya, wrote, "Almost three months in Israel working in what I had dreamed of all my life . . . The only thing I regret is that I cannot write to you in Hebrew, but I promise I will do so in another fifty or sixty years. I think that by then I will know something about this crazy language, my only problem in Israel (I think that my case will make history because I have no complaints and every day I feel happier than the day before)."[54]

The housing shortage in Israel during the 1970s allowed Argentine immigrants who were better off in terms of social and economic capital to organize collective protests and push for better locations or larger apartments. At the same time, there is no doubt that housing difficulties among the factors that encouraged the return of many Argentine migrants whose energies and savings were depleted by multiple moves, bureaucratic labyrinths, or uncomfortable living conditions. Even for those who, after a long period, received a suitable apartment, container storage at the port represented a huge financial burden and had psychological implications for their sense of self. Each person's identity is sustained by a network of social and material elements, and for an immigrant, possessions brought from abroad provide a sense of "stability to the self."[55] The 1967 economic boom accelerated the process of social class differentiation in Israeli society, and as in other countries housing functioned as a permanent reminder of a person's social status. Staying in an absorption center was like being at the entrance of Israeli society without experiencing what it was like inside.

After six months at the center, the new immigrant was expected to find a job and a home, and most immigrants did so. However, for a portion of them, the experience was difficult enough to motivate them to return to their country of origin during this initial stage of settling in Israel. For others, the absorption center created the conditions necessary to meet people in a similar situation, typically immigrants from the same country or region, with whom they could compare the benefits they obtained with those received by other groups, and to organize protests if the former were found lacking. Before the Six-Day War, collective protests had been less frequent, even though some had taken place at the ports or on the ships on which the immigrants had arrived and become sadly notorious.[56] In the early 1970s, the expansion of the absorption centers, the housing shortage, and high expectations fueled by the Israeli economic boom, combined with Argentine immigrants who aspired to continue their social mobility in Israel, created fertile ground for collective Latin American protests led by Argentines.

The increased professionalization of sectors within the absorption system that came about with the creation of the Absorption Ministry combined with the popularization of the absorption centers to create a client-provider approach in which Zionism was still present in rhetoric but "services" were evaluated in terms of cost and benefit by both parties. Argentine immigration to Israel in 1973 was driven strongly by long-term aspirations of political stability and sustained economic prosperity. The sacrifices demanded by Zionist ideology during previous decades and the social stigma against those leaving the country were waning. Paradoxically, the fact that recently arrived immigrants considered it their right to protest in the name of Zionism marked the success of the State of Israel. Its message to Diaspora Jews that they were a part of Israel had been effective. It was as part of that message that they expected to receive a proper home and did not know about the challenges the state faced to provide it. The housing shortage would worsen following the Yom Kippur War, which caused deep trauma and a long-term economic recession that exacerbated existing social tensions. The war also had an immediate impact on Argentine migration to and from Israel.

## STUDENTS FEEL SAFE IN ISRAEL IN SPITE OF WARS

On October 6, 1973, an Arab coalition led by Egypt and Syria attacked Israel; although the Yom Kippur War would last until only October 22, the national trauma would produce lasting consequences. Leaders glorified for their role in the Six-Day War were now accused by the Israeli people of irresponsibility, and the Agranat Commission was created to investigate their role in the debacle.[57] The economy was seriously damaged and, despite the Diaspora's solidarity with Israel, there was a sharp decline in the number of immigrants arriving from anywhere (table 4.7).[58] Conversely, emigration increased and the future looked bleak for new immigrants, as an official report explained: "The relative calm felt in Israel in the years 1967–1973 has been shattered and since the Yom Kippur War there is a deep awareness of the possibility of a new war . . . ; the Israeli economy is in a state of stagnation, if not recession. The situation is difficult for all Israeli citizens but particularly so for new immigrants who are endeavoring to build a new life in a strange country with a rapid rate of inflation and difficulties with housing, employment, and social integration."[59]

Immediately following the war, several articles with data on Argentine immigration to Israel in 1972 were published in Argentine newspapers. The Middle Eastern conflict was incorporated into local political struggles within the Peronist movement, and the Arab League organized an anti-Israel campaign.[60] These events aroused the concern of Kalman Grossman, head of the JA office in Buenos Aires, who wrote an assessment of the impact of the war on migration trends. "There is bleak news coming out of Israel via newspapers and letters and, in general, things are inflated in a negative way," he observed. "A decrease in the number of files opened for aliyah has been noted . . . On the other hand . . . visits to our office are more 'determined,' that is: there are fewer 'turnabouts' during a first, second, and third interview with the emissary for general information and more immediate resolution at the first or second meeting. The willingness to initiate the aliyah process has increased lately in the provinces more than in Buenos Aires."[61]

It seems that after the outbreak of the war only the more ideologically motivated, those with nothing to lose, or those that had already decided to leave Argentina continued to leave for Israel. Therefore, they did not need several

**Table 4.7. Migrants to Israel by Origin and Year of Arrival (January–November)**

| Region | 1973 | 1974 | 1975 |
|---|---|---|---|
| USSR | 30,422 | 16,033 | 7,607 |
| US and Canada | 4,479 | 3,162 | 2,648 |
| Latin America | 4,132 | 2,694 | 1,583 |
| Romania | 3,234 | 2,860 | 1,919 |
| West Europe | 3,023 | 2,735 | 2,371 |
| Other | 5,008 | 2,682 | 1,829 |
| **Total** | **50,298** | **30,317** | **17,826** |

Source: U. Narkis to Board Members, December 15, 1975, 506/5, ISA, 186.

interviews. In addition, the relatively higher number of prospective migrants coming from the provinces could be explained by the greater vulnerability of regional economies and the escalation of political violence during that decade, issues that would later affect the entire country. From its office in Córdoba, headed by Yosef Arazi, the JA focused its efforts on Neuquén, Tucumán, Paraná, Bahía Blanca, Córdoba, Mendoza, Rosario, and Concordia. In December, Arazi reported that prospective immigrants in the region were having difficulty selling their property due to economic fluctuations. He added, "I am not exaggerating if I say that the decline continues regarding everything connected to Jewish affairs. An additional negative [factor] . . . is the arrival of letters from relatives in Israel that not only discourage aliyah but also cause a mood and discussion that are difficult to counter."[62]

Grossman's report from December mentioned similar issues and elaborated on the impact of the letters that arrived from Israel to relatives in Argentina. Their "negative influence" continued to grow, he wrote; most of the letters contained grim and embellished news. He reported that while the Jews were willing to listen to the emissaries explain the Israeli situation, most behaved as if "business [was] as usual" and many left the big cities for vacation spots during the summer holidays.[63] To witness the Jewish Argentines living their lives "as usual" upset the emissaries. They found it hard to understand how easily political violence and general instability in Argentina were accepted, a fact already observed by JA emissaries in the previous decade when the military's internal divisions led to armed street battles.[64] Moreover, they were disappointed by Jewish Argentines' relative indifference to Israeli needs in the aftermath of the Yom Kippur War.[65] This reality should not be surprising, however, as Jewish Argentines were rooted in Argentine society and were familiar with the entire spectrum of political ideas and movements of their time and as such were comfortable navigating and even thriving within the context of the country's instability. This reality was captured by the *American Jewish Year Book*, which mentioned two synagogue gatherings organized to demonstrate support for Israel; nevertheless, it also reported that

> it was a source of no little consternation that many leftist and unaffiliated Jews were persuaded not only not to support Israel's cause but also actively voiced opinions and attitudes unfavorable to Israel. A large part of the medical staff at the Hospital Israelita Ezrah refused to back a demonstration in support of Israel, and when funds were finally raised, they were donated to the Red Cross rather than to Israel. Many Jewish teachers in Jewish schools were dismissed for refusing to back the Israeli war effort in the classroom and openly opposing Israel's position. Although no figures were available on the funds raised, it was admitted by some of the foremost communal leaders that the amounts fell short

> of expectations. All these symptoms indicated the harsh reality of the creeping advance of the assimilation of Argentine Jews and the lack of forceful leadership to stem this tide.[66]

It is clear, then, that notable circles of Jewish Argentines were influenced or intimidated by the leftist winds that characterized the period. At least by that period of their life, many avoided supporting Israel publicly, did not feel attached to Israel, or were even to demonstrate against the country. Between them and those who decided to relocate to Israel there was a wide range of Jews who just wanted to live their lives "as usual." This sociological reality was a much stronger factor working against migration to Israel than the negative effect of the letters arriving from those who had already migrated. Moreover, Jewish Argentines did not only consume news about the war through letters from Israel: such news arrived in Argentina through the press, radio stations, and national TV (Channel 7), all of which the Jewish Argentines would have been exposed to. Another source of information was the Spanish-language Israeli newspaper *Aurora*, which published a series of articles dedicated to Latin Americans leaving Israel between February and April 1974. In an interview to the newspaper, Yitzhak Harel, the JA's vice director for immigration and absorption, stated that Latin American emigration from Israel was beginning to show signs of slowing down. He explained that while the war had destroyed Israeli economic and housing conditions, the economic situation in some Latin American countries had improved, as a result of which relatives' letters from the country of origin encouraged return.[67]

Such letters, and the information provided to migrants before and after migration, were not the only factor to consider. Despite some clichés about the inadequate information they received, OLEI president Geula Javkin offered some illuminating comments about the emigrants. She maintained that emigration (which she described as holding at a "normal 9 or 10 percent") had begun with the war because typical problems had become more severe. Salaries were insufficient, people were working extra hours in factories, and labor conditions left little time to study Hebrew. Those older than fifty had been fired as a result of the postwar recession, creating a "desperate" situation for many. She also distinguished between two kinds of return migrants, making sarcastic references to those who left to avoid conscription. "There is no doubt that currently there are several issues caused by the Yom Kippur war . . . Many olim feared and remain fearful of being forgotten due to the country's problems. In addition, there are people at the age of military service or with kids at the right age to be called up. So, here comes the 'weather issue.' It seems that many people notice now that the weather here is not good for them and leave."[68]

Javkin claimed that some immigrants had entered Israel as "temporary residents," instead of becoming Israelis with "new immigrant" status, so that their children could avoid military service. She considered ideology to be a decisive factor in determining a person's desire to live in Israel.[69] Nonetheless, she expressed her respect and understanding for those who were leaving. Many did not sell their homes in Israel, she said, and might return.[70] There is no doubt her statements were based on real cases she knew about, and some testimonies of returnees support her arguments. For example, José C., whose family's story appears in the introduction to this book, arrived in Israel at age fifteen together with his family six months before the war. It was his second time as an immigrant. His father died soon after the war from heart failure. Affected by the death of the head of the household, as well as by the national trauma, José's elder sister and mother persuaded him to return to Argentina: "It was a family crisis . . . We were going through a kind of Greek tragedy . . . We had no idea what to do. . . . My sister and mother were experiencing a sort of guilt because they had decided to go to Israel and I was going to be recruited by the army. Therefore, they started suggesting that I return to Argentina, at least for two years, to think about it carefully, and to decide on my own."[71]

While José returned to Argentina, the war affected other Argentine immigrants in Israel differently. For example, Saúl S. decided to get Israeli citizenship precisely as a consequence of the Yom Kippur War. While his pregnant wife spent much of the time in an underground shelter, he felt uncomfortable as a civilian living in Israel: "I used to take the bus and there were all women. There was not a single man and I used to feel tremendously guilty. Kind of, what am I doing here?" After getting Israeli citizenship, Saúl was conscripted into the army.[72] Moreover, many young people suffered the consequences of war without being responsible decision makers. Daniel F. had arrived in Israel at the age of four in 1972. His parents were active in the Zionist movement and the family settled in a northern kibbutz. Daniel experienced the war before returning to Argentina in 1974. After many years of soul-searching, he realized he had very few memories and was not even sure which ones were genuine; however, his feelings and political views were marked by what he had undergone during the war. "I used to have a memory of a sort of . . . great happiness about the kibbutz swimming pool. How we used to swim . . . My psychologist used to tell me, 'Talk to your parents to see what the hell happened in that swimming pool' . . . Then I asked them and it happened that the pool was . . . fucked up by a bomb during the Yom Kippur War. I have some images of life in the bunker on mattresses."

His parents also told Daniel that he had had an accident during the war. As they were running for shelter into the bunker, his mother spilled boiling water on his back. He had been taught that kibbutz Jews were strong and therefore did not permit himself to cry. Instead, he repeated continually, "I am strong, I am strong" [*Ani hazak, . . .* ] until he lost consciousness. He still has a scar on his back and he has never returned to Israel, either as a tourist or scholar, even though he has received several invitations. He is aware of being "doubly angered" both at the political and personal level. Nevertheless, he would be happy if his children visited the country as part of the *Taglit* (Birthright) program.[73]

These three stories demonstrate the challenges Argentine immigrants faced in their attempts to adapt to Israeli culture. The families' difficult decisions took place against a background of national and economic distress. In this context, *Haaretz* reported the departure of nine Latin American professionals, a report reproduced by *Aurora*. Confirming this information, OLEI representative Jenny Grinberg explained that jobless lawyers, architects, and engineers were "wandering" around the country. In some cases, she said, their unemployment had lasted six months; housing was also a relevant factor. "Last year, there was a similar wave of bitterness and many Latin American families returned to their countries," she concluded.[74] Argentine newspapers published similar news. In March 1974 Grossman wrote, "Newspapers and radio here carry news about large numbers of [citizens who are making] yerida. Even the very influential *La Opinión*, considered the most pro-Israel newspaper, published the results of a survey that appeared in *Haaretz* according to which 11.6 percent of the population are considering the possibility of yerida. In a number of radio shows, they referred to this news, labeling it 'an exodus' from Israel. This kind of news, that someone here cares to inflate . . . has a devastating effect everywhere, and particularly in provincial towns and small communities where the Jews . . . tend to believe everything that circulates in newspapers and on the radio."[75]

Ironically, according to the survey published by *Haaretz*, the majority of potential emigrants were aged eighteen to twenty-nine, precisely the population referred to by JA representatives in Argentina as being more inclined to migrate to Israel. Both types of information reflected the leading place that young people generally occupied within immigration streams due to the perceived advantages of relocation. It is also interesting to note Grossman's paternalistic tone and his underestimation of Jewish Argentines' capacity to judge the political scenario themselves. Another irony relates to the alleged negative role of exaggerated news and letters in counteracting the Zionist goal of attracting immigrants. Indeed, official Zionist publications might have provoked similar consequences. The monthly bulletin of Tnuat Aliyah included a section for immigrants' letters sent to the large "family" of activists. In general, the letters referred to firsthand experiences during the absorption process but, after the war, activists who had arrived in Israel just days before gave their impressions. For example, an immigrant named Dubo wrote a letter on the third day of the war announcing that he had gone to Kibbutz Harel and was enjoying the swimming pool when an army truck arrived. "Half an hour later the kibbutz was 'pandemonium.' Phantoms jets flashed past, helicopters, . . . tanks starting to move south, everything in such an orderly and quiet manner that it makes one feel part of a community of heroes; we feel no fear at all . . . this is the Israel that received us on September 29 and which, exactly six days after our arrival, offers us this opportunity to act in . . . another page of our peoples' heroism . . . Many of the problems and issues that we considered before our aliyah, apartment, containers, clothes, etc. seem so minor now . . . I hope to see you here soon. Israel needs [you] and I am sure that . . . we will build this tough and beautiful *medina* [nation]."[76]

Dubo's letter is one of an activist imbued with Zionist ideology. His references to "heroism" might have been appealing to his colleagues who had remained in Argentina, many of whom may have joined him later. However, his description most likely dissuaded less ideologically motivated people from immigrating to Israel. Most potential immigrants did not want to be heroes or to build a nation; they simply wanted to have a job and own a home in a country that was already built. In another letter, Alicia and Arnaldo described the "really dramatic moment" when they heard the anti-aircraft alarm and had to rush to shelters. They took the necessary precautions and prepared the house for total lockdown by covering all the windows and crisscrossing them with tape, using candles in order to avoid any light escaping. The night, they wrote, was "desolate" due to the complete darkness. "The children felt the impact of the surprise and much patience was necessary to keep them quiet . . . Classes at primary school were suspended during the first two days of war . . . On the other hand, secondary school students were gathered at schools for voluntary tasks . . . In the streets and stores, there are only women, the elderly, and children . . . There is no fear at all about the result of the war; but anguish is felt for those that are on the frontlines . . . All our friends are mobilized (the age limit is fifty-five) and in most cases fathers and sons are in the army."[77]

Potential migrants did not need to receive a dramatic letter from a relative or friend in Israel to feel concern, alarm, or doubts about immigration to Israel. The stories from Zionist circles would have been enough to dissuade a person whose main reason for emigration was the search for better living standards. Israel was at a very difficult juncture and Jewish Argentines knew this, even from Zionist leaders such as Jenny Grynberg, who had been in Argentina during the war and, once back in Israel, published her impressions after the conflict. Declaring she had found "a completely different country," she explained that for the first time in her life she understood the meaning of "the survival of Israel."[78] Possibly, the letters that arrived from Israel exaggerated the situation because many new immigrants would have tended to view the war with more concern than a native-born Israeli raised in a society used to military conflict. However, the Yom Kippur War did represent a serious threat and official references to "survival" may have been enough to discourage a potential immigrant to Israel from committing to the move.

In addition, while the Yom Kippur War generated a dramatic turnabout from the golden period inaugurated by the Six-Day War, the changes in Argentina also had a negative impact on emigration rates from the Zionist perspective. In his annual report, Grossman offered two main conclusions. First, he wrote, "The expectations of an absolute increase in the number of olim from Argentina in 1973 were not realized. [This] is related to three causes: (a) Argentina's improved economic situation . . . since the Peronists' accession to government, and belief in a continuation of this trend; (b) the impact of the Yom Kippur War; and (c) negative echoes about absorption in Israel that have arrived in Argentina through letters from olim and relatives."[79] Grossman's words demonstrate his awareness of the relevance of the interplay between the Argentine and Israeli contexts in driving fluctuations in the number of migrants. Crucially, Grossman did not mention either Zionist ideology or a Jewish education in Argentina as factors relevant to immigration. Instead, Grossman, who had previously reported apprehension about Peronism among certain Jewish circles, explained that the government had not undertaken any anti-Jewish measures and that the Peronist government's economic policy benefited many sectors of society, including prospective migrants to Israel. His second conclusion dealt with changes among this population. Namely, "The increase in the relative proportion of youth in the general aliyah continues. It is reasonable to assume that this trend is a strongly motivated aliyah and we will dedicate efforts during the current year to activities supporting the aliyah of this population."[80]

According to Grossman, there were 2,506 immigrants in 1973, a number 4.5

**Table 4.8. Number of Files Opened for Argentine Migrants to Israel during the Five Months after the Yom Kippur War by Age Group (One File per Household)**

| Age Group | 1973 | | | 1974 | | |
|---|---|---|---|---|---|---|
| | Oct. | Nov. | Dec. | Jan. | Feb. | Total |
| 17–25 | 80 | 71 | 55 | 59 | 30 | **295** |
| 26–30 | 18 | 8 | 7 | 2 | 4 | **39** |
| 31–35 | 15 | 5 | 5 | 5 | - | **30** |
| 36–40 | 10 | 9 | 5 | 2 | 1 | **27** |
| 41–45 | 14 | 16 | 4 | 6 | 1 | **41** |
| 46–50 | 6 | 7 | 4 | 3 | 3 | **21** |
| 51–55 | 7 | 5 | 2 | - | 1 | **17** |
| 56– | 14 | 16 | 8 | 13 | 9 | **60** |
| **Total** | **164** | **137** | **90** | **90** | **49** | **530** |

Source: K. Grossman to U. Narkis, March 3, 1974, TLC, 220232.

*Only the householder is reflected in the table.

percent lower than in 1972 (that year saw 2,624 immigrants).[81] The decline resulted from cancelations and delays following the October war. A comparison of two consecutive years, for December only, sheds light on this fact: 301 immigrants in 1972 compared with only 183 in 1973. Referring to the increased proportion of younger people, the report emphasized that half of the total in 1973 were below the age of twenty-six. Grossman analyzed the decline and the changes in a separate document, with data relating to the period from October 1973 to February 1974. These five months accounted for 530 emigration files, including 1,007 people (211 families and lone immigrants). Almost 70 percent of householders were between the ages of seventeen and thirty-five, and only 10 percent were above the age of fifty-six (table 4.8).[82]

Grossman noted that the number of students immigrating to Israel did not decrease in October when the war began (table 4.9). On the contrary, their numbers increased over three consecutive months. This group only began to diminish in number when the academic year was about to open in Argentina and the student emigration "season" ended. This conjuncture of events suggests that their emigration was not thwarted by the war; rather, students willing to migrate to Israel had left according to their own schedule. Another revealing insight from table 4.9 concerns the population of "industrialists." Their number was already low in relation to the total number of immigrants in October when

**Table 4.9. Number of Files Opened for Argentine Migrants to Israel during the Five Months after the Yom Kippur War by Type of Profession (One File per Household)**

| Profession | 1973 | | | 1974 | | |
|---|---|---|---|---|---|---|
| | Oct. | Nov. | Dec. | Jan. | Feb. | Totals |
| Academics | 15 | 13 | 8 | 7 | 1 | **44** |
| Technicians | 20 | 19 | 5 | 6 | 5 | **55** |
| Merchants | 23 | 16 | 9 | 13 | 4 | **65** |
| Students | 35 | 39 | 40 | 39 | 21 | **174** |
| Industrialists | 10 | - | 1 | - | - | **11** |
| Liberal professions | 32 | 26 | 16 | 11 | 10 | **95** |
| Physicians | 9 | 7 | 1 | 2 | 2 | **21** |
| Other | 20 | 17 | 10 | 12 | 6 | **65** |
| **Total** | **164** | **137** | **90** | **90** | **49** | **530** |

Source: K. Grossman to U. Narkis, March 3, 1974, TLC, 220232.

Observations: Only the householder is reflected in the table. The category of, "academics" includes lawyers, engineers, etc.; "technicians" includes construction workers, programmers, etc.; "liberal professions" includes teachers, officials, general directors, etc.; "physicians" includes dentists; "other" includes housewives, retirees, or those without a defined occupation.

the war started and Perón took office; it became nil after the war. Prospects for industrialists became complex in an Israeli economy seriously damaged by the war. Conversely, Perón's government favored local producers. Its emphasis on domestic consumption also benefited people involved in commerce. As a result, Grossman reported, "only" sixty-five merchants had migrated to Israel. No doubt, he was used to seeing them figure more prominently.

Students and industrialists represent two opposite poles in relation to ideology and material motivation, and this is reflected in their immigration to Israel. Usually, students consider their material circumstances after completing their studies. At the time examined in this book, immigrant students were typically single, did not need a high income, and might have been imbued with idealism. On the other hand, an industrialist had first to weigh the material aspects of emigration even more than a professional would. Industrialists were subjected to the peculiarities of the local economy and its regulations and might also be dependent on certain equipment, materials, and logistical issues. In other words, industrialists were much more reliant than students on the economic structure of the country where production took place. Conversely, students might be considered as "lightweight" migrants, with several options to continue studying after some bureaucratic paperwork.

The Yom Kippur War, short-term improvements in the Argentine economy, and political violence which increased steadily after Perón's death in July 1974 shaped the context within which the immigrants' profile was consolidated: a young population, comprising mostly students and university graduates. Moreover, JA emissaries tended to depict Jewish Argentines as wealthy and continued mentioning the difficulties prospective immigrants faced in selling their property.[83] Therefore, while Jewish Argentine immigrants of 1974 could not expect the economic opportunities that their predecessors of 1973 had enjoyed prior to the Yom Kippur War, they were not in economic need and were driven mostly by push factors operating in Argentine society. The preeminence of such factors, notably life-threatening political violence, is evident in the increased proportion of university students who departed for Israel in 1974.

A comparison of immigrant data during the first half of 1973 and 1974 supports this picture. The decrease in Argentine immigration to Israel is clear (tables 4.10 and 4.11). The reports did not include numbers of families and singles; however, the data shows a variation in the ratio of people to files opened for each family group. While in 1973 there was a file for every 2.11 persons, in 1974 the ratio was 1:1.68. Thus, 1974 included a larger proportion of singles. Most 1974 immigrants were younger than thirty-six (table 4.12); in fact, their proportion within the group was almost 70 percent, as it was in 1973 (table 4.13).

The percentage of Jewish Argentine students between ages eighteen and twenty-five who were planning to continue their studies in Israel increased from

### Table 4.10. Migrants to Israel from Argentina by Month and Year

| Month | 1973 | 1974 |
|---|---|---|
| January | 283 | 200 |
| February | 293 | 191 |
| March | 460 | 217 |
| April | 83 | 277 |
| May | 212 | 106 |
| June | 166 | 64 |
| **Total** | **1,497** | **1,055** |

Source: K. Grossman to U. Narkis, August 9, 1974, TLC, 220757.

### Table 4.11. Files Opened for Immigration by Month and Year

| Month | 1973 | | 1974 | |
|---|---|---|---|---|
| | Files | People | Files | People |
| January | 143 | 302 | 91 | 141 |
| February | 78 | 157 | 49 | 78 |
| March | 124 | 260 | 76 | 120 |
| April | 73 | 168 | 33 | 50 |
| May | 126 | 314 | 65 | 109 |
| June | 177 | 325 | 38 | 75 |
| **Total** | **721** | **1526** | **341** | **573** |

Source: K. Grossman to U. Narkis, August 9, 1974, TLC, 220757.

### Table 4.12. Number of Migrants to Israel by Age Group for 1974

| Age Group | Numbers |
|---|---|
| 0–5 | 88 |
| 6–12 | 123 |
| 13–17 | 108 |
| 18–25 | 272 |
| 26–35 | 127 |
| 36–50 | 176 |
| 51–60 | 76 |
| 61+ | 85 |
| **Total** | **1,055** |

Source: K. Grossman to U. Narkis, August 9, 1974, TLC, 220757.

**Table 4.13. Percentage of Immigrants by Age Group for 1973 and 1974**

| Age Group | 1973<br>Percent | 1974<br>Percent |
|---|---|---|
| 0–17 | 28.53 | 30.23 |
| 18–25 | - | 24.92 |
| 26–35 | - | 12.03 |
| **0–35** | **70.74** | **67.18** |

Source: K. Grossman to U. Narkis, August 9, 1974, TLC, 220757.

57.19 in 1973 to a remarkable 79.41 in 1974. There was also a sharp proportional rise in university graduates. They represented 23.7 percent in 1973 and 35.8 percent in 1974, becoming the most prominent difference between these two datasets in the category of "occupation" (table 4.14). This is not a surprise considering that these populations were among the main victims of Argentine political violence. They had good reasons to look for a new horizon.[84]

Finally, before ending this discussion a few words should be said regarding other categories of immigrants to Israel from Argentina at this juncture. There was a notable increase of retirees: if 1973 saw the departure of eighty-six retirees, or 3.43 percent of the total, in the first half of 1974 there were eighty-five, representing 8.14 percent of the total. The rise in immigrating retirees suggests they were heading to Israel to join family members who had already settled there. Lastly, twenty-three Jewish Argentines who had migrated to Israel in the past

**Table 4.14. Immigrants by Occupation in the First Halves of 1973 and 1974**

| Occupation | Jan.-June, 1973<br>Percent | Jan.-June, 1974<br>Percent |
|---|---|---|
| Liberal professions (university graduates*) | 23.7 | 35.82 |
| Technical and arts | 24.22 | 15.82 |
| Commerce and services | 24.55 | 27.46 |
| Clerical work | 19.63 | 15.82 |
| Needlework and leatherwork | 6.94 | 3.88 |
| Agriculture | 0.9 | 1.20 |
| **Total** | **100** | **100** |

Source: K. Grossman to U. Narkis, August 9, 1974, TLC, 220757.

*The actual proportions in this category should be considered even larger because many graduates were included in other categories.

did so a second time in the first half of 1974. In all likelihood, they were guided by long-term considerations and opted for the external threats faced by Israel instead of living with the internal ones that marked everyday life in Argentina. Nevertheless, they were a minority among Jewish Argentines; moreover, the war triggered a noticeable stream of Argentine returnees from Israel.

The role played by the economy in the case of the 1973 immigrants was related more to their future expectations than to their intermediate requirements. Push factors operating in Argentina were a necessary condition for immigration to Israel but were not sufficient. Israel needed to offer prospects of economic prosperity and security because the Argentines who arrived in 1973 had experienced a trend of social mobility and aspired to continue advancing in their new home. They were better equipped with cultural and economic capital compared with the immigrants of ten years earlier, and many of them expected to own a home according to their preferred schedule and style. However, the Yom Kippur War thwarted the rising immigration trend that had begun in Argentina toward the year 1969 and changed the immigrants' profile. The violence escalated after Perón's death in July 1974 and the interplay of these variables contributed to the emigration of a young population, comprising mostly students and university graduates.

The next chapter analyzes the noticeable stream of emigrants from Israel to Argentina as a consequence of the Yom Kippur War, in parallel with the immigration to Israel of Jewish Argentines affected by state terrorism and the consequences of economic liberalization pursued by the military. It also looks at the frustrated expectations of Israeli and Zionist leaders who anticipated a historical arrival of Argentines in 1978.

## METHODOLOGICAL APPENDIX TO CHAPTER 4

Comparing the occupational distribution of Jewish Argentine immigrants of 1963 with that of 1973 required consideration of two different scenarios. This methodology was necessary due to the use of different labels in the categorization of immigrants in 1963 and 1973. Five of the six labels used for the occupational categories elaborated by Grossman in 1973 do not match those used by Klor in his study of Argentine immigrants during the 1960s (table 4.15). Therefore, in order to compare the two sets of data, it is necessary to consider the subcategories contained in Grossman's report regarding 1973 (table 4.16). The problem with this document is that it mixes labels related to people, such as "nurse," with those related to occupations or disciplines, such as "graphology," within the same category, in this case, the so-called academic professions.

Due to the lack of information regarding occupations within categories 1 and 5, they are counted in groups A and B in two different scenarios (table 4.17). This is because category 1, needlework, cleaning, and leather, might include employees working as cutters, furriers, etc., or alternatively, small business owners who provided jobs to others in the textile industry. Category 5, commerce and services, includes a main subcategory, merchants, which is comparable with the category of the same name used in the classification of 1963 immigrants.

**Table 4.15. Argentine Immigrants in Israel by Occupational Group and Occupation Expressed in Number, Percentage, and Percentage of Economically Active Immigrants (EAI), 1963**

| Group | Occupation | Number | Percent | Group Percent | Percent of EAI |
|---|---|---|---|---|---|
| A | Artisans | 468 | 12.42 | 22.26 | 47.22 |
| | Skilled craftsman | 191 | 5.07 | | |
| | Farmers | 28 | 0.74 | | |
| | Unclassified | 152 | 4.03 | | |
| B | Liberal professionals | 342 | 9.07 | 24.88 | 52.78 |
| | Clerical workers | 367 | 9.74 | | |
| | Merchants and industrialists | 229 | 6.07 | | |
| C | Pupils | 1,165 | 30.92 | 52.86 | - |
| | University students | 59 | 1.58 | | |
| | Housewives and widows without Profession | 752 | 19.98 | | |
| | Retired | 14 | 0.38 | | |
| | **Total** | **3,767** | 100 | 100 | 100 |

Source: Sebastian Klor, "Database 10,487" (unpublished, provided to author by Sebastian Klor).

**Table 4.16. Number of Argentine Immigrant Arrivals in Israel in 1973 by Occupational Category**

| Occupational Categories | N |
|---|---|
| **Needlework, Cleaning, and Leather**<br>Sewing, knitting, weaving, and cutting (41), clothing manufacture (11), furriers (7), laundry and ironing (4), hats (2) | 65 |
| **Agriculture**<br>Agriculture (8), poultry (1) | 9 |
| **Academic Professions***<br>Education* (78), medicine* (76), psychology and sociology (17), pharmacy and biochemistry (16), law* (9), physiotherapy and speech therapy (7), economy (6), optics (5), agronomy (5), journalism (2), graphology (1), nurse (1) | 223 |
| **Technical and Artistic**<br>Building and architecture (61), metal (41), electricity and electronics (37), drivers (19), textile (16), carpenters (9), leather work (8), industry (7), photo and films (4), drawing and graphics (4), practical engineers (3), plumbers (3), programmers (3), dancers (3), musicians (3), painters (2), shoemakers (2), cooks (1), guards (1), air industry (1) | 228 |
| **Commerce and Services**<br>Merchants (176), agents (including travel agents) (18), watchmakers and silversmiths (14), butchers (9), decorators (7), salesmen (6), baker (1) | 231 |
| **Clerical Workers**<br>Clerks (including managers and accountants) (181), hoteliers (2), rabbi (1), mohel (1) | 185 |
| **Total** | 941 |

Source: K. Grossman to U. Narkis, March 19, 1974, TLC, 220756.

*The category academic professions that Grossman and his colleagues used included a variety of occupations related to university studies, not all of them strictly "academic." Therefore, I preferred to maintain this imprecise label, translated literarily. University graduates were also included in other categories.

However, it is impossible to know whether those within the group of watchmakers and silversmiths were shop owners or skilled craftsmen employees. Therefore, the two possibilities are considered. Categories 2, 3, and 6 are comparable directly with their counterparts used to classify the 1963 immigrants, despite label differences in the cases of 2 and 3. Both scenarios presented here take category 4 as equivalent to the so-called skilled craftsmen and artisans in relation to 1963 immigrants, although there is insufficient information to take this for granted. Many householders counted in this category, for example, in the subcategories textile, electronics, metal, or building, might have been small business owners or merchants. That is why the two scenarios estimating variations in the proportion of Group A and Group B occupations from 1963 to 1973 presented in the discussion in chapter 4 are conservative. Table 4.17 shows the occupational distribution of economically active immigrants from Argentina who arrived in Israel in 1973 classified in Groups A and B, using two scenarios:

**Table 4.17. Number and Percentage of Economically Active and Inactive Argentine Immigrants**

| | All Immigrants | |
|---|---|---|
| | Number | Percent |
| **Economically Active** | 941 | 41.58 |
| Needle, cleaning, and leather | 65 | 2.87 |
| Agriculture | 9 | 0.39 |
| Academic professions | 223 | 9.85 |
| Clerical workers | 185 | 8.17 |
| Technical and artistic professions | 228 | 10.08 |
| Commerce and services | 231 | 10.22 |
| **Economically Inactive** | 1,321 | 58.42 |
| **Total** | 2,262 | 100 |

Source: K. Grossman to U. Narkis, March 19, 1974, TLC, 22075.

in 1973 by Occupational Group, Using Alternative Scenarios (Not Including Children under Six)

| | Economically Active Immigrants | | | |
|---|---|---|---|---|
| | Scenario 1 | | Scenario 2 | |
| | Group A | Group B | Group A | Group B |
| | 65 | - | - | 65 |
| | 9 | - | 9 | - |
| | - | 223 | - | 223 |
| | - | 185 | - | 185 |
| | 228 | - | 228 | - |
| | 55 (agents [18], salesmen [6], watchmakers and silversmiths [14], butchers [9], decorators [7, baker [1]) | 176 (merchants [176]) | 17 (butchers [9], decorators [7], baker [1]) | 214 (merchants [176] agents [18] salesmen [6] watchmakers and silversmiths [14]) |
| Total number | 357 | 584 | 254 | 687 |
| Total percent | 37.93 | 62.07 | 26.99 | 73.01 |

# 5

# IN TIMES OF ARGENTINE STATE TERRORISM

Israel's economic and social problems were aggravated by the Yom Kippur War. Immigrants were particularly vulnerable to the situation and some of the Argentines among them began to return to their country of origin, a phenomenon that gathered steam in 1974. Seeking to escape the violence of war in the Middle East, they found their Latin American homeland severely affected by political violence. Yet, this circumstance did not lead to a spike in immigration to Israel, either among new potential migrants or those who had returned to Argentina due to the Yom Kippur conflict. After the death of President Perón, as violent internecine strife increased, JA emissaries in Buenos Aires and Córdoba noted with surprise that immigration to Israel did not surge. Moreover, they observed

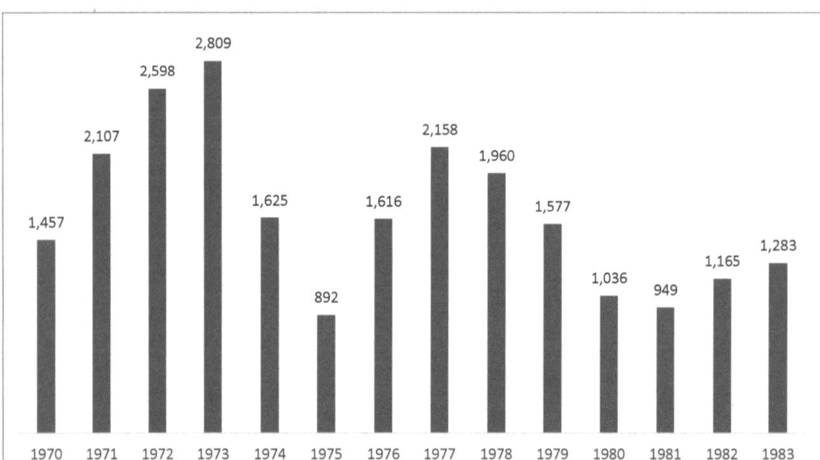


**Figure 5.1** Number of Argentine migrants to Israel by year, 1970–1983. Source: Israeli Central Bureau of Statistics, "Total Immigration to Israel by Select Country by Year," Jewish Virtual Library. The graph does not include returning citizens.

with apprehension that Zionist Jewish Argentine youth did not find Zionism to be an attractive ideology. While the emissaries' assessments about Argentina tended to be accurate, they failed to accept that at this juncture most Argentine Jews were fully integrated into society and were not willing to consider immigration to Israel. The third Peronist government devalued the currency by 100 percent, a move that harmed wide sectors of society, particularly salaried workers and those with modest savings. When the new military regime took power in March 1976, it carried out political repression and liberalized the economy. Thereafter, the negative effects of the economic program and state terrorism caused a clear increase in the number of immigrants (figure 5.1). However, it was not as large as expected by Zionist leaders, who created a special committee to boost immigration from Argentina; the committee failed to attain its goals. Moreover, even during the darkest times of human rights violations, Jewish Argentines continued to return from Israel.

## BAD TIMES FOR ARGENTINE ZIONISM: BETWEEN LEFTISTS AND RETURNEES

1974 saw a noticeable rise in Argentine returnees from Israel. They had left a country suffering the consequences of the Yom Kippur War, returning to a place where the situation was far from peaceful but where Jews were well-rooted and integrated in all spheres of national life. In January, Yosef Arazi, the JA emissary in Córdoba, lamented that recruitment of candidates for immigration had decreased due to the recent war and described the Jews in the province as (1) established families that enjoyed a "comfortable social and financial situation" and were less likely to migrate; (2) the elderly, who needed to be invited by relatives in Israel; (3) young couples (who constituted the highest potential for immigration); (4) and teenagers and youth. Arazi wrote, "[The Jews] are far from Judaism and Israel because they lack education about them and . . . motivation. They have their own views; in particular, in a number of *garinim* [youth groups; lit., kernels], there is no talk of aliyah . . . they are simply not interested."[1]

If this was the situation within organized Jewish youth groups, what was happening to Jewish Argentines unaffiliated with Jewish organizations? Their weak connection to Zionism and Judaism evidenced a decline of Zionist ideology and the primacy of Jewish ethnic bonds as the reverse side of the coin of successful integration into society. Arazi deplored the letters from relatives in Israel who discouraged immigration and reflected on what Argentine historiography calls the Navarrazo, a provincial coup d'état in Córdoba.[2] Arazi was referring to the "anarchy"—the closure of businesses and the shootings involving various armed groups and state organizations that had forced him to close his office.[3] In the midst of this new escalation of violence, the Jewish community of Córdoba adopted a lower profile, reducing social activities and organized gatherings and holding home meetings and even the Kabbalat Shabbat in daylight.[4] Violence also escalated in Buenos Aires, where JA emissary Kalman Grossman reported on right- and left-wing Peronist struggles, illegal organizations, and kidnappings for ransom in the context of the start of a new inflationary cycle.[5] Because José Ber Gelbard, the economics minister, was Jewish, Grossman wrote that some Jews feared they would be blamed for his programs' failures. However, they were trying to behave as if business was as usual, while news coming from Israel through letters and the press discouraged their emigration.[6]

Despite the emissaries' frequent references to letters and news from Israel, there were more powerful and vivid testimonies about the difficulties that Israel posed to Jewish Argentines: the returnees. In March 1974 Grossman reported that "fresh yordim" had arrived and were influencing prospective candidates against immigration to Israel.[7] In Córdoba, letters sent by immigrants satisfied with their treatment in Israel were being read to youth still taking part in community activities as a means of counteracting the stories told by the returnees and promoting immigration to Israel. However, most of the youth were attracted by Argentine politics instead of Zionism and divided by ideological differences. Arazi reported, "The youth problem continues to worry and disturb: they are divided and separated into different sectors which cannot find common ground; leftist ideas are growing and moving this youth far from all interest in Israeli issues. The lack of an Israeli *sheliach* [in this case, an emissary dedicated exclusively to youth education] sharpens a problem that is not only an educational issue but also a very significant and dangerous one."[8]

While JA officials believed that the lack of emissaries was a problem, *La Luz* expressed the opposite view. It referred to the large number of emissaries as a "plague" of "horrific" influence on the Jewish Argentine community and blamed them for creating divisions according to each emissary's partisan interests. Moreover, the magazine accused the emissaries of introducing Jewish youth to "Third World philosophies," which were contrary to Zionist and Jewish values.[9] *La Luz*'s criticism demonstrates that the emissaries' view of Jewish Argentine problems and needs was contested. Nevertheless, from a historical perspective we know that Jewish Argentine involvement in local politics was not the responsibility of a single person or organization. Youth political radicalization was taking place in Western European societies, the United States , and South America due to generational changes. Wide sectors of the youth were willing to demonstrate, some of them even violently, against things they considered injustice. At the same time, the alienation of most of the youth they were trying to promote was not the only problem for JA emissaries. The agency was also under criticism in Israel due to its allegedly large number of emissaries, inflated budget, and the emissaries' lack of ideological motivation and commitment to their mission.[10]

In Argentina, meanwhile, tensions had continued to rise since the rupture between Perón and the left wing of his movement, which decided to return to armed struggle. Within this context, Grossman approached immigration from a realistic perspective that did not even mention ideologies. Forecasting that immigration figures would depend on the security and economic situation in Argentina and Israel, he described two opposing trends affecting Jewish Argentines and elaborated on the returnees' attitude: "On the one hand, the general feeling of 'business as usual' has a great influence on the Jewish middle class; on the other, they continue to be concerned about the deterioration of the political situation, internal security, and an increase in anti-Semitic expressions . . . Despite these facts, there is considerable caution and indifference of many toward aliyah. The yordim who have recently returned from Israel have considerable influence today; some of them slander Israel, apparently to justify their yerida."[11]

Jewish Argentines thinking about leaving for Israel in 1974 had to contend with other considerations, as well. At this juncture and for the first time, the escalation of political violence directly targeted organized Jewish immigration to Israel. The Italmar navigation company had been hired by the JA to transport one hundred people to Israel on board the *Colombo*, scheduled to depart on April 20. The night before, the federal police informed the captain that the ship would be bombed by terrorists if they took the passengers. The company wanted to cancel the departure and only after pressure from the JA, the captain and his crew, advised by their union representative, agreed to the ship's departure. The incident persuaded the JA to consider using a pool of companies and to vary the dispatch of future immigrants by air and sea.[12]

In this context, the Israeli government began paying more serious attention to the question of Argentine returnees. On July 2, 1974, a day after Perón's death, the communication unit of Israel's Ministry of Foreign Affairs asked JA officials in Argentina about the estimated number of "yordim" living in the country.[13] Three weeks later, Grossman received a letter of complaint from his colleague Tzvi Tzvik, a JA representative in the economic unit who was also based in Buenos Aires. "We have received several requests from relatives of olim asking us to take care of their yerida to Argentina," Tzvik wrote. "In most cases, the person is sent by you to our office so we have no option other than to receive them and to withstand the pressure of people that are demanding our authority in this matter."[14] Tzvik added that he would like to avoid "unpleasant discussions" with the relatives. Possibly, he was referring to a number of Argentines in Israel who wanted to return and did not have the means to do so. Being in distress, they may have contacted their relatives in Buenos Aires, who had tried to secure help for them from the office where their immigration had begun.

Migration between Israel and Argentina, then, was a two-way street and there were even those who went back and forth more than once, an "outstanding fact" that Tzvi Rivkin, the emissary in Córdoba, reported in October. A number of "yordim" had asked for assistance to remigrate to Israel. References like this continue to appear in future reports throughout the decade. Rivkin also reported hearing gunfire "sometimes every day" and, like many before him, thought that escalated violence would drive Jewish Argentines to Israel.[15] However, this forecast paralleled reports of an opposite trend, "the weakening of Jewish national values, apathy and assimilation."[16] In November, like his predecessors in the job, Rivkin called for strengthening of the Zionist youth commitment.[17] Some Jewish youth, Grossman explained to his superiors in Israel, had celebrated former president Héctor José Cámpora's victory.[18] "Vast sectors of this youth have adopted leftist positions, which characterize Argentine youth in general, including the vision of Israel as the 'aggressor' that oppresses Palestinian rights. The rightist orientation of the Peronist government caused frustration and confusion among Argentine youth and the influence of this atmosphere is well entrenched among Jewish youth."[19]

In fact, the Peronist Left adopted the terms "oppressor" and "Third World" as defined by the New Left; consequently, Argentina and the Palestinians were perceived as allied in the global fight against imperialism.[20] Jewish Argentines were also protagonists of this cultural and political mix. There had been chants at a Zionist youth gathering in the main synagogue of Buenos Aires during the Yom Kippur War, which combined support for Israel with leftist and Peronist terminology. Slogans included "Fuera los Yankees de America Latina, pero también de Israel y Palestina" (Yankees, get out of Latin America but also out of Israel and Palestine) and "Venga, venga, venga, venga compañero, que acá se está luchando por la paz del mundo entero" (Come, come, come, come, comrade, here we are fighting for world peace).[21] Leftist ideas and other Argentine political notions permeated Jewish and Zionist organizations. And while large portions of youth and students were attracted by local politics and culture, Jewish Argentine adults were also a source of disappointment for JA officials. In December 1974 Grossman reported that in spite of high inflation and "two hundred assassinations since July," Jews in commerce and industry enjoyed the "atmosphere of 'prosperity' that prevails in the consumer goods market at Christmas and New Year's Eve."[22] As such, they were unlikely candidates for emigration to Israel.

Toward the end of 1974 and beginning of 1975, Rivkin commented on the government's success in its offensive against guerrilla groups in Córdoba and indicated that the numerous anti-Semitic publications had no influence on the number of prospective immigrants.[23] He continued to be apprehensive regarding the risky position of Jewish youth continued. "A number of key people in the Jewish community in Córdoba and local institutions are very worried about the activity of groups of young people who are involved with the radical Left, which many young Jews have joined," he wrote. "It was decided that the presence of a special youth emissary is urgently required to be fully dedicated to the problem and to connect the youth to Zionism and Jewish affairs."[24]

While interest in Zionism was in clear decline, immigrant absorption in Israel continued to receive unfavorable publicity. Several Argentine families had complained because the housing they expected was not being provided and people were stuck in absorption centers. According to *Aurora*, these immigrants were being left without answers.[25] On the other hand, the integration of Jewish Argentine youth, which reflected their alienation from Zionism, was clear in 1974 to the compilers of the *American Jewish Year Book*, who wrote, "Writers, journalists, lecturers, and Jewish community leaders seemed to agree that in 1974 the crisis of Argentine Jewish life was more acute than ever before. The inroads by extreme leftist political organizations among Jewish youth were repeatedly decried. This tendency reached its zenith in the latter part of the year when Jewish youth painted on the walls and blackboards of many Jewish schools and organizations such slogans as, 'For a Free Palestine,' 'Freedom for the Palestinians,' and 'Down with American Imperialistic Zionism.'"[26]

These were turbulent times, in which people were increasingly losing their lives. After Perón's death on July 1, 1974, there were 170 acknowledged political murders in the country and more than 200 people were killed in armed clashes with the police.[27] As the Peronist right wing had the upper hand, the man who had been Perón's private secretary, López Rega, became the strongest political figure in a decaying government.[28] Violence increased in Córdoba, where several Jews had been among those kidnapped for ransom. Consequently, Zionist leaders there created a new group named Amos, offering the youth a Jewish option to channel their demands for social justice.[29] One of its leaders was attacked and threatened for his Zionist activities. The group promoted immigration to Israel and numbered twenty members, a roster that did not indicate strong interest on the part of the supposed constituency.[30] Rivkin expressed his concerns about a community that was trying to live a normal life despite the danger. He wrote, "Most of the Jews here are increasing their capital and are not interested in looking at the situation as it is."[31] As a Zionist, he found it hard to understand their decision to stay in Argentina in such circumstances.

Evincing a different perspective, *La Luz* reported on high emigration rates from Israel; these, according to Pinchas Sapir, who had been Israeli minister of finance and chairman of the JA, were greater than those registered during the recession of 1966.[32] Moreover, return migration from Israel to Argentina continued despite the spread of violence. By mid-1975, a message sent to all JA emissaries in Latin America presented JA deputy director Yitzhak Harel as someone with the experience to halt yerida and the person to contact in the event of potential return.[33] His efforts, however, did not meet with unmitigated success. For example, Saúl S. had migrated to Israel in 1965; his wife was pregnant during the Yom Kippur War. In 1975 their Israeli son was a year old and they decided to return to Argentina in order to receive support from the family network in raising the child. They arrived during the last stages of the Peronist government's collapse, after the Rodrigazo, a series of financial measures applied by Economy Minister Celestino Rodrigo in June 1975, the most salient of which was a 100 percent devaluation of the national currency, which led to an inflation rate of almost 800 percent.[34] Saúl's memories reflect the challenges he faced:

> Argentina was a mess: López Rega, the guerillas, Montoneros . . . we felt much less safe here [in Argentina] than in Israel because here you were stopped on the street [by security forces]; you had to get out of the car and put your hands up . . . It was a terrible atmosphere of fear. We had leftist friends and hid many of them in our home for days or weeks. Let's say that in Israel, the enemy was outside, and here it was inside. That was the great difference . . . I tried to work in my profession, but here it was cheaper to pay a harvest worker and my expertise was in making harvesting machines . . . it was a terrible time . . . I went to the National Institute of Industrial Technology and machine factories, but the [technological] backwardness compared with Israel was considerable.[35]

As Saúl's testimony demonstrates, Jewish Argentines' bond with their native country was strong enough to encourage some of them to return from Israel even in the midst of dangers and economic uncertainty. The devaluation hit most Argentines severely and had an impact on Jewish organizations. Jewish schools suffered due to their dependence on monthly fees and the teachers launched a strike.[36] Paradoxically, however, as already mentioned, although the years 1974 and 1975 were among the most chaotic in Argentine contemporary history, there was no surge in immigration to Israel; in fact, in 1975 it reached the lowest point in over a decade. Moreover, according to the *American Jewish*

**Table 5.1. Number of Petitions Submitted by Returning Citizens by Region Representing Number of People and Percentage**

| Region | Petitions | People | Percent |
|---|---|---|---|
| US and Canada | 427 | 1200* | 51.5 |
| Europe | 310 | 871* | 37.4 |
| South America | 34 | 95* | 4.1 |
| Others | 57 | 160* | 7 |
| **Total** | **828** | **2328** | **100** |

Source: "Yerida from Israel: Research," ISA, 506/5, 141.

*Estimated figure based on total number of people and petitions.

*Year Book*, "many Argentines returned to their native country as yordim."[37] At the same time, it is true that the converse phenomenon of remigration to Israel continued throughout the decade, although statistics are scarce. Between June 1975 and February 1976, thirty-four householders submitted a petition from Latin America to return to Israel as immigrants (table 5.1).

Unlike in the 1960s, when push factors operating in Argentina were sufficient variables to explain a surge in immigration to Israel, after the Yom Kippur War, mounting guerrilla and paramilitary activities and the historical devaluation of 1975 did not produce a growth in immigration rates to Israel.[38] Until the war, Israel had attracted Jewish Argentines who sought to leave behind the political mayhem and economic instability in the expectation of a sustained path of prosperity. Thereafter, although the violent upheavals in Argentina worsened, circumstances in Israel deteriorated and the number of immigrants decreased, in part because the pool of potential candidates was smaller but mainly because the Argentine economy was in the expansion phase of its cycle. As noted, the 1973 peak was unique in the history of Jewish Argentine immigration to Israel because people were not driven by pressing economic need. The reduced number of those who migrated in 1974 had similar socio-demographic characteristics and their desire to leave behind increasing Argentine violence overcame their reluctance to move to a country seriously damaged by the Yom Kippur War. Overall, the negative effect of the Yom Kippur War on Argentine immigration to Israel began to shift only in 1976, with the ascendance of a criminal military regime.

## A SHELTER, NOT A PROMISED LAND: ESCAPING DICTATORSHIP

The military regime that ousted María Estela Martínez de Perón lasted from March 24, 1976, to December 10, 1983. During this period, Argentina experienced some of the darkest moments in its history. In a climate dominated by the Cold War doctrine of national security and struggle against leftist guerrillas, the military government systematically violated human rights in order to annihilate political opponents. State terrorism and an economic program aimed at the destruction of the country's domestic industry led to rapidly declining living conditions for vast sectors of the population and forced many into exile. Political repression, commonly called the Dirty War, was particularly violent during the first years of the dictatorship and, due to censorship in Argentina, news about it was more accurate and abundant abroad.[39] The entire society underwent deep transformations, which affected Jewish organizations and their bond with Israel. On July 22, 1976, five JA emissaries and three local activists were detained in Córdoba. The Israelis were members of the Socialist Zionist Hashomer Hatzair (the young guard) and had sought to convince members of Amos to return to

Zionism after they had been drawn to the People's Revolutionary Army (ERP). The detainees were tortured for twelve days. Israeli society was shocked and left wondering who really was in danger in Argentina.[40]

At the same time, the "pauperization of the middle-class" and its harmful effect on the "Jewish community" began to be reported in Jewish Argentine newspapers.[41] Moreover, the integration of the younger generations into national life produced a vacuum in Jewish organizations, which failed to adapt. In a letter to the World Zionist Organization executive Josef Almogy, DAIA secretary Nehemias Resnizky argued that the Zionist Organization of Argentina had become "merely a sum of rubber stamps," implying that the organization was active only formally, without substantial membership or meaningful activity. Resnizky complained that young Jews remained passive regarding "Jewish life, meaning they were not active in the Zionist movement and/or were unaffiliated with Jewish organizations."[42] Asserting his goal of preventing Jewish organizations from becoming an "army of mediocre generals without soldiers," Resnizky added that the "emptying of Jewish knowledge" was not irreversible; he argued instead that it had been caused because "any vigorous and creative freedom of thought is disqualified as if it were heresy."[43] His military references and use of the term "heresy" seem to have been inspired, whether consciously or not, by a military dictatorship that repressed intellectual freedom. His assessment of institutions that no longer represented the interests and beliefs of the majority of Jewish Argentines was accurate. The banning of electoral processes caused an additional problem for institutional life, with Jewish leaders being unsure about the ban's applicability to their organizations.[44] Such was the fear and uncertainty prevailing in Argentine society.

A report written by Israel's ambassador in Buenos Aires, Herzl Inbar, depicted in detail the new challenges that Jewish organizations and many unaffiliated Jews faced. In the report, Inbar referred to an invitation received by the chief rabbi to join an official banquet at Government House, Casa Rosada, in October 1976. In his view, the banquet was a governmental tactic to promote a pluralistic image of the military regime. He explained that the chief rabbi, Abraham Fisherman, did not speak Spanish and consequently was not supported by other leaders. Therefore, the Jewish leaders maneuvered to send Rabbi Schlomo Ben Hamu in his stead. Ben Hamu's presence at the lunch would be presented years later by Jewish Argentines and other sectors of society as proof of the community's alignment with the regime.[45] According to another interpretation, accepting such an invitation was not optional; rather it was an obligation supported by an underlying threat. (This was the contention, for example, made by tango composer Astor Piazzolla, who met with the regime's leaders while his daughter was in exile.)[46] Inbar added in his report that there were "questions and doubts" because it was the first time that the community was described by an Argentine government as a "religious" group. However, despite their uneasiness, Jewish Argentine leaders tried to use the banquet to establish a channel of communication with the government. According to Inbar, "As a gesture of the government, following its celebration [of the banquet] and an additional request from DAIA and the rabbinate to the Interior Ministry, the former president of DAIA-Córdoba, [Jaime] Pompas, was released from detention, which had lasted for several months, without any express accusations (his daughter was active in the underground)."[47]

At the end of 1976, in an attempt to become better acquainted with the people they formally led and represented, Jewish Argentine leaders ordered a study based on interviews with householders affiliated with Jewish institutions.[48] According to the researchers, one-third of the member database was outdated, an observation as eloquent as the study's results. Both revealed signs of institutional weakness. Potential immigration to Israel was low and the researchers considered Jewish education key to explaining the lack of interest. They found there was a tendency against sending children to Jewish schools because these latter provided no "marginal benefit." In addition, only 25 percent of those affiliated with Jewish institutions had practiced any kind of activism during the previous five years, with half of these considering a donation as a form of activism. Membership in sports clubs, researchers noted, was larger, but less ideologically committed. In fact, the size and development of Jewish sports clubs made them a salient Jewish Argentine particularity. There is no other country where affiliated Jews give the sports club such a relevant role. Originally designed as places to spend the weekends in green spots in the suburbs, some of these organizations have turned into private neighborhoods and many members left their homes in the capital to live there permanently. Clearly, at the beginning of military rule Zionist ideology and immigration programs had no place in the lives of those affiliated with Jewish Argentine organizations, and most unaffiliated Jewish Argentines were even further from Zionism. Zionist motivation would not produce favorable changes in the migration trend.

What did begin to have an impact on immigration to Israel was the systematic annihilation of people defined as subversive by the military. In early 1977 a JA representative based in Argentina listed the following problems: increasing abandonment of Jewish life; a lack of appropriate leadership to deal with ongoing problems; conflicts within and between Jewish organizations; and crises in Jewish education due to the lack of trained teachers. The same official noted an increase in migration to Israel: "In 1976, there were approximately 1,900 olim compared with approximately 1,000 the previous year. It is thought that the [problem with] this aliyah stems from the fact that the majority are young people fleeing regime persecution because they were leftists or relatives of leftists."[49]

Indeed, the increase in immigration figures was driven by state terrorism rather than a sudden strengthening of Zionist commitment. However, the cumulative effects of a deteriorating economy also need to be considered. It was within this context that General Yitzhak Pundak arrived from Israel to head the fifty JA emissaries in Argentina, four of whom dealt with immigration. Apart from JA emissaries, Israel's ambassador, Ram Nirgad, who was a skilled diplomat, provided keen insights into the changes taking place.[50] He noted that the main Jewish organizations were losing their centrality in relation to other Jewish groups because they defined themselves as Orthodox and Zionist, while most Jewish Argentines did not subscribe to such categorizations. In his view, Jewish Argentines were reassessing their identity, as well as their connection to Judaism, Israel, and Argentina. Thus, a number of independent, conservative, and reform communities opened their own schools, synagogues, cooperatives, community centers, and sports clubs. Nirgad believed that the majority of Jews were now wealthy and no longer consisted mainly of workers and craftsmen. Despite this, donations to Israel had been unsatisfactory the previous year, and there was almost no investment in Israel on the part of the Argentines. Making matters worse, in his view the Jewish educational network was facing a financial crisis, lacked the appropriate manpower, and was rife with ideological confusion. Nirgad concluded, "The community and its leaders have almost no relations with the heads of the [Argentine] government and, in that sense, the embassy constitutes a bridge that is often needed . . . Domestically, many areas [education, etc.] receive material support from Israel."[51]

Nirgad's observations reflect the powerlessness of Jewish Argentine community leaders under military rule and the weakening of their traditional organizations. After the return to democracy, these leaders came under harsh criticism from Jewish Argentines whose relatives were victims of the repression. They believed that Jewish organizations could have contributed more toward the rescue of the "disappeared." Journalists and academicians tended to single out the DAIA, interpreting the organization's actions and omissions as evidence of a clear alignment with the military regime. Based on Nirgad's description, however, one could argue that such criticism ignored the real weakness of Jewish institutions in the face of the military, which had no hesitation in committing the most heinous crimes against the country's citizens, foreigners, and members of the Catholic Church. In a book that came out in Hebrew, Marcel Zohar criticized the role of Israel and of Ambassador Nirgad and praised Rabbi Marshall Meyer and JA emissary Daniel Recanati for helping victims of state terrorism.[52] Nevertheless, Meyer described Nirgad as "a credit to Israel" and declared that his own accomplishments would not have been possible without the ambassador's support and advice. Recanati dismissed as "ridiculous" Zohar's allegation that Nirgad did not help Jewish Argentines facing government oppression.[53]

For his part, Nirgad reported at the time that while military rule was not harming the Jews directly, the clandestine struggle had undermined the rule of law, making life more difficult for them as well as for everyone else in Argentina. He listed five issues for consideration: (1) traditional "Nazi" propaganda and bombings, both anonymously targeting Jews; (2) Nazi elements within the repressive forces, evident in the detention of Jews suspected of connections with guerillas; (3) the overrepresentation of Jews in underground groups compared with their representation in society as a whole, while the presence of Jews in key Peronist [left-wing] positions was used by anti-Semitic elements to defame all the Jews; (4) government regulation of the marginal activities of Nazi groups in accordance with its own international and national interests; and (5) the Jews' unwillingness to consider themselves truly endangered as a group. Instead, their main worries were "Jewish youth, in particular, those attracted by leftist movements and the underground; also, assimilation and mixed marriages, which have reached 35 percent in the countryside."[54] Regarding increased immigration to Israel, Nirgad wrote, "Aliyah during the past year was a consequence of the situation regarding security as already described. Many among the olim found in Israel a shelter . . . and their connection to Judaism and the Israeli nation is questionable."[55]

Israel's leadership was also assessing the Argentine situation. Two months after Nirgad's report, the JA found itself working on a four-year plan for Argentine immigration elaborated by Raanan Weitz, the director of its settlement department.[56] The discussion on ways to increase this immigration was brought to the JA board, and a meeting of former JA emissaries to Argentina was organized to gather information and ideas for future action.[57] Israeli leaders' intentions did not necessarily correspond with Jewish Argentines' own goals, however. Moreover, Jewish Argentine leaders had their own views about what was happening in Argentina and how to deal with it publicly. In June, General Pundak implied on Israel's state radio, Kol Israel, that the Jewish Argentine community was in danger. His statements were considered "inappropriate and inaccurate" by DAIA, which protested to Israel's foreign minister, Moshe Dayan.[58] While visiting Israel in August 1977, a group of Jewish Argentine leaders demanded Pundak's replacement, arguing that the two sides shared no common ground. They made clear that anti-Semitism was not supported officially in Argentina and demanded a better selection of emissaries with expertise in Jewish education.[59] Their interest in strengthening Jewish education in Argentine meant that immigration to Israel was not their priority.

In order to understand the source of the disagreement between Pundak and Argentine leaders, it is necessary to reconstruct a series of major events. On April 15, 1977, Jacobo Timerman was kidnapped from his home by security forces.[60] A Jew and a Zionist, he was the owner of one of the leading newspapers, *La Opinión*. His Jewishness had been enough to attract the attention of paramilitary groups that had carried out anti-Semitic campaigns even before the onset of the dictatorship. Later, the regime accused Timerman of being connected to another Jew, David Graiver, who had administered money for the Peronist guerrilla group Montoneros and appeared to be the main financial backer of *La Opinión*.[61] While anti-Semitic publications, bombings, and threats had been part of the general upheaval several years prior to the Timerman affair, the kidnapping provoked an increase in anti-Semitic activities. At the DAIA board meeting of May 2, Resnizky denounced these actions by providing names of some of the people responsible. His speech was published in the Jewish Argentine newspaper *Nueva Sion* and the *New York Times*.[62] The events that followed could have been perceived as confirmation of an anti-Semitic campaign in Argentina by Jewish leaders there and abroad, as well as by portions of the Jewish Argentine population.[63] While the distinction between official and unofficial anti-Semitism seemed important to DAIA, it was regarded as meaningless in the United States and Israel.

On June 20 the wife of Jacobo Kovadloff, the American Jewish Committee's (AJC) representative in Buenos Aires, answered the telephone in their home and heard an unknown voice say, "Tell your husband that if he does not leave the country, the same thing that happened to Timerman will happen to him."[64] The next day Kovadloff received a note: "Traitor, you're overdoing your duplicitous game. Go before it is too late. We don't want Yankee or Jewish offices." There were two more calls that day and Kovadloff left for Brazil. His family departed the following day. They were escorted to the airport by a US embassy car, searched so thoroughly that their plane was delayed by half an hour, and a uniformed official crushed the lenses of Kovadloff's son's eyeglasses.[65] The AJC decided to close its office in Buenos Aires, which had been open for twenty-nine years. In the United States, AJC president Richard Maass declared that the Argentine government had "subversive and antidemocratic forces within its own structure" and that a large number of extreme right-wingers in positions of authority had launched a campaign against the Jews in order to embarrass President Videla.[66] B'nai B'rith's *Messenger* asserted that the closure was no surprise since the Jewish community of Argentina was "living in a climate of fear."[67]

On July 27 Marcos Resnizky (aged twenty-two), son of the DAIA secretary Nehemias Resnizky, was taken from his home and tortured for days.[68] The abduction was not mentioned in the Israeli or Argentine press, but Jewish Argentine leaders including Mario Gorenstein and Marcos's father issued statements during a visit to the United States. Nehemias Resnizky hoped that the kidnappers would release his son and expected to "spare the community the knowledge of yet another outrage." He also declared that while the government itself was not anti-Semitic, there were "obscure and pogromist forces" at work in the country.[69] Marcos's rapid release turned out to be one of the most controversial episodes in contemporary Jewish Argentine history. Individuals such as Sara Brodsky, the mother of a disappeared person who received no support from DAIA in locating and rescuing relatives, argued that Nehemias Resnizky used his influence to get his son back and did not care about others.[70] Generally, critics believe that DAIA could have dealt with the government more effectively regarding the disappeared. Journalistic investigations and recent academic studies have strengthened this view, based on the fact that Resnizky had a meeting at the Interior Ministry.[71] According to Resnizky's detractors, he negotiated institutional silence regarding the crimes of the military rule in exchange for the life of his son. After his release, Marcos and his sister migrated to Israel, while Resnizky continued as DAIA president, for which he has been also criticized.[72]

The idea that Resnizky's son was released as a result of his father's meeting with Interior Ministry officials overestimates his personal influence, that of DAIA, and the potential effects of US Jewish organizational pressure on the military regime. Public denunciation of anti-Semitism in the United States, which was the only way to influence the regime, was independent of DAIA's will; it began before Marcos's kidnapping and did not end with that incident. DAIA's attitude toward US criticism was irrelevant. Second, the teenage daughter of the president of DAIA-Córdoba, Alejandra Jaimovich, was also kidnapped, tortured, and disappeared. However, the institutional position of her father had no effect on the actions of the criminals.[73] Moreover, military rule was based on the division of the nation into three areas, between the three military arms, which included within them factional divisions; at the bottom of the pyramid was a multitude of soldiers, policeman, gangsters, hooligans, and regular criminals.[74] Within this structure, even people with direct influence on the president could not guarantee that they could locate or recover a disappeared person. Resnizky was not the only Jew who met with Interior Ministry officials regarding the abduction of a family member; nor was Marcos the only Argentine who survived illegal detention. A wide range of factors might have led to his release, including random, unknown ones. Lastly, the military regime had no problem disappearing French nuns (in Deember 1977) and many other foreigners (including Dagmar Hagelin, a young Swedish-Argentine woman who vanished in January 1977). Sweden closed its embassy in Buenos Aires in protest while US president James Carter and Pope Jean Paul II pressed for Dagmar's release.[75] Moreover, in both cases the French and Swedish governments claimed they had a solid case against a specific suspect, Captain Alfredo Astiz, including eye witness accounts; however, the military rulers simply denied the facts. France and Sweden did not even get a chance to question Astiz despite their repeated demands.[76] In this atmosphere, neither Resnizky nor DAIA were in a position to influence the dictators.

The described incidents, which could be interpreted as part of an anti-Semitic campaign, were compounded when an influential journalist, Mariano Grondona, published an article in a mainstream political magazine arguing that the Jews were an unresolved problem in Argentina because they were not assimilated into the national fabric.[77] At the end of 1977, an article published in the *New York Times* presented an assessment of anti-Semitism in Argentina in the context of political repression.[78] It argued that, given the anti-Semitic actions committed by members of the security forces, it was clear that President Videla did not have a monopoly on repression. Repressive forces were acting with impunity and Videla's declarations and meetings with Resnizky were insufficient to offset the sense of insecurity among many Jews. Moreover, the Jewish leadership in Argentina was wrong in arguing that anti-Semitic threats like those against Kovadloff were committed by right-wing groups outside of the official security forces.

In addition, it appears some sectors of the repressive forces believed the Jews were deeply involved in left-wing guerrilla activities. The *New York Times* article stated, correctly, that the majority of Argentine Jews were not affected directly by security operations; however, according to an anonymous Jewish source, about six hundred Jews, mostly young people, were among the eight thousand people killed, arrested, or kidnapped from March 1976. Interestingly, these figures are compatible with those established by various organizations dealing with the issue in contemporary Argentina, a fact that debunks the argument that the population was unaware of the crimes at the time. The total number of Argentine disappeared registered by the National Commission for the Investigation of Disappeared People (CONADEP) was 8,961.[79] The number of Jewish Argentine disappeared is estimated at some thirteen hundred for the entire period of military rule.[80] The article also mentioned accounts from people who testified they had been detained by security personnel just because they were Jews; it also noted reports of swastikas and photographs of Hitler seen at detention centers. Lastly, the *Times* explained that for Argentine security forces, any suspicion of a connection with groups regarded as "left-wing" or "subversive" was sufficient cause for a "secretive arrest, violent interrogation, and a summary execution."[81]

During the Argentine dictatorship, Jewish Argentine leaders agreed unofficially on the characteristics of anti-Semitic incidents that were occurring in the country. At the same time, both the general and the Jewish press in the United States were reporting on Jewish affairs in Argentina. Jewish leaders in the United States and in Israel were well aware of Jewish youth involvement in leftist groups. From the point of view of Israeli and North American Jewish organizations, the distinction made by Jewish Argentine leaders was less relevant and the question was rather about the degree and characterization of the dangers that threatened Jewish Argentines. While in the United States Jewish organizations publicly denounced anti-Semitic incidents, in Israel discussion focused on how to increase Jewish Argentine immigration. Toward that goal, the interests of the Jewish state and the Zionist ethos coincided. However, most Jewish Argentines did not see themselves as refugees in need of a safe haven.

The first two years of military rule were the worst in terms of the implementation of state terrorism and resulted in a new surge of immigration to Israel. Many people who were in danger due to their political activities and were aware of the human rights violations committed by the dictatorship found a haven in Israel. In addition, the series of anti-Semitic actions described in this section certainly influenced the decision of Jewish Argentines uninvolved in politics to opt for immigration to Israel. Lastly, the year 1977 registered an additional increase in Argentine immigration to Israel compared with 1976, reflecting the accumulated effects of the dictatorship's state terrorism and its economic program. Once again, Zionist and Israeli leaders expected an imminent escalation in Argentine immigration.

## STILL AWAITING ARGENTINE IMMIGRANTS

On August 22–23, 1977, a delegation of Jewish Argentine leaders representing various sectors of the organized Jewish Argentine community visited Israel. They included Nehmias Resnizky (DAIA secretary), Mario Gorenstein (AMIA president), Rabbi Schlomo Ben-Hamu (AMIA chief rabbi), Rabbi Marshall Meyer (Conservative movement), Jaime Barilko (director of the Central Committee for Jewish Education of Argentina), Simon Felenbok (Maccabi president), representatives of three main sports clubs (Club Náutico Hacoaj, Sociedad Hebraica Argentina, and Club Atlético Sefaradí Argentino), and a representative from OLEI. During the visit, the rabbis presented a program to strengthen the connection with Israel; Rabbi Ben Hamu arranged for the selection of 250 students to receive rabbinical instruction there; and Rabbi Marshall Meyer shared views on how to bolster communication between the younger generations in Israel and the Diaspora.

At the heart of the visit was a four-year plan conceived by settlement department head Ranaan Weitz, which was presented to the delegates at the headquarters of the JA. Its goal was to reach a target of three thousand Argentine immigrants in 1977. As part of this plan, an absorption program for five hundred families had begun functioning in Beersheba, and three hundred families had already arrived there. Similar programs were being prepared for Jerusalem, Carmiel, Migdal HaEmek, Nazareth Illit, Eilat, and Kiryat Gat. Special training programs were established for dentists, furriers, accountants, marketing specialists, salesmen, and workers in the clothing and hotel industries. The plan included the construction of two Argentine moshavim, each for 120 families, and an Argentine-style country club in Jerusalem. The ambitious scheme also included training for people who aspired to set up small- and medium-size businesses, as well as the absorption of three hundred students. Seven JA emissaries were assigned to the task of recruitment in Buenos Aires, one in Córdoba, and another was scheduled to arrive in Rosario. Additional staff would travel to Argentina on short visits to promote specific projects. As requested by the Argentine delegation, the JA was considering a program for young couples and families consisting of various options, including a volunteer period in a kibbutz or a development town. The program would be modeled on Tapuz ("orange"), which had been set up during the Yom Kippur War to bring young people to orchards to harvest fruit while Israel's human resources were directed to the war effort.

The visitors tasked with organizing a "committee for aliyah" in Argentina, including representatives from all the Jewish organizations, in order to strengthen and rejuvenate Zionist leadership. The JA's immigration and absorption departments considered it possible to aim for a record high that would surpass that of 1963: five thousand Jewish Argentine immigrants in one year. At the same time, the Argentine leaders also shared their own challenges, complaints, and interests. They criticized Yitzhak Pundak, head of the JA in Argentina. They also explained that Zionist promotional material had to be carefully reviewed in order to avoid the regime's censorship. Moreover, some of the delegation members suggested changing the name and purpose of the traditional fundraising campaign for Israel, due to the regime's restrictions on money transfers. Instead of Keren Hayesod (United Israel Appeal), it should be called "community fund," which would be available "in the event of local needs." The suggestion was not naive. The donation of money and immigration to Israel were integral parts of the material connection between Israel and the Diaspora. Israel, in turn, supported Jewish education and Zionist activities. Now Jewish Argentine leaders wanted to raise money in order to sustain Jewish continuity in line with their own perspective.

Prime Minister Menachem Begin met with the Argentine group twice, once at the beginning of their visit in the company of other leading officials, and once alone at the end. The visit protocols reflect how most of the visitors supposedly changed modified their thinking following conversations with Begin and other ministers. At the first meeting, the Argentines put forward their views about the political situation in Argentina, painting a gloomy and worrisome picture. Begin expressed his deep concern and called to work for "greater aliyah." The visitors' first reaction to Begin's idea was as follows: "Although most of the speakers shared views regarding the situation, not everyone arrived at the same . . . solution to the problem. There were those (the minority) who agreed with the Prime Minister's approach and those (the majority) who emphasized the need for action on long-term issues such as education, a focus on Jewish identity, and tradition. In relation to aliyah, there were comments about the need to improve absorption in Israel."[82]

Clearly, during the first meeting, only a minority viewed immigration to Israel as the solution to the challenges facing Jewish Argentines and preferred, instead, to work on strengthening local aspects of their organizations. This was reflected in the idea to transform fundraising for Israel into a local endeavor. However, at the second meeting, the leaders moved closer to agreeing with Begin. According to the protocols, this change was the result of their conference with the absorption minister, who presented new programs. The official visit closed with a personal message from Begin, calling for the leaders to convey to the Jewish people of Argentina the need for a "massive aliyah." Another account of the visit, also official but evidently written by a different representative, emphasized that the delegation was not homogeneous, especially in regard to a "solution to the problems of their community."[83] Accordingly, Begin asked the delegation to make a great effort to promote immigration in the face of a "fragile situation" that included kidnappings, torture, and assassinations. Nevertheless, although assimilation represented the biggest danger in the delegates' view, they professed themselves "impotent about it."[84] Moreover, following their visit to absorption centers and new development towns for Argentine immigrants, they "emphasized that emissaries from leftist [Israeli] parties conduct activities in Argentina that endanger the Jewish community and which, on more than one occasion, brought the youth under their supervision to incarceration. They referred to the awful absorption in Israel, due to which figures of aliyah are low and there is a considerable percentage of yordim who are disappointed with their treatment."[85]

Thus, while Begin emphasized the dangers posed by political repression and suggested that immigration to Israel was the best response, Argentine leaders (the protocols do not specify which ones) blamed leftist Israeli emissaries for their influence on youth, criticized immigrant absorption in Israel, and pointed to disappointed returnees as the reason for low immigration rates. Reading between the lines, Argentine leaders appear to have felt criticized for not being Zionist enough because, despite the dangerous Argentine context, immigration to Israel was not as high as expected. Their reaction was to blame Israel both for low immigration rates and Jewish youth involvement in politics. Both sides in the discussion were avoiding a central point: Jewish Argentines were well integrated into Argentine society. Because they identified as Argentines and cared about Argentine society, Jewish youth sought to become more involved in politics and the majority of Jews wanted to continue their lives in Argentina. This was a historical fact independent of Israeli or local Jewish leaders' actions.

Notably, the Israeli press did not cover disagreements within the delegation and their initial opposition to Begin's proposal. Although some articles referred in passing to the discord, the headlines set the official tone. *Maariv* published an article titled "Jewish Argentine Leaders Say That an Increase in Aliyah Is the Solution for Their Community," with a subheading stating that they intended to bring five thousand new immigrants in one year. Quoting Josef Almogy, president of the Zionist Executive, the article explained that while they disagreed on the issue at the beginning of their visit, in the end they decided that Begin's call was the best solution to their problems.[86] A different perspective on Latin American Jews and immigration to Israel, closer to the localism expressed by the delegation's first negative reaction toward Begin's proposal, had appeared in *Haaretz* half a year earlier. At the time, the paper reported on a disappointed Shimon Shofty from Kibbutz Ramat HaShofet, who had served as an emissary in Latin America. Once back in Israel, Shofty declared that Zionist activities were ineffective and that young Latin American Jews and their new intelligentsia believed that it was possible to continue living as Jews without a connection to Israel.[87]

In addition to Begin's clear interest—both ideological and official—in Jewish immigration, circumstances on the ground led to the belief that Jewish Argentines truly were in danger. As noted, the first period of the military regime was the most aggressive in committing human rights violations. All segments of Argentine society were immersed in a process of violence that had escalated years before, and the country had simply become used to it. Moreover, while denouncing anti-Semitic actions, Jewish leadership argued that such acts were not sponsored by the regime. On the other hand, for a traditional Zionist leader like Begin, whose family was murdered by Nazis, anti-Semitism was the historical tragedy from which the Jews had to be rescued. Anti-Semitic actions in Argentina were occurring in a broader context of human rights violations constituting a vital part of the military's plan to "reorganize" society.

The Argentine labor movement had been a powerful social actor that managed to resist several attempts at economic reform. The military regime's economic plan was aimed at weakening domestic industry in favor of financial valorization as a means of disciplining society. As the majority of Argentines, and particularly the organized labor movement, depended on the domestic market, their power would be diminished since their economic base would be destroyed.[88] Thus, Argentine society and its labor movement would be prevented from continuing their long tradition of organized struggle to protect their jobs and interests. José Alfredo Martínez de Hoz, Argentina's economy minister, opened up the country to imports of industrial products and deregulated the financial market. As a result, import substitution industrialization was abandoned. New financial options such as short-term bonds were created, and speculation became more profitable than investment in industry.[89] The long-term effects of the new economic program would be reflected years later in a debt crisis and worsening social and development indicators. In the short term, the program was unable to halt inflation, resulting in the erosion of the living standards of the working and middle classes.[90]

The effects of such a program on Jewish Argentines became evident in the profile of a portion of the candidates for immigration to Israel during the second half of 1977. Based in Córdoba, JA emissary Yoav Koifman reported that the relative calm in guerrilla and military operations had brought "mental tranquility" and therefore "unwillingness to emigrate." At the same time, he elaborated on the effects of inflation and its relation to Jewish immigration to Israel. "[Inflation] hurts the Jewish community badly because most are shopkeepers. The continuous rise in prices brings them many losses when you consider that consumer power decreased steeply . . . A phenomenon that we have begun to see lately, but that will . . . increase is distress among young couples . . . holding academic degrees and coming to us. It is difficult for them to attain their parents' [living] standard because their salary [is less than] their daily expenditures. These couples are seriously interested in . . . possibilities in Israel."[91]

Koifman emphasized that the economic situation of salaried educated people was "going downhill;" in his view, this trend would cause an increase in immigration to Israel.[92] Indeed, over a four-month period, forty-eight people migrated to Israel from Córdoba and for ten of them it was not the first time; they already held Israeli citizenship. He also depicted the community in Córdoba as weakened, as many leaders had emigrated and even the current community president was planning to migrate to Israel. He lamented that the Zionist activities he tried to organize "did not flourish as expected, due to the fear and reservations that still exist within the community."[93] Possibly, the connection of Zionist movements to leftist organizations, which could be seen clearly in Córdoba, prevented people from associating with the movement. Indeed, the dismantlement of social bonds within Argentine society was one of the main goals of state terrorism.[94] On the other hand, it could be that Jewish Argentines in Córdoba simply did not find Zionist activities attractive.

Koifman's report reflected the period when Argentine state terrorism and the liberalization of the economy operated in tandem and the number of Jewish Argentine migrants to Israel rose; more left in 1977 than in 1976. Encouraged by this increase, a committee under the Prime Minister's Office and an interministerial committee were created in Israel in early 1978. These bodies would be in charge of the absorption of Jewish Argentines, on the understanding that "in light of what is going on [there] is an urgent need to activate programs as soon as possible."[95] Those comprising the prime-ministerial committee gathered for the first time on April 12, at which time they expressed varied, even discordant views.[96] Haim Aron (OLEI) observed that many Jewish Argentines had migrated to countries other than Israel, adding that a number of Israeli absorption initiatives had failed. Yeshayahu Anug, a government representative, believed that Argentine Jewry was not experiencing economic distress and was not in an emergency situation requiring emigration. In a later meeting, they agreed on the need to gather information, research available locations for absorption, and offer specific projects for each target group as soon as possible.[97]

Two weeks later, the committee concluded that Carmiel, Arad, Kiryat Gat, Beersheba, Jerusalem, and Netanya were the best options for the absorption of Argentines and decided to begin printing promotional brochures in Spanish. However, economic, social, and housing programs in these cities were not yet in place.[98] The committee discussed a dossier compiled by the Absorption Ministry about Latin American experiences in Israel, which emphasized that Argentines represented more than half of those immigrating from the region. Their immigration had increased since the end of 1975, the dossier explained, due to political changes in Latin American countries. Still, this rise was "disappointing" in relation to expected goals.[99] According to the report, which compared "Latin Americans" with "all immigrants," Latin American absorption was satisfactory even though during certain periods their return rate had reached 24 percent. In conclusion, it stated, "It is a high percentage in relation to all the olim but low in relation to other immigrants from the West. The yerida rate is particularly high among single people, who constitute some 40 percent of Latin American olim. Yerida is lower among families."[100]

On May 30, 1978, fourteen people took part in a meeting of the Committee for the Immigration of Argentine Jews, including representatives of Israel's main ministries, the JA, and OLEI. Moshe Yagar (Prime Minister's Office) emphasized the urgent need for jobs and housing for immigrant absorption. JA director Uzi Narkis said that Israel envisaged the arrival of more than three thousand Argentines in 1978, but the information he provided contradicted his own statement. No doubt, expectations were mostly a reflection of the prime minister's wishful thinking while, as in the case of Argentine leaders, the lower echelons of the Israeli absorption system did not really believe it was possible. Indeed, absorption in Beersheba had ceased after the arrival of 350 families due to the lack of jobs. Regarding Argentina, Narkis used the outdated figure of "about 400,000 Jews," arguing that only 30 percent considered themselves members of the Jewish people, and an even smaller share defined themselves as Zionists.[101] Very few were thinking of immigrating to Israel. "The reaction of the Jews of Argentina to the difficult situation there is not as we would like it to be: there is much assimilation [mixed marriages] and there are no conversions [to Judaism], the communities in the provinces are shrinking and deteriorating, the leadership is leaving . . . We should remember that aliyah costs money and that the potential difficulties in Israel seem greater than those of the Jews there."[102] Clearly, Narkis recognized the gap between the expectations of Zionist leaders and the situation on the ground, as well as the economic obstacles that immigration posed to potential candidates.

Eliyahu Ben-Elieser, another committee member, was even more skeptical, stating that Argentine Jewry did not feel they were in danger. He believed Jewish and Zionist feelings in the country to be weak and that the potential for immigration was low. Nevertheless, he agreed to do his best to maximize the numbers of immigrants. There were already forty projects under examination, including the creation of new industries. The Israeli officials decided to work toward receiving three thousand families within two to three years and to "relocate a community" instead of individuals.[103]

The committee also discussed the socioeconomic profile of potential immigrants. According to available information, these were mainly individuals involved in commerce (38.5 percent), industry (31.8), and services (26.3 percent). However, three factors were operating against their immigration: (1) a lack of housing that would meet their expectations; (2) a desire for an independent source of income, such as owning a shop; and (3) a lack of familiarity with the Israeli economy. The first point was critical because at the time there were only a small number of apartments available in a limited number of locations for immigrants in general: Carmiel (370), Kiryat Gat (130), Arad (20), Maalot (55), and Jerusalem (700).[104] The housing shortage was not new, nor was it a secret. While the committee was discussing how to accommodate thousands of future immigrants, those already in Israel were complaining about their living conditions. For example, twenty-two Latin American families residing in the environs of Netanya but working in the city center sent a petition to the Absorption Ministry, stating, "As 'new Israelis' we have the right to [send] this petition . . . From the moment of our aliyah we accepted all the obligations coming from the State of Israel; we offered our entire professional talent, creativity, our sons and hopes, without doubts, hesitation, or conditions, (some of us serve in the IDF reserves), because our unique objective is a Jewish life in our country, for the first time in our lives."[105]

The signatories explained that they had been in a difficult situation for more than two years and were aware of the problem of "increased yerida." Stressing that they had jobs, they defined themselves as Zionists and OLEI activists working to bring "all the Jews" to the country. They wanted either a mortgage of "at least IL 400,000" or to obtain new immigrant housing in buildings regulated by the Absorption Ministry in Netanya. The petitioners numbered seventy-three individuals, mostly adult professionals. Wanting the best of both worlds, they defended their right to petition as Israelis but were doing so as Latin American immigrants. They demanded a personal meeting with officials from the Absorption Ministry and, in the final paragraph, hinted that leaving the country was an option: "There is a bitter feeling regarding the lack of solutions to our problem, a sense that our absorption in Israel could be endangered."[106]

In short, following Begin's initiative, Israel had created the committees to boost immigration; however, absorption problems, which had become evident at the beginning of the decade, were still present. Another case from 1979 is illustrative of this point. A Zionist Argentine activist complained that he was advised to stay in Argentina because there were no apartments in Jerusalem, where he and his wife wanted to reunite with their daughter who was already in Israel. While the housing shortage was real, the activist regarded the situation with distrust; this suspicion was reinforced by the fact that the couple had lived in Israel twice, in 1954 and 1970. "I expected some kind of difficulty but not such ill-intentioned treatment," he wrote. "Either they are testing us to see if we are convinced and how far are we willing to go to defend our rights, or is it that they only want to take our daughter and break the family apart?"[107]

Material limitations, state policies, and bureaucratic misunderstandings were usually taken personally by the immigrants, who did not see or cared little about the broader picture and felt their rights were being violated. Argentine immigration in the second half of the 1970s was characterized by various profiles: professionals seeking to take advantage of the possibilities for social mobility, perceived as impossible in Argentina; people who saw their living standards eroded by Argentina's economic liberalization; and those escaping from political repression. The complexity of the Argentine immigrant population and the sudden fluctuations that characterized the Argentine economy explain why they were described alternatively as wealthy or middle class, and why some observers considered them to be in need of rescue while others did not. In any event, the weight of Begin's views did not alter reality.

The governmental bodies for boosting Argentine immigration failed to achieve their goals, and 1977 remained the peak year for the arrival of such migrants during the military dictatorship. The skepticism expressed by several committee members and Argentine delegates discussed earlier was more realistic than the goal of a new record in Argentine immigration. Moreover, Argentine return migration from Israel did not stop at any point during the decade, although there were variations between different periods (table 5.2). The data available refers to "Latin American leaving rates" from Israel, which was not exactly equivalent to "Argentine return." However, the influence of Argentine immigrants on the general trend is clear. For instance, the economic and political causes for the high return rate of those who arrived in Israel in 1970 and left by 1973 included the still relatively low level of political violence in Argentina combined with the effects of the Yom Kippur War and its associated recession. In the case of the high leaving rate of those who arrived in Israel in 1978 and left by 1981, the main reason was that the numbers in this immigration had risen substantially as a result of state terrorism. Many of the Argentines left Israel for Europe as soon as possible, having used the Jewish state as a temporary refuge.

**Table 5.2. Percentage of Latin Americans Who Left Israel by Year of Arrival, Measured after One, Two, Three, Four, and Five Years**

| Year of Arrival | Number of years after arrival 1 | 2 | 3 | 4 | 5 |
|---|---|---|---|---|---|
| 1970 | 13 | 17 | 20 | - | - |
| 1971 | 7 | 12 | 18 | - | - |
| 1972 | 5 | - | 16 | - | - |
| 1973 | 9 | - | 17 | - | 25 |
| 1974 | 6 | - | 16 | - | - |
| 1975 | 7 | - | - | - | - |
| 1976 | 7 | - | - | - | - |
| 1977 | 5 | - | - | - | - |
| 1978 | 12 | - | 23 | - | - |
| 1979 | 10 | - | 21 | - | - |

Source: Riki Mandelzweig, "Klita and Yerida One Year after Arrival in Israel," 1985, TLC 225341.

Others returned to Argentina when military rule weakened.[108] Nevertheless, each immigration group included a proportion of people who returned to Argentina for various reasons. Under constant circumstances, their share would have remained stable. Therefore, changes in the trend reveal the influence of political and economic events affecting Argentine and/or Israeli society.

Besides the main trajectories described, others included return migration to Argentina during the most dangerous years of the military government. The most radical of such cases was that of young people involved in political activities who had never been happy in Israel and felt guilty about the difficult situation of their compatriots and friends in Argentina.[109] Their return, which in most cases led to their torture and death, was noted in 1978 by José Itzigsohn in the Zionist journal *Dispersión y Unidad*.[110] Nevertheless, they were not the only ones who went back during the dictatorship; many people chose to resume their lives in Argentina despite their awareness of the political repression that was taking place. For example, Silvia R., whose brother had been kidnaped and tortured by the military, returned because as a psychoanalyst she preferred to build her career in Argentina, while Ricardo A. and his partner decided to go back because otherwise they would soon be called up for Israeli military service.[111]

Adrián Merajver was one of the hundreds who arrived in Israel in 1978 but without any intention to stay. He had been legally jailed for his activities as a member of a Marxist guerilla group and planned to leave Israel as soon as possible. Nevertheless, he slowly began to feel comfortable and even served in the army during the 1982 Lebanon War. In 1984 he returned to Argentina, where he noticed how much he had acquired a taste for Israeli food, music, the people and the lifestyle. He told me, "I never made a long-term plan because I always thought about returning to Argentina . . . I was always just living the moment and not getting settled so as to be able to leave. When I returned to Argentina I noticed that I was uprooting myself a second time. I had uprooted myself when I left Argentina for Israel, and somehow, even though I did not notice, there were many things that I had incorporated [in Israel] and, somehow, returning to Argentina was a second uprooting. A second exile."[112]

Adrián's story demonstrates that even for a person who arrived without ideological motivation or an emotional attachment to Israel, his sojourn in the country created new cultural bonds and left an enduring imprint. In fact, he continued his professional life in Argentina working for a Jewish organization; one of the reasons he chose the job was the opportunity to continue speaking Hebrew and to stay in touch with Israel. He considers himself Israeli as well as Argentine, has visited Israel several times, and continues to live between two homelands.

Although the years 1974 and 1975 were among the most chaotic in Argentine contemporary history, Jewish Argentine migration to Israel reached the lowest point of the decade. As a result of the distress caused by the Yom Kippur War, Israel was not an attractive destination. Moreover, in 1974 returnees from Israel began to be noticeable and their presence embarrassed JA emissaries promoting immigration. As had been the case in 1973, those who left Argentina for Israel in 1974 were not driven by pressing economic need. Now they were driven by increasing political violence. Migration between the two homelands was a two-way street.

Argentine society underwent deep transformations, which had an impact on Jewish organizations and their bond with Israel. Israeli leaders believed that Jewish Argentines were in danger, a notion that accorded with their policy of maximizing immigration to Israel. Nevertheless, most Jewish Argentines did not see themselves as people in need of a safe haven. The truth was that Jewish Argentines were well integrated into Argentine society—which explains why the special committee created to boost their immigration did not meet its goal for 1978. Moreover, Argentine return migration from Israel did not stop at any point during the years of state terrorism and massive human rights violations.

The incongruity of the Zionist leadership's expectations regarding Jewish Argentine immigration to Israel continued in the decades after the return of democracy. Moreover, while Zionist ideological pressure waned, it became clear that Argentina's declining economy was the main driving force behind immigration to Israel. Two hyperinflationary peaks in the period from 1989 to 1990 were accompanied by immigration peaks. Throughout the 1990s, most

Argentine migrants left only after they had lost everything. Similarly, the largest ever emigration from Argentina to Israel took place in the early 2000s, when Argentines suffered the most catastrophic economic, social, and political decline in the country's history. As in 1966, the return to Argentina in 2003 of substantial portions of these migrants became evident, though Israeli officials argued that press reports about it were exaggerated.

# EPILOGUE

From the 1980s to the early 2000s, the profile of Jewish Argentine immigrants arriving in Israel became increasingly defined as those dramatically affected by economic decline. At the same time, the return of some Argentines continued and was increasingly accepted as part of the migration process. During the 1980s, those leaving Israel for Argentina included a number of young people who had previously migrated to Israel for political reasons during the dictatorship. Their return began when the dictatorship started to weaken and continued during Argentina's democratic "spring" that followed in 1983.[1] Of the total number of those who immigrated in 1978, about 21 percent had returned to Argentina by 1981, and about 23 percent of those who moved to Israel in 1979 had returned by 1982.[2] However, none of these waves of return were ever officially acknowledged as such, and only one Argentine departure was reported by the Israeli press after 1982: that of the journalist Jacobo Timerman, who had been disappeared by the military and who returned to Argentina in 1984.[3] Argentine democracy was fragile, and that was not the only problem in the country. Inflation became part of Argentines' everyday life. Governmental programs to lower it failed and from 1986 it grew steadily. Thereafter, the number of Argentines who left for Israel corresponded to the inflationary trend, a pattern that can be seen in figure E.1, where the years 1989 and 1990 tally with two hyperinflationary peaks of over 3,000 percent and 2,000 percent, respectively.[4] Each of these events was marked by a tremendous devaluation of the nation's currency, driving thousands of Argentines into poverty.[5]

In the run-up to the first peak, Jewish Argentine leaders made repeated requests for financial aid from Israeli and international Jewish organizations. In one case, in addition to expounding on the crisis in Jewish schools, due to the families' inability to pay the fees, they argued that the funds would be used for the implementation of "an aliyah project which would include 300 families of yordim wishing to return to Israel [and] have no . . . means to finance their return. They do not enjoy the same rights as olim. To return the yordim (about 1,000) and increase aliyah in general, we need a budget of $1,500,000."[6]

While the number of returnees willing to remigrate to Israel mentioned in this appeal seems unrealistic, the fact that they were mentioned demonstrates that this kind of migrant was known within Jewish Argentine organizations. In addition, the claim of an inability to pay for their travel to Israel was accurate. In most cases, Israel became an option precisely at moments of penury. A letter sent by a thirty-five-year-old man from Buenos Aires to his relative, Zionist leader Simcha Dinitz, is illustrative. They had not been in touch before, but due to the circumstances, the Argentine decided to write: "I have a wife and a three-year-old daughter . . . My parents passed away four years ago and I . . . felt the need to write to you because you are one of the few relatives I have. I know that you are much appreciated in 'our Israel' . . . [We] wonder if we could get a stable and secure job through your mediation and go live in the city. I know that it sounds rude, but having a little girl, I would like to travel with 100 percent certainty that I will have a job . . . Here in Argentina, we are having a very hard time because I am unemployed . . . I worked as a textile salesman, but I am in such need that I am willing to take any job . . . I apologize for writing now that I am in trouble and not before . . . Shalom!!!"[7]

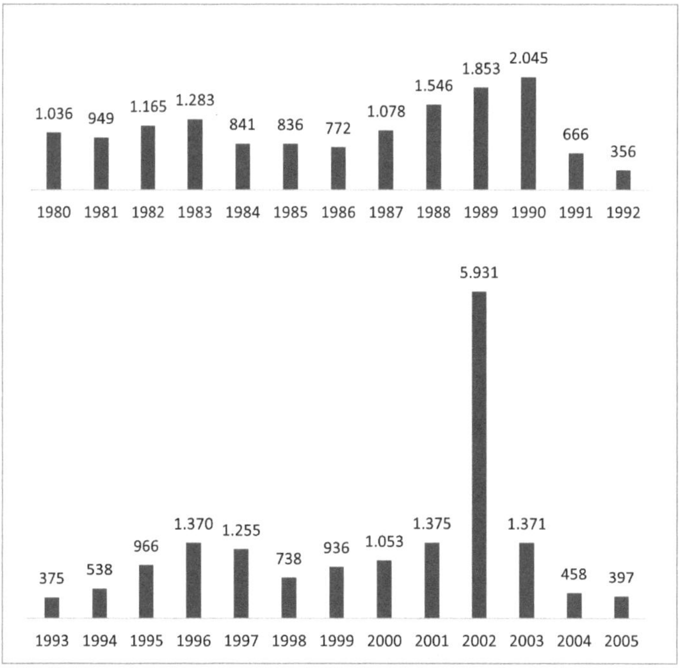


**Figure E.1** Number of Argentine migrants to Israel by year, 1980–2005. Source: Israeli Central Bureau of Statistics, "Total Immigration to Israel by Select Country by Year," Jewish Virtual Library. The graph does not include returnee citizens.

The letter represented the situation of large segments of the Argentine population. A 1989 WZO report described the situation of unemployed Jews and those living on a devalued salary: "An increasing number of Jews affected by the economic crisis have reached the point of having nothing to eat and have sold their belongings to feed their families. There are many cases of Jews who were forced to leave their apartments because they could not afford the rent and moved to housing in inferior conditions. A considerable number of Jewish families passed a difficult winter without electricity due to a lack of money to pay their bills. Many families took their children out of Jewish schools because they could not pay the fees. The numbers of people coming to the community's welfare office increased substantially . . . They are Jews in such economic need that they have overcome the 'shame barrier' to request money from the community."[8]

The effects of hyperinflation and the associated increase in immigration to Israel merely foreshadowed events that would come twelve years later. In 1991 a new economic program in Argentina halted inflation and immigration to Israel plummeted. Under the convertibility law, the Argentine peso was fixed to the dollar at a one-to-one exchange rate. The Central Bank was obliged to hold one dollar for each Argentine peso in circulation.[9] However, the inflation rate was curbed at a very high cost. Vast sectors of the population gained access to imported goods, holidays abroad, and credit in dollars with a low interest rate, at the expense of domestic industry and rising unemployment.[10] Besides privatizing state-owned companies, the convertibility program was based on foreign debt and short-term direct foreign investment.[11] It widened the gap between rich and poor and eroded the standard of living of vast sectors of the population. Unresolved structural vulnerabilities became evident in 1995–96, as the negative spillover of the 1994 Mexican devaluation, known in the region as "the tequila effect," accelerated economic deterioration and unemployment. These were the causes of the pronounced surge in immigration to Israel from 1994 to 1996 (figure E.1). On the other hand, the impact on immigration of two major terrorist attacks was marginal: In March 1992 a bomb was detonated at the Israeli embassy, resulting in 22 dead and 242 injured, while in July 1994 a second bomb destroyed the AMIA building, taking 85 lives and injuring 300.[12] Despite these possible push factors, contemporary observers had no doubt that Jewish Argentines were motivated to migrate for economic reasons. According to Aliza Arieli, a JA emissary in Buenos Aires, Zionist ideology held weak sway in Argentina. "Hundreds and thousands of Jews from the middle class . . . lost their assets, they were fired, or they liquidated their businesses. The vast majority of our olim have nothing and they arrive in Israel with nothing . . . It makes me feel sad to say that what was not attained by two murderous terrorist attacks in Argentina will be accomplished by the economic crisis."[13]

Meanwhile, during the 1990s, there was a constant stream of Argentine return migration from Israel (table E.1). It was not a noticeable wave, and as such the subject was not raised either by the press or in public discourse. A thorough analysis of variations in return rates during those years goes beyond the focus

**Table E.1. Immigrants from Argentina by Year of Arrival: Number and Percentage of Those Who Left by the Third Year, by the Fifth Year, and by 2004**

| Year | Immigrants | Number and Percent of Those Who Left Israel by | | |
|---|---|---|---|---|
| | | Year 3 | Year 5 | 2004 |
| **1989** | 1,892 | 102<br>5.4% | 185<br>9.8% | 352<br>18.6% |
| **1990** | 2,154 | 212<br>9.8% | 387<br>14.2% | 457<br>21.2% |
| **1991** | 665 | 74<br>11% | 91<br>13.7% | 152<br>22.8% |
| **1992** | 330 | 54<br>16.6% | 69<br>21% | 89<br>27% |
| **1993** | 364 | 38<br>10.4% | 54<br>14.8% | 69<br>19% |
| **1994** | 552 | 34<br>6.2% | 52<br>9.4% | 81<br>14.7% |
| **1995** | 1,013 | 78<br>7.7% | 123<br>12% | 172<br>17% |
| **1996** | 1,434 | 137<br>9.5% | 195<br>13.6% | 223<br>15.5% |
| **1997** | 1,318 | 183<br>13.9% | 237<br>18% | 237*<br>18% |
| **1998** | 788 | 80<br>10.2% | - | 95<br>13.05% |
| **1999** | 984 | 111<br>11.3% | - | - |
| **2000** | 1,115 | - | - | 102<br>9.2% |
| **2001** | 1,428 | - | - | 81<br>5.7% |
| **2002** | 6,224 | - | - | 113<br>1.8% |

Source: Schmuel Adler, "Yerida among Olim from Argentina who Immigrated within the Period 1/1/1989 to 31/12/2002," Ministry of Absorption, Israel, March 2004, 6.

*It seems odd that there was no variation between the number of those who arrived in 1997 and left in 2002 and 2004. This might be due to a typing error in the original or an accurate representation of an equal number of emigrants. Argentina was just beginning its economic recovery after a historical crisis. Therefore, the table captures these numbers from the highest peak in history. However, it does not include their return rates beyond 2003.

of this book and will be presented in a separate work. Nevertheless, it is worth stressing that even when economic conditions in Argentina were extremely unfavorable, many immigrants decided to return from Israel. For instance, more than 10 percent of those who arrived in Israel in 1997 left for Argentina within the first three years, just as the country approached the most severe economic, social, and political collapse in its history. Many of those choosing to return were likely affected by the deterioration of the security situation in Israel following the assassination of Prime Minister Yitzhak Rabin. Further, there is no doubt that cultural and personal motives, the impact of which is more difficult to gauge than that of political events and economic trends, were powerful driving forces underlying return migration. Homesickness, language difficulties, and the desire for typical foods or leisure activities, as well as many other noneconomic or political factors, also contributed to the return migration of Jewish Argentines. In any event, Argentina's economic situation has undoubtedly played a much more powerful role as a push factor than as a pull one. Most Jewish Argentines migrating to Israel have tended to do so because of the state of the Argentine economy while most of those who have returned to Argentina have done so in spite of it.

The immigration zenith of 1996 to 1997 was caused by the emergence of the Argentine "new poor," the phenomenon of people born and raised as middle class and used to a middle-class lifestyle who were now suddenly destitute.[14] Their appearance toward the mid-1990s foreshadowed events that occurred in 2002. The end of the convertibility program became evident in December 2001 when the government limited the amount of cash people could withdraw from their savings accounts at banks and ATM machines.[15] Witnessing the de facto confiscation of their savings, wide sectors of urban populations joined the vast numbers of unemployed Argentines who had been protesting for years. While the organizations of unemployed, led by former workers and experienced unionists, blocked roads throughout the country, the middle class protested by banging their pots and pans in Buenos Aires' Plaza de Mayo and in other cities.[16] The state of siege decreed by the president exacerbated the situation, and tens of thousands took to the streets chanting "¡Que se vayan todos!" (Go home, all of you!), expressing their frustration against politicians.[17] At least thirty people died in confrontations with the police throughout the country, including nine children.[18] President Fernando de la Rúa resigned on December 20, 2001, and within eleven days, five different presidents took office. Social and economic indicators were at dramatically low levels never before experienced. Unemployment and poverty affected half the population as the phenomenon of the new poor devoured wide sectors of the middle class. Even people who owned more than one property found themselves without money to buy food.

Even before the collapse, emigration from Argentina had attracted the interest of the media, which showed queues of people waiting at various embassies in order to obtain European passports by claiming their Italian or Spanish ancestry. The emigration of Jewish Argentines was also noticed in this context. Unlike the peak of 1963, in the early 2000s it was clear to any observer that the economy was the main force driving Jewish Argentine immigration to Israel. The immigrants themselves offered eloquent testimonies in that regard and their stories were less ornamented with Zionist or Jewish symbolism than in the past. For instance, interviewed after his arrival in Israel, a forty-eight-year-old man and former secretary of the Sociedad Hebraica Argentina sports club reported, with tears in his eyes, that a short time earlier he had been the owner of an advertising agency. Now he was living in Israel, together with his wife and four children. The family had completed the entire immigration process, from making the decision to their arrival in Israel, in just ten days. He did not hide his economic motive: "None of my clients were paying their bills, and I couldn't pay my suppliers . . . Our last month there was downright dramatic . . . We just couldn't go on anymore."[19] Moreover, the relaxation of Israeli restrictions and controls for new immigrants, together with the weakening of ideologies in general and the waning of Zionism in particular, contributed to an open admissions process. There was less ideological pressure surrounding in the arrival of Argentines in Israel; furthermore, the new immigrant could also leave the country without any official permits or stigmatization.[20]

In addition, as economic need had become the immigrants' most obvious characteristic, the JA decided to counter this undesirable image by "improving the image of aliyah," presenting it as the option of the "successful."[21] Publicity cannot change reality, however, and the generalized perception by Jewish Argentines of the immigrants as bankrupt or unemployed was accurate. In fact, the unemployed represented almost 20 percent of the total and half of the immigrants of working age (table E.2). An equal part was represented by "self-employed and craftsman," whose financial situation was hardly better (table E.3).

The peak of Argentine immigration to Israel in 2002 was the highest in history until today; nevertheless, it fell short of previous Israeli estimations. The JA had expected sixty-five hundred immigrants during that period when, among many other benefits, the absorption package included a special grant of $20,000 to be used for mortgages.[22] In addition, the abrupt halt of Argentine immigration to Israel in 2003 was accompanied by the noticeable return of a substantial portion of Argentines. This occurred mainly because the coincidence of the Argentine collapse and the Second Intifada put many Jewish Argentines in a difficult position.[23] More than one thousand Israelis and several thousand Palestinians died in the intifada. As a result, tourism in Israel declined sharply and the entire economy contracted. Making matters worse, many victims of suicide attacks were Argentines who had arrived over the decades.[24]

**Table E.2. Percentage of Argentine Migrants to Israel in 2002 by Occupation**

| Occupation | Percent |
|---|---|
| University students | 25 |
| Self-employed and craftsmen | 18 |
| Retired | 12 |
| No profession / unemployed | 18 |
| Under 18 | 27 |

Source: "JA Department of Immigration and Absorption, Summary Meeting of Year 2002," March 16, 2003, TLC, 343489.

**Table E.3. Percentage of Argentine Migrants to Israel in 2002 by Age Group**

| Age Group | Percent |
|---|---|
| 5–17 | 27 |
| 18–34 | 24 |
| 35–54 | 28 |
| 55–64 | 9 |
| 60+ | 12 |

Source: "JA Department of Immigration and Absorption, Summary Meeting of Year 2002," March 16, 2003, TLC, 343489.

In contrast, Argentina seemed to be recovering quickly from the economic conflagration, at least in the short term. In the aftermath of the 2001 crisis, the Peronist party took office again, first, through a transitional government, which imposed a 300 percent currency devaluation, and, later, through two leaders who won over wide sectors of the population and governed the nation for twelve years. Néstor Kirchner was elected in 2003, and his wife Cristina Fernández was elected in 2007 and reelected in 2011.[25] The effects of devaluation and high commodity prices in international markets favored Argentina and a new expansive cycle of its economy began. Exports and local production increased, helping to reduce poverty. Many Argentines decided to return from abroad, including from Israel. By the end of 2003, there were several press reports about Argentines leaving Israel, focusing on their frustrations regarding the job market and security concerns. As had occurred during the 1960s, the real number of returnees became a topic of debate, with the quantitative gap between official and press estimates echoing the discussions of Argentine returnees during the 1966 Israeli recession. An article in *Maariv* argued that one thousand Argentines who had arrived in 2001 to 2002 had left Israel, while according to the Absorption Ministry and OLEI, these numbered fewer than five hundred. Moreover, rejecting the notion that many immigrants were suffering penury in Israel, the ministry and OLEI representatives argued that such difficulties affected mainly single-parent families, the elderly, and the sick. Meanwhile, many immigrants were using an Argentine expression equating poverty with starvation to explain their decision, and the newspapers reproduced their reasoning: "If the choice is between dying of starvation here or in Argentina, I prefer to do it there, where at least I know the language."[26]

The available figures regarding return rates among immigrants who arrived in Israel from Argentina in 2000, 2001, and 2002 were elaborated in 2003. The chaotic situation prevailing in Argentina, where political stability and economic recovery resumed only toward the end of 2003, explains the relatively small number of returnees. Nevertheless, it is remarkable that 9.2 percent of those who arrived in 2000 had left Israel by 2004. Undoubtedly, that number continued increasing over time. Moreover, a portion of those returnees from Israel decided to leave Argentina and relocate to Israel a second time. Indeed, having met several of them, I will share their stories in a separate work.

The most pronounced peaks in Jewish Argentine immigration to Israel were caused by economic decline, which acted as a push factor in Argentina. Accordingly, each time an immigration peak took place, it was followed by the return to Argentina of a portion of the migrants and, among those returnees, an unknown but non-negligible number later remigrated to Israel. Apart from the noticeable streams of return that followed those crests, remigration to Argentina continued throughout the years in small numbers. Therefore, return rate is better reflected when the studies consider a longer period of time between arrival and departure. Each time that Argentina was undergoing a difficult economic or political situation, the JA and Israeli officials in charge of immigration and absorption overestimated the number of immigrants that would arrive. Regarding the return to Argentina of a portion of the migrants, JA and other Israeli officials have argued consistently that their numbers are half of those provided by the press.

By means of a transnational and nonlinear approach to immigration and return migration, the data, testimonies, and stories included in this book challenge Zionist narratives regarding the reasons Jewish Argentines migrated to Israel and demonstrate that their connection to the country did not end when they left. Indeed, many of them migrated to Israel a second and even a third time, while those who remained in Argentina continued to be culturally, socially, emotionally, and/or professionally attached to Israel. Approaching Jewish Argentine migration to Israel as a cycle that might include return and remigration several times in the life of an individual allows for a better understanding of the migration experience and broadens the perspective on Israel-Diaspora relations. In times of fast and affordable transport and communications, migrants can move more than ever before, and living between two homelands has become much easier than it used to be. Moreover, Israel's departure from an ideological approach toward immigration and absorption policies to a pragmatic one has removed many emotional, economic, and legal burdens from the shoulders of migrants who want to leave Israel or want to settle there a second time.

I have referred to three historical moments when the return of Jewish Argentines from Israel became noticeable: during the Israeli economic recession of 1966; in the aftermath of the Yom Kippur War; and toward the year 2003 during the Second Intifada. Such visible streams of return migration demonstrate the power of economic crisis, war, and terrorism as push factors operating in Israel against the absorption of Argentine immigrants. Nevertheless, while these crises triggered rapid and perceptible waves of emigration from Israel, we should bear in mind that Jewish Argentine return has been a continuous phenomenon that, in the long term, evidences a relatively stable rate. While these return streams reflect external forces that mitigated in favor of migration, a long list of circumstances, though less observable and measurable, motivated individuals and families to return to Argentina. Homesickness, dissatisfaction with the Israeli lifestyle, and difficulties in continuing schooling or a professional career in Hebrew are just a few examples of the variety of factors underlying the continuous trickle of Argentine migrants beyond the brief duration of each of the three waves of return analyzed in this book.

In addition, there are similarities and differences between the three cases. First, Jewish Argentine immigration to Israel has surged each time Argentina has undergone an economic crisis. The landmark mass arrivals of 1963 and 2002 are exemplary here; both were followed by a counterwave of return migration to Argentina when the Israeli economy declined. Indeed, Argentine immigrants pushed from Argentina by economic factors were liable to return for those same reasons. Moreover, the visibility of the counterwaves of return migration correlated with the large numbers of Argentines who had taken part in the previous immigration. Having noticed their immigration, it was impossible not to discern their departure. Conversely, the daily emigration of a single person or family, which in the long term would equal the leaving rate of all the counterwaves, remained unnoticed. Many of the 1966 and 2003 returnees might have gone back anyway, and the Israeli economic recession just catalyzed their decision.

On the other hand, the return stream of 1974, caused by the Yom Kippur War, demonstrates the disruptive effects of military conflict—a central element in cultural adaptation and a subject that deserves further research. This time the departure of Argentine returnees had not been preceded by a mass immigration wave. Therefore, while documented in the Israeli press in Spanish and in JA files, it was just another small expression of the national drama that affected all Israelis. Interestingly, in the same manner that continuing economic decline did not prevent the return of Argentines who had left Argentina because of this factor, political violence and state terrorism did not preclude the return of those who migrated to Israel for these reasons. Therefore, clearly, migration placed people in new circumstances that allowed them to make new decisions based on information and experience they had not possessed previously. Moreover, for many, the migration experience was so meaningful that their beliefs, priorities, and values were reassessed and modified.

While available data is not as complete and detailed as keen researchers and readers would like, it provides a clear picture. After the immigration peak of 1963, official statistics, which considered only "self-declared" returnees, reported that 850 Argentines out of 11,780 who arrived between 1948 and 1964 had returned to Argentina.[27] However, this 7.21 percent did not reflect the actual number of returnees. First, they dated from before the economic recession of 1966, when the return of substantial numbers of Argentines became evident. Thereafter, OLEI sources referred to an 11 percent return rate of Latin Americans.[28] Even more importantly, a secret report recognized what everyone knew: the majority of those leaving the country made no formal declaration.[29] Official numbers were less than half of the actual leaving rate, which might have been 20 percent or more. Regarding the 1970s, the emigration of Latin Americans from Israel, with Argentines representing the majority, was measured more systematically and included those who were not in Israel after a certain period, without requiring an official declaration. For those who arrived in the years 1970, 1971, 1972, 1973, and 1974, the leaving rate measured three years later was 20, 18, 16, 17, and 16 percent, respectively, and 23 and 21 percent for 1988 and 1989, respectively. In addition, 25 percent of those who arrived in Israel in 1973 had left by their fifth year in the country.[30] Finally, 18.84 percent of the immigrants from Argentina who arrived in Israel between 1989 and 1998 had left by 2004.[31] Available data suggest that in the long term, the return rate of Argentines from Israel was around 20 percent and that it continued to increase each time a survey was conducted. The percentage of Jewish Argentines who migrated to Israel more than once remains unknown. At the beginning of the research that resulted in the present book, I was surprised to learn of people who had relocated from Argentina to Israel twice. After interviewing many such migrants, I now know that repetition of the migration cycle was not at all unusual even in times when the families had to make a three-week voyage, carrying with them all their belongings. It has become even more prevalent nowadays.

Although return migration from Israel was largely ignored during most of Israel's history, it is an integral component of Israel-Diaspora relations. Moreover, the case of Jewish Argentine returnees demonstrates that return migration has had a meaningful influence on Israel's bond with Jewish Argentines and their organizations, on the one hand, and, on the creation of a multiplicity of links between Argentine and Israeli societies in general, on the other. In addition, except for the short period between the Israeli recession, which peaked in 1966, and the Six-Day War, when the return of Argentines had a negative impact on Argentine immigration numbers, return migration has been beneficial for Jewish Argentine relations with Israel. Within this context, a portion of the returnees decided to remigrate to Israel, making the decision based on firsthand experience. In other cases, their children, who were raised in Argentina and bore Hebrew names or simply had grown up with cherished memories of Israel transmitted by their parents, were inspired to migrate.

Moreover, returnees from Israel turned out to be a valuable human resource for Jewish organizations in Argentina. Many among the people I interviewed worked for a Jewish organization after their return to Argentina or still work there. When I began creating a list of potential interviewees using the snowball methodology, I was surprised by the large number of returnees from Israel employed, for instance, in various roles in Tarbut, a Jewish high school located in northern Buenos Aires. An extensive survey targeting the entirety of professionals and lay leaders employed at Jewish Argentine organizations would probably demonstrate that return migration has contributed strongly to shaping the daily life, structures, and goals of these institutions. Just considering the role of teachers in Jewish schools would suffice to demonstrate that the traditional Zionist view on the returnee as a failure or even as a traitor to the Jewish cause was not only unfair but also radically inaccurate. All of the returnees who have worked in Jewish organizations have become, in one way or another, channels of communication between the two homelands.

Many people who once lived in Israel have played a prominent role in Argentine society. Well-known examples in the political and cultural spheres include former foreign minister Héctor Timerman, who lived in Israel as a teenager during his family's exile in the 1970s, and Fernando Sokolowicz, founder of the progressive newspaper *Página 12*, who lived in Israel during the final period of Argentine military rule. They also include Mario Blejer, whose academic work is quoted in this volume: he studied at the Hebrew University of Jerusalem and later became director of the Argentine Central Bank. The complete list of Argentines who lived in Israel and returned to their country of origin would include thousands of names in a range of jobs and social classes and holding a variety of political views. In addition, their experiences reflect the four types of migrant relations with Israeli and Argentine culture elaborated by Berry and noted in the introduction to this volume: (1) migrants who feel comfortable in both countries; (2 and 3) those who feel they belong to only one of them;

and (4) those who feel they belong in neither Israel nor Argentina. Moreover, among the returnees some identified with Israel each time it was involved in an armed conflict, like influential writer Marcelo Birmajer, or became well known for their criticism of Israel, like journalist Pedro Brieger. Thousands of returnees became, in one way or another, channels of communication between Israeli and Argentine culture. While conducting research for this book I was surprised to find a large number of academics teaching, for example, in the Faculty of Social Sciences at the University of Buenos Aires. Indeed, returnees have brought what they learned in Israel to every sphere of Argentine life. From the graduate of the Technion who established several companies in Argentina to the many who have continued listening to Israeli music, reading Hebrew books, or preparing Israeli foods—all have incorporated aspects of their Israeli experience into Argentine society. While returnees developed a variety of views about the time they spent in Israel and differing emotional connections to that country, all my interviewees agreed that their time there was a meaningful experience in their lives. In fact, given that people's identity is the result of their accumulated experience, the returnees' sojourn in Israel influenced the way they and their families evolved. Throughout the process of identity formation, the migrants were influenced by the cultures of their two homelands and their ties with Argentina and Israel changed over time.

Thus, a foundation has been laid for an initial discussion about the impact of the Israeli experience on return migrant identities. I advance the idea that they developed multilayered identities due to their connections with Argentina and Israel. At the same time, migrant testimonies demonstrate that a lot can still be learned about cultural integration, or the lack thereof, in Israel as well as in Argentina following the Israeli experience. In the following, I will mention some relevant topics to be considered in this regard.

According to Tzvetan Todorov, culture is common memory and a guide for living together; we learn the same language, history, and traditions, and we speak in order to be understood and behave in accordance with society's rules.[32] Clearly not every cultural element is based on language, but language is at the heart of every culture. Language is critical for building a rich social life and for entering the job market. Moreover, adaptation to a new language affects the immigrant's psyche.[33] The Hebrew language appeared in the stories of every interviewee as an obstacle that Argentine immigrants face in Israel. However, it is equally important to consider how the Hebrew language continued, or did not continue, to be an important part of the migrant's life once they returned to Argentina. Many of the interviewees told me that prolonged use of Hebrew had affected the way they spoke Spanish, due to their different accent and pronunciation. As returnees from Israel they were often asked where they came from. The long-lasting effect of the Hebrew language on many people was what made it possible for me to meet José C., whose story is quoted in this book. It was 2011 and a man who was reading a book in Hebrew on the exercise bike next to me in a Buenos Aires gym aroused my curiosity. When I asked him about it, he told me that since his childhood in Israel he had never stopped reading Hebrew literature.

In another example, the story of Demián is telling regarding the effects of Hebrew and Israeli culture on young children. He was born in Israel after his mother, Susana M., moved there as a political exile in the 1970s. The family returned to Argentina once democracy had been restored, when Demián was four. He found the switch in languages confusing, and after visiting a therapist, his parents were told, "You should talk to him about Israel; it's his identity . . . He has another identity, an Israeli one." So, his parents created a photo album and sent him to a Jewish school in Buenos Aires to continue his connection to Hebrew.[34]

Other key aspects that deserve further research are the gender-based differences that characterize the entire migration experience, which require attention as a subtopic of Argentine participation in the Israeli job market.[35] Two examples are worth mentioning. Silvi B. felt unable to leave her husband while they were living in Israel during the 1980s. However, once they returned to Rosario the economic and emotional support from her family helped her get a divorce in 1988.[36] Miriam K. became pregnant while a student in Jerusalem and although she and her husband loved each other they had not planned to have a family. Abortion was illegal in Argentina but legal in Israel under certain circumstances. Miriam had to present her case to a special committee, which included a rabbi a doctor, and a social worker. She told me that during that difficult time, she felt the state had taken care of her and provided her with the possibility of carrying through her decision to abort under safe conditions.[37] A third story is relevant here too. A young couple's life is always transformed by the arrival of the first child. As new immigrants, Mariano and Marina felt the lack of a family network to help support them in Israel. When they decided to return to Argentina, Mariano suffered a partial paralysis of his face due to the emotional and psychological pressure he felt. He would have preferred to stay in Israel, but he recognized that doing so would be unfair to his wife: the baby had changed the couple's balance.[38]

The impact on Mariano's body and mind caused by the stress of his prospective return to Argentina leads to the following question: How does Argentine society perceive Argentine returnees from abroad? The answer lies beyond this work, but one of the most popular Argentine tango lyrics, immortalized by the voice of Carlos Gardel, refers precisely to the fears caused by return and to the nostalgia and love for a country where most people die in the same city, or even neighborhood where they were born.

I imagine the flickering
of the lights that in the distance
will be marking my return.
They're the same that lit,
with their pale reflections,
deep hours of pain
And even though I didn't want to come back,
you always return to your first love
The tranquil street where the echo said
yours is her life, yours is her love,
under the mocking gaze of the stars
that, with indifference, today see me return.

To return
with withered face,
the snows of time
have whitened my temples.
To feel . . . that life is a puff of wind,
that twenty years is nothing,
that the feverish look,
wandering in the shadow,
looks for you and names you.
To live . . .
with the soul clutched
to a sweet memory
that I cry once again

I am afraid of the encounter
with the past that returns
to confront my life
I am afraid of the nights
that, filled with memories,
shackle my dreams.
But the traveler that flees
sooner or later stops his walking
And although forgetfulness, which destroys all,
has killed my old dream,
I keep concealed a humble hope
that is my heart's whole fortune.

To live . . . with the soul clutched

> to a sweet memory
> that I cry once again[39]

Global and national transformations have forced Israel to change its formerly ideological approach to immigration in favor of a more professional one. While the Zionist narrative is present during the immigration process of Jews to Israel, it is more a folkloric background that invites the immigrant to be part of the national saga rather than to make an ideological commitment. In addition, immigrants can leave the country without explanation or any special requirement as early as the day after their arrival. Besides the particular benefits that each group of migrants to Israel can receive in accordance with their circumstances, their experiences are taking place in an era when dual nationality gives many people the possibility of living between two homelands. The Zionist project aimed to put Jews on an equal footing with people with a state of their own. The twenty-first century has witnessed a proliferation of states that allow dual citizenship, and people have taken advantage of regimes that make additional citizenship possible by utilizing their ancestry. These factors, together with changes in the global economy, raise new questions about migration in relation to ethnic and national identities. For example, in what sense is the experience of Jewish Argentine immigration and return from Israel different from that of non-Jewish Argentines who moved to Spain or Italy? And what about Jewish Argentines who preferred destinations other than Israel? Did Argentine immigrants in other countries use their multiple identities to present their case when complaining about something? What about the cultural imprint that the migration experience left on people? Did Argentines who returned from a country other than Israel make that experience a strong part of their identities as Jewish Argentines returning from Israel did? These questions are among many that further research may answer.

This volume is an attempt to contribute to migration studies by throwing new light on changing relations between Israel and the Jewish Diaspora. It also aims to fill a void regarding a particular aspect of Jewish, Argentine, and Israeli history. While this book was being written, the Argentine economy entered a new recession and inflationary trend, aggravated by the global impact of the coronavirus crisis, whose duration and consequences remain unknown. New groups of Argentines will no doubt be displaced and will be forced to lower their standard of living as a result of unemployment and poverty. The severity of Argentina's approaching crisis will determine the number of Argentines who will emigrate, the proportion that will choose Israel, and the share that will return to Argentina. All of them will have the opportunity to repeat the migration cycle along the road that separates their two homelands, in the footsteps of generations of Jewish Argentines.

# NOTES

## Introduction

1. Interview with José C., April 23, 2016.

2. Interview with Susana C., Buenos Aires, August 4, 2016.

3. Interview with Susana C.

4. Interview with Hector J., Buenos Aires, July 26, 2016.

5. Interview with Susana C.

6. The Hebrew word *mezuzah* means "doorpost." Denotatively, the word refers to a small, sometimes decorative box traditionally affixed to the doorpost at the entrance to a Jewish home as well as to each of the interior rooms (except for bathrooms). The mezuzah contains a small parchment scroll (*k'laf*) inscribed with two biblical passages.

7. Interview with Susana C.

8. Steven Gold and Rona Hart, "Transnational Ties during a Time of Crisis: Israeli Emigration, 2000 to 2004," *International Migration* 51, no. 3 (June 2013): 196.

9. Argentine immigrants who left Israel for a third country, participants in one-year educational programs, or kibbutz volunteers are not included. The remigration of Argentines from Israel to third countries could be incorporated in future comparative studies. For an approach to a remigration case, see Eduardo Faingold, *Exile from Argentina: A Jewish Family and the Military Dictatorship (1976-1983)* (Charlotte, NC: Information Age, 2008).

10. Jonathan D. Sarna, "The Myth of No Return: Jewish Return Migration to Eastern Europe, 1881-1914," *American Jewish History* 71, no. 2 (December 1981): 256, 268.

11. On Jewish emigration from Palestine during the pre-state period, see, for example, Yehoshua Kaniel, "Emigration from Palestine during the Period of the First and Second Aliyot," *Cathedra* 73 (September 1994): 115–38; Gur Alroey, *An Unpromising Land: Jewish Migration to Palestine in the Early Twentieth Century* (Redwood, CA: Stanford University Press, 2014).

12. Yinon Cohen, "Migration Patterns to and from Israel," *Contemporary Jewry* 29, no. 2 (August 2009): 119.

13. Mario Blejer and Yitzhak Goldberg, "Return Migration: Expectation versus Reality. A Case Study of Western Immigrants to Israel," *Research on Population Economics* 2 (1980): 433–49; Michael Beenstock, "Failure to Absorb: Remigration by Immigrants into Israel," *International Migration Review* 30 (Winter 1996): 950–78; Chaim Waxman and Michael Appel, *To Israel and Back: American Aliyah and Return Migration* (New York: American Jewish Committee, 1986); Gerald Engel, "Comparison between Americans Living in Israel and Those Who Returned to America: Part II, Israeli Background," *Journal of Psychology* 75, no. 2 (1970): 243–51; Engel, "Comparison between Americans Living in Israel and Those Who

Returned to America: Part I, American Background," *Journal of Psychology* 74, no. 2 (January 1970) : 195–204; Engel, "Comparison between Americans Living in Israel and Those Who Returned to America: Part III, Predictions About America and Israel," *Journal of Psychology* 76, no. 1 (July 1970): 117–23.

14. Steven Gold, "From Nationality to Peoplehood: Adaptation and Identity Formation in the Israeli Diaspora," *Diaspora* 13, nos. 2–3 (Fall–Winter 2004): 331–58; Yinon Cohen, "Economic Assimilation in the United States of Arab and Jewish Immigrants from Israel and the Territories," *Israel Studies* 1, no. 2 (Fall 1996): 75–97; Yinon Cohen and Yitchak Haberfeld, "The Number of Israeli Immigrants in the United States in 1990," *Demography* 34, no. 2 (May 1997): 199–212; Yinon Cohen and Andrea Tyree, "Palestinian and Jewish Israeli-Born Immigrants in the United States," *International Migration Review* 28, no. 2 (Summer 1994): 243–55; Yinon Cohen and Yitchak Haberfeld, "Self-Selection and Return Migration: Israeli-Born Jews Returning Home from the United States during the 1980s," *Population Studies* 55, no.1 (August 2001): 79–91.

15. Yossi Harpaz, "Ancestry into Opportunity: How Global Inequality Drives Demand for Long-Distance European Union Citizenship," *Journal of Ethnic and Migration Studies* 41, no. 13 (May 2015): 1–24; Larissa Remennick, "Transnational Lifestyles among Russian Israelis: A Follow-Up Study," *Global Networks* 13, no. 4 (October 2013): 478–97; Gold and Hart, "Transnational Ties during a Time of Crisis."

16. On the contrary, many personal accounts and literary works reflect Jewish Argentine return migration from Israel. For some personal accounts, see David Horacio Nillni, *Guerrillero y soldado: Una vida entre La Plata y Beer Sheva* (Buenos Aires: AMIA, 2015); José Itsigsohn, *Una experiencia judía contemporánea: Memorias y reflexiones* (Buenos Aires: Editorial Paidós, 1969); Bruria Elnecavé, *Crisol de vivencias judias* (Buenos Aires: Ediciones La Luz, 1994). Argentine returnees have also expressed their Israeli experience in literary works. See, for example: Ricardo Feierstein, *El caramelo descompuesto* (Buenos Aires: Ediciones Nueva Presencia, 1979); Mauricio Goldberg, *Donde sopla la nostalgia* (Buenos Aires: Grupo Editor Latinoamericano, 1985). In addition, returnees from Israel have appeared in literary fiction, for example: Marcelo Birmajer, *Tres mosqueteros* (Buenos Aires: Debate, 2001), and in documentaries and movies, for example: *El abrazo partido*, directed by Daniel Burman (2003; Buenos Aires: Bd Cine, 2003) and the documentary *El año que viene . . . en Argentina*, directed by Jorge Gurvich and Shlomo Slutzky (National Center for Jewish Films, 2005).

17. Luis Roniger and Deby Babis, "Latin American Israelis: The Collective Identity of an Invisible Community," in *Identities in an Era of Globalization and Multiculturalism*, ed. Judit Bokser Liwerant et al. (Boston: Brill, 2008), 297–320.

18. Rebeca Raijman and Ariane Ophir, "The Economic Integration of Latin Americans in Israel," *Canadian Ethnic Studies* 46, no. 3 (December 2014): 77–102.

19. See, for example, Luis Roniger et al., *Exile, Diaspora, and Return: Changing Cultural Landscapes in Argentina: Chile, Paraguay, and Uruguay* (New York: Oxford University Press, 2018).

20. Ori Yehudai, "Displaced in the National Home: Jewish Repatriation from Palestine to Europe, 1945–48," *Jewish Social Studies* 20, no. 2 (Winter 2014): 69–110; Marcos Silber, "Immigrants from Poland Want to Go Back: The Politics of Return Migration and Nation Building in 1950s' Israel," *Journal of Israeli History* 27, no. 2 (September 2008): 201–19.

21. Jeffrey Lesser and Raanan Rein, "Challenging Particularity: Jews as a Lens on Latin

American Ethnicity," *Latin American and Caribbean Ethnic Studies* 1, no. 2 (November 2006): 249–63.

22. Beatrice D. Gurwitz, *Argentine Jews in the Age of Revolt: Between the New World and the Third World* (Leiden: Brill, 2016); Emmanuel Kahan, *Memories That Lie a Little: Jewish Experiences during the Argentine Dictatorship* (Leiden: Brill, 2018).

23. Haim Avni, *Argentina and the Jews: A History of Jewish Immigration*. Tuscaloosa: University of Alabama Press, 1991; Leonardo Senkman, "El antisemitismo bajo dos experiencias democráticas: Argentina 1959/1966 y 1973/1977," in *El antisemitismo en la Argentina*, ed. Leonardo Senkman (Buenos Aires: CEAL, 1989), 117–90; Natán Lerner, "Las raíces ideológicas del antisemitismo en la Argentina y el nacionalismo," in Senkman, *El antisemitismo en la Argentina*, 191–218.

24. Sergio DellaPergola, "National Uniqueness and Transnational Parallelism: Reflections on the Comparative Study of Jewish Communities in Latin America," in *Judaica Latinoamericana—Estudios históricos, sociales y literarios*, ed. M. Bejarno, F. Goldberg, and E. Zadoff, vol. 7 (Jerusalem: AMILAT-Magnes, 2013), 73–100.

25. Nir Cohen, "From Overt Rejection to Enthusiastic Embracement: Changing State Discourses on Israeli Emigration," *GeoJournal* 68, nos. 2-3 (June 2007): 267–78; Cohen, "From Nation to Profession: Israeli State Strategy toward Highly-Skilled Return Migration, 1949–2012," *Journal of Historical Geography* 42 (October 2013): 1–11; Cohen, "Come Home, Be Professional: Ethno-Nationalism and Economic Rationalism in Israel's Return Migration Strategy," *Immigrants and Minorities* 27, no. 1 (December 2009): 1–28; Cohen, "State, Migrants, and the Negotiation of Second-Generation Citizenship in the Israeli Diaspora," *Diaspora: A Journal of Transnational Studies* 16, nos. 1–2 (Spring–Fall 2007): 133–58; Cohen, "Rights beyond Borders: Everyday Politics of Citizenship in the Israeli Diaspora," *Journal of Ethnic and Migration Studies* 37, no. 7 (May 2011): 1137–53.

26. Yinon Cohen, "Israeli-Born Emigrants: Size, Destinations and Selectivity," *International Journal of Comparative Sociology* 52, nos. 1–2 (February 2011): 46.

27. Reuben Lamdani, "Emigration from Israel," *Economic Quarterly* 11, no. 116 (April 1983): 462–78.

28. Alroey, *Unpromising Land*.

29. Sebastian Klor, *Between Exile and Exodus* (Detroit: Wayne State University Press, 2017).

30. Jeffrey Lesser and Raanan Rein, eds., *Rethinking Jewish-Latin Americans* (Albuquerque: University of New Mexico Press, 2008).

31. Jean-Pierre Cassarino, "Theorising Return Migration: The Conceptual Approach to Return Migrants Revisited," *International Journal on Multicultural Societies* 6, no. 2 (December 2004): 255.

32. See, for example, Takeyuki Tsuda Gaku, "Ethnic Return Migration and the Nation-State: Encouraging the Diaspora to Return 'Home,'" *Nations and Nationalism* 16, no. 4 (October 2010): 616–36; Rainer Silbereisen, Peter Titzmann, and Yossi Shavit, eds., *The Challenges of Diaspora Migration: Interdisciplinary Perspectives on Israel and Germany* (New York: Routledge, 2014).

33. Alessandro Portelli, *The Death of Luigi Trastulli, and Other Stories: Form and Meaning in Oral History* (New York: SUNY Press, 1991), i.

34. Raanan Rein, *Argentine Jews or Jewish Argentines? Essays on Ethnicity, Identity, and Diaspora* (Leiden: Brill, 2010), 3.

35. Lesser and Rein, "Challenging Particularity," 3-4.

36. John W. Berry, "Psychology of Acculturation: Understanding Individuals Moving between Cultures," in *Applied Cross-Cultural Psychology*, ed. Richard W. Brislin (Newbury Park, CA: Sage, 1990), 232–53.

37. Rein, *Argentine Jews or Jewish Argentines*, 28; Avni, *Argentina and the Jews*; Boleslao Lewin, *Cómo fue la inmigración judía en la Argentina*, 2nd ed. (Buenos Aires: Plus Ultra, 1983).

38. Rein, *Argentine Jews or Jewish Argentines*, 27.

39. The number of Jewish victims is still unknown. Victor A. Mirelman, "The Semana Trágica of 1919 and the Jews in Argentina," *Jewish Social Studies* 37, no. 1 (Winter 1975): 61–73.

40. Raanan Rein, *Argentina, Israel, and the Jews: Peron, the Eichmann Capture and After* (Bethesda: University Press of Maryland, 2003).

41. Their names were Edgardo Trilnik and Graciela Sirota. See Rein, *Argentine Jews or Jewish Argentines*, 77, 85.

42. Rein, *Argentine Jews or Jewish Argentines*, 193.

43. Rein, *Argentine Jews or Jewish Argentines*, 31. See also Haim Avni, "The Impact of the Six-Day War on a Zionist Community: The Case of Argentina," in *The Six-Day War and World Jewry*, ed. Eli Lederhendler (Maryland University Press, 2000), 137–65.

44. Israeli Central Bureau of Statistics, "Total Immigration to Israel by Select Country by Year," accessed April 19, 2019 (online).

45. Sergio DellaPergola, "World Jewish Population, 2019," in *American Jewish Year Book, 2019*, ed. Arnold Dashefsky and Ira M. Sheskin, vol. 119 (Dordrecht: Springer, 2020), 263–353; DellaPergola, *Jewish Demographic Policies: Population Trends and Options in Israel and in the Diaspora* (Jerusalem: Jewish People Policy Planning Institute, 2011).

46. A person who has at least one Jewish grandparent and who has not converted from Judaism to another religion is eligible under the Law of Return.

47. Adrián Jmelnizky and Ezequiel Erdei, *La población judía de Buenos Aires: Estudio sociodemográfico* (Buenos Aires: Centro de Documentación e Información sobre Judaísmo Argentino Marc Turkow, JDC-Meida, 2005). According to the survey, approximately 3,416 Jewish Argentines had once lived in Israel. However, their total number was undoubtedly larger: (1) The study's statistical method assumed that its degree of accuracy decreased the more it referred to a specific subuniverse such as returnees from Israel. (2) A considerable number of returnees had died by the time of the survey. (3) The survey was conducted just two years after the highest immigration peak of Jewish Argentines to Israel ever registered and the return of a considerable portion of them was just beginning. (4) The area under examination did not include people living outside of Buenos Aires.

48. C. Wright Mills, *The Sociological Imagination* (New York: Oxford University Press, 2000).

49. "Argentina GDP per Capita 1960–2020," Macrotrends, accessed July 20, 2020 (online); "Israel GDP Per Capita 1960-2020," Macrotrends, accessed July 20, 2020 (online).

50. César Tcach Abad, *Arturo Illia: Un sueño breve—El rol del peronismo y de Los Estados Unidos en el golpe militar de 1966*, ed. Celso Rodriguez (Buenos Aires: Edhasa, 2006); Thomas M. Millington, "President Arturo Illia and the Argentine Military," *Journal of Inter-American Studies* 6, no. 3 (July 1964).

51. Cyrus Stephen Cousins, "General Onganía and the Argentine Military Revolution of

the Right: Anti-Communism and Morality, 1966-1970," *Historia Actual Online* (Fall 2009): 65–79.

52. Sergio Moreno, *La noche de los bastones largos* (Buenos Aires: EUDEBA, 2016).

53. Ana Castellani, "Privileged Accumulation Spaces and Restrictions on Development of State-Business Relations in Argentina," *American Journal of Economics and Sociology* 72, no. 1 (January 2013): 90–121.

54. Avni, "Impact of the Six-Day War," 139.

55. Zvi Gitelman and David Naveh, "Elite Accommodation and Organizational Effectiveness: The Case of Immigrant Absorption in Israel," *Journal of Politics* 38, no. 4 (November 1976): 963–86.

56. Ruth Tamar Horowitz, "Immigrants in Transition: The Israeli Absorption Center," *International Migration* 15, no. 4 (October 1977): 288–99.

57. Guido di Tella, *Argentina under Perón, 1973–76: The Nation's Experience with a Labour-Based Government* (New York: St. Martin's, 1983).

58. On Gelbard's economic program and the challenges of Peronism during their third government, see Óscar Landi, "La tercera presidencia de Perón: Gobierno de emergencia y crisis política," *Revista Mexicana de Sociología* 40, no. 4 (October–December 1978): 1353–410; Ronaldo Munck, "The Crisis of Late Peronism and the Working Class 1973–1976," *Bulletin of the Society for Latin American Studies* 30 (April 1979): 5–34; Robert L. Ayres, "The 'Social Pact' as Anti-Inflationary Policy: The Argentine Experience since 1973," *World Politics* 28, no. 4 (July 1976): 473–501; Cecilia Vitto, "Plan económico del tercer gobierno peronista: Gestión de Gelbard (1973–1974)," *Problemas del Desarrollo* 171, no. 43 (October–December 2012): 111–34.

59. Marcelo Diamand, "La estructura productiva desequilibrada Argentina y el tipo de cambio," *Desarrollo Económico* 12, no. 45 (April–June 1972): 25–47; Martín Fiszbein, "La economía del stop and go: Las ideas estructuralistas en la Argentina, 1945-1976," *Desarrollo Económico* 55, no. 216 (September–December 2015): 187–210.

60. On Gelbard, see Leonardo Senkman, "Populismo y empresarios judíos: Actuación pública de Horacio Lafer y José B. Gelbard durante Vargas y Perón," *Araucaria: Revista Iberoamericana de Filosofía, Política y Humanidades* 15 (January/June 2006): 46–76; Raanan Rein and Claudio Panella, eds., *La segunda línea: Liderazgo peronista 1945-1955*, (Buenos Aires: Universidad Nacional de Tres de Febrero, 2013); María Seoane, *El burgués maldito: Los secretos de Gelbard, el último líder del capitalismo nacional* (Buenos Aires: Editorial Sudamericana, 2002). On Jews and Peronism, see Raanan Rein, *Los muchachos peronistas judíos: Los argentinos judíos y el apoyo al justicialismo* (Buenos Aires: Sudamericana, 2015).

61. Senkman, "El antisemitismo bajo dos experiencias democráticas." For an account of anti-Semitic episodes, see Nissim Elnecavé, "Latin America," in *American Jewish Year Book* (New York: American Jewish Committee, 1972), 438.

62. Alfredo A. Triana, "Argentina: La política como cultura o los años del GAN. La primacía de la política. Lanusse, Perón y la nueva izquierda en tiempos del GAN," *Sociohistórica* 7, no. 7 (January–June 2000).

## Chapter 1

1. Joseph W. Esherick, Hasan Kayali, and Eric Van Young, *Empire to Nation: Historical Perspectives on the Making of the Modern World* (Lanham, MD: Rowman and Littlefield, 2006).

2. Theodor Herzl, *The Jewish State* (New York: Dover, 1988); Arthur Hertzberg, *The Zionist Idea: A Historical Analysis and Reader* (New York: Jewish Publication Society, 2014).

3. Anita Shapira, *Israel: A History* (Waltham, MA: Brandeis University Press, 2012), 103.

4. Herbert S. Lewis, *After the Eagles Landed: The Yemenites of Israel* (Boulder, CO: Westview Press, 1989).

5. Ben Halpern and Jehuda Reinharz, "The Cultural and Social Background of the Second Aliyah," *Middle Eastern Studies* 27, no. 3 (July 1991): 487–517.

6. Yehoshua Kaniel, *Continuity and Change: Old Yishuv and New Yishuv during the First and Second Aliyah* (Jerusalem: Yad Ben-Zvi, 1981); Yoseph Gorny, "Changes in the Social and Political Structure of the Second Aliyah between 1904 and 1940," in *Essential Papers on Zionism*, ed. Jehuda Reinharz and Anita Shapira (New York: New York University Press, 1996), 371–421; Aaron Bar Adon, "The Contribution of the Second Aliyah to the Revival of Hebrew: Perceptions and Reality," in *Proceedings of the World Congress of Jewish Studies: Hebrew and Jewish Languages* (Jerusalem: World Union of Jewish Studies, 1985), 63–70.

7. Shapira, *Israel*, 30–31

8. Shapira, 103.

9. Shapira; Tamar Wolf-Monzon, "Uri Zvi Greenberg and the Pioneers of the Third Aliyah: A Case of Reception," *Prooftexts* 29, no. 1 (Winter 2009): 31–62; Zachary Lockman, "The Left in Israel: Zionism vs. Socialism," *MERIP Reports* 49 (July 1976): 3–18; A. Ben-Porat, "Class Consciousness before Class: The Emergence of a Jewish Working Class in Palestine," *Theory and Society* 16, no. 5 (September 1987): 741–69.

10. Casmir Dadak, "National Heritage and Economic Policies in Free and Sovereign Poland after 1918," *Contemporary European History* 21, no. 2 (May 2012): 193–214.

11. Shapira, *Israel*, 106.

12. Shapira, 104, 115.

13. David Yisraeli, "The Third Reich and the Transfer Agreement," *Journal of Contemporary History* 6, no. 2 (April 1971): 129–48; Hava Eshkoli-Wagman, "Yishuv Zionism: Its Attitude to Nazism and the Third Reich Reconsidered," *Modern Judaism* 19, no. 1 (February 1999): 21–40.

14. Michael J. Cohen, "Appeasement in the Middle East: The British White Paper on Palestine, May 1939," *Historical Journal* 16, no. 3 (September 1973): 571–96; Yehoyada Haim, "Zionist Policies and Attitudes towards the Arabs on the Eve of the Arab Revolt, 1936," *Middle Eastern Studies* 14, no. 2 (May 1978): 211–31.

15. The term Aliyah Beth uses the second letter of the Hebrew alphabet, which is also the beginning of the Hebrew word "illegal."

16. Bernard Reich, *A Brief History of Israel*, 2nd ed. (New York: Checkmark Books, 2008), 39–40.

17. Paul Rivlin, *The Israeli Economy from the Foundation of the State through the 21st Century* (New York: Cambridge University Press, 2010), 21-22.

18. In 1970 those rights were extended to people with one Jewish grandparent and the spouse of a Jew, whether or not the spouse was considered Jewish under Jewish religious law, *Halakha*, which defines a Jew as a person whose mother is Jewish. Consequently, there are two different criteria defining who is a Jew: according to the Law of Return, and according to the religious authorities that regulate marital issues in Israel.

19. Rivlin, *Israeli Economy*, 35.

20. Gur Alroey, "The Jewish Emigration from Palestine in the Early Twentieth Century," *Journal of Modern Jewish Studies* 2, no. 2 (August 2003): 111–31.

21. Rein, *Argentine Jews or Jewish Argentines?* (see intro, n. 34).

22. David Spector, "Days of Worry," *Al HaMishmar*, January 18, 1953; David Ben Israel, *De América Latina a Israel, Al Kibutz* (Merhavia: Merhavia Press, 1978); Florinda Goldberg and Iosef Rozen, eds., *Los Latinoamericanos en Israel: Antología de una aliá* (Buenos Aires: Contexto, 1988); Shlomo Bar-Gil, *We Started with a Dream* (Beer Sheba: Ben-Gurion University, 2005).

23. "Olim from Argentina Celebrate Funding like a Prize," *Herut*, March, 18, 1955. When Manguel was close to finishing his mission and the village was inaugurated, the library was named after him.

24. "Agro-Industrial Village Built for Argentine Jews," *Davar*, November 4, 1952. See also Klor, *Between Exile and Exodus*, 170 (see intro, n. 29).

25. "The *Jerusalem* Sails to the USA," *Davar*, January 18, 1954.

26. Yaacov Yosef Nidina, "And the Apostates Should Not Have Hope," *Davar*, April 5, 1954.

27. "263 Olim Arrive; 200 Yordim Leave," *Al HaMishmar*, October 25, 1954.

28. M. Shmiriahu, "15,000 Voters Escape," *Maariv*, July 12, 1955.

29. Baruch Karo, "Book of Argentina," *Haboker*, August 26, 1955.

30. "Yishuv 'Acharon,'" *Maariv*, November 11, 1958.

31. Rafael Bashan, "They Did Not Question Our Stand on Jerusalem," *Maariv*, August 7, 1959.

32. "Departures in July Set Record," *Jerusalem Post*, August 14, 1957. See also "Nearly 8000 Exited Israel in July," *HaBoker*, August 14, 1957, Central Zionist Archive (henceforth CZA) S60/334; "Emigration from Israel, Record in July," *Herut*, August 14, 1957; "Record in Number of Emigrants," *Davar*, August 14, 1957, CZA S60/334. Some articles criticized the role of the JA and the government, for example, "Symposia about Absorption of Academicians: Lack of Coordination between Government and Agency Causes Yerida," *LaMerhav*, n.d., CZA S60/334.

33. Kalman Levin to Dov Yosef, February 2, 1959, CZA, S60/334.

34. Bar Yehuda to Dov Yosef, January 22, 1959, CZA S60/334.

35. Dov Yosef to Bar Yehuda, December 23, 1958, CZA S60/334.

36. *Research about Yerida from the Country: Summary Report*, October 1959, Hebrew University of Jerusalem, 3, CZA S6/6563.

37. See Chaim I. Waxman, "Critical Sociology and the End of Ideology in Israel," *Israel Studies* 2, no. 1 (Spring 1997): 194–210.

38. *Research about Yerida*, 7

39. *Research about Yerida*, 10; "Findings of the Commission for the Research of Yordim Problems," n.d., CZA S60/334.

40. *Research about Yerida*, 88

41. S. Z. Shragai to Dov Yosef, October 19, 1959, CZA S60/334.

42. B. Duvdevany to Dov Yosef, March 3, 1961, CZA, S60/334. In the telegram, Duvdevany introduced Yitzhak Cohen as an emissary with expertise in yerida due to his job in Canada.

43. M. Sharett to Y. Cohen, April 11, 1961, CZA, S65/187.

44. Y. Sar to Y. Dominitz, April 14, 1961, CZA, S65/187.

45. S. Z. Shragai to M. Sharett, August 1, 1961, CZA S65/187.

46. In the case of Brazil, there was a controversial project, supported by the American Jewish Joint Distribution Committee and the Hebrew Immigrant Aid Society, to relocate Holocaust survivors who did not adapt to Israel. See Yehudai, "Displaced in the National Home" (see intro, n. 20); Yehudai, "Forth from Zion: Jewish Emigration from Palestine and Israel, 1945–1960" (PhD diss., University of Chicago, 2013).

47. A. Hadar to E. Dovkin, June 12, 1962, CZA, S65/187.

48. E. Dovkin to A. Hadar, June 11, 1962, CZA, S65/187.

49. B. Yahir to A. Chisling, December 7, 1961, CZA, S65/187; Y. Cohen to M. Sharett, July 12, 1961; Y. Cohen to M. Sharett, May 25, 1961, CZA, S65/187.

50. "Con valiosa carga humana zarpó el *Flaminia* rumbo a Jaifa," *La Luz*, March 15, 1963.

51. "The Group of Immigrants," *Davar*, March 21, 1963. See Raanan Rein, "The Eichmann Kidnapping: Its Effects on Argentine-Israeli Relations and the Local Jewish Community," *Jewish Social Studies* 7, no. 3 (Spring–Summer 2001): 101–30.

52. "The Latin American Aliyah," *Hatzofe*, April 1, 1963.

53. "Aboard the Immigrant Ship was the Body of the Youngster Assassinated in an Anti-Semitic Attack in Montevideo," *Hatzofe*, April 1, 1963. On anti-Semitism in Uruguay, see Clara Aldrighi, ed., *Antisemitismo en Uruguay: Raíces, discursos, imágenes (1870–1940)* (Montevideo: Ediciones Trilce, 2000).

54. Moshe Sharett, "The Unification of Two Trends," *Davar*, April 4, 1963.

55. "The People of the *Flaminia* and Their Journey," *Hatzofe*, April 8, 1963.

56. See Rein, "Eichmann Kidnapping."

57. See Rein, *Argentine Jews or Jewish Argentines*, 77, 85.

58. See Rein, *Argentine Jews or Jewish Argentines*, 193.

59. Israeli Central Bureau of Statistics, "Total Immigration to Israel by Select Country by Year" (see intro., n. 44).

60. Rein, *Argentine Jews or Jewish Argentines*, 31. See also Avni, "Impact of the Six-Day War on a Zionist Community" (see intro, n. 43).

61. Luis Alberto Romero, *A History of Argentina in the Twentieth Century* (University Park: Pennsylvania State University Press, 2002), 207–8.

62. Klor, *Between Exile and Exodus*, 136.

63. Klor, 137.

64. Klor, 138.

65. Klor, 142, 199.

66. Anna Rovner, "Los Srugos Invaden Israel," *Aurora*, February 6, 1964.

67. "La industria a las puertas del Negev"; "Fabrica de pelotas de futbol 'Argentina'"; "Fabrica de artículos de plástico 'Avergros'"; "Fábrica de muebles Argentina"; *Aurora*, special issue on Beer Sheba, October 29, 1964.

68. Ezequiel Adamovsky, *Historia de la clase media Argentina* (Buenos Aires: Planeta, 2009), 366.

69. "42 *Olim* Return to South America," *Davar*, December 17, 1963, CZA, S62/316.

70. "OLEI Eighth Territorial Congress in Tel Aviv," Conference Proceedings, June 29, 1966.

71. Teodoro Ducach, "Convención de Latinoamericanos en Tel Aviv," *La Luz*, July 22, 1966.

72. J. R. from Beersheva, "Nadie se alimenta de Sionismo," *Aurora*, July 9, 1964. The Israeli

pound or lira (IL) replaced the Palestine pound in 1952 and was replaced by the Israeli shekel in 1980.

73. The term "absorption capacity" has its origins in the beginnings of Zionist thought; the British Mandate administration also used it as a central element to regulate immigration to Palestine. Hence, the concept was used in political dispute: the British used it as part of their arguments to limit Jewish immigration to Palestine, while the Zionists recruited and hired teams of professionals from several disciplines, from archeology to economics, to demonstrate that Palestine was able to receive Jewish immigrants and provide them with economic opportunities if properly administered. See Ilan Troen, "Calculating the 'Economic Absorptive Capacity' of Palestine: A Study of the Political Uses of Scientific Research," *Contemporary Jewry* 10, no. 2 (September 1989): 19–38; Lily Weissbrod, "Economic Factors and Political Strategies: The Defeat of the Revisionists in Mandatory Palestine," *Middle Eastern Studies* 19, no. 3 (July 1983): 326–44.

74. Herzl, *Jewish State*, 38.

## Chapter 2

1. Fiammetta Martegani, *The Israeli Defence Forces' Representation in Israeli Cinema: Did David Betray His Soldiers?* (Newcastle upon Tyne: Cambridge Scholars, 2017), 33

2. Maya Balakirsky Katz, "The De-Politicization of Israeli Political Cartoons," *Israel Studies* 18, no. 1 (Spring 2013): 20.

3. Romero, *History of Argentina*, 162 (see ch. 1, n. 61).

4. Elizabeth Montes Garcés, "Sentido de lugar y género en Condorito y Mafalda," *Revista Canadiense de Estudios Hispánicos* 43, no. 1 (2018): 26.

5. Fiszbein, "La economía del stop and go," 187–210 (see intro, n. 59).

6. Romero, *History of Argentina*, 154.

7. Guillermo A. O'Donnell, *Modernization and Bureaucratic-Authoritarianism: Studies in South American Politics* (Berkeley: University of California, 1973), 169-72.

8. Alain Rouquié, *Poder militar y sociedad política en la Argentina: Práctica y mecanismos del poder militar. Anatomía del poder militar, ensayo de interpretación* (Buenos Aires: Hyspamérica, 1986).

9. Rivlin, *Israeli Economy* (see ch. 1, n. 17).

10. "The Reparations Agreement with Germany—General Debate and Decision: Knesset Sessions 38-40, 7-9.1.1952," in *The Reparations Controversy: The Jewish State and German Money in the Shadow of the Holocaust 1951–1952*, ed. Yaakov Sharett (Berlin: De Gruyter, 2011), 161–272; Frederick Honig, "The Reparations Agreement between Israel and the Federal Republic of Germany," *American Journal of International Law* 48, no. 4 (October 1954): 564–78; Kenneth M. Lewan, "How West Germany Helped to Build Israel," *Journal of Palestine Studies* 4, no. 4 (Summer 1975): 41–64.

11. "The Current Regime Is Not Prepared to Absorb South American Immigrants," *Herut*, December 2, 1965, CZA, S62/351.

12. Israel Inbari, "Olim from South America Who Turned into Yordim," *Davar*, June 3, 1966.

13. "Preocupa la crisis de la *'aliya'* en Israel," *La Luz*, July 8, 1966.

14. "Is" Macrotrends, accessed May 14, 2020.

15. "Tel Aviv-Jaffa, Israel Metro Area Population 1950–2020," Macrotrends, accessed May 15, 2020 (online).

16. "Buenos Aires, Argentina Metro Area Population 1950–2020," Macrotrends, accessed May 15, 2020 (online).

17. *Censo nacional de población 1960* (Buenos Aires: Dirección Nacional de Estadísticas y Censos, 1960).

18. Romero, *History of Argentina*, 153.

19. Mariano Ben Plotkin, "Freudian Slips: On the Complicated—and Lingering—Legacy of Psychoanalysis in Argentina," *World Policy Journal* 35, no. 1 (Spring 2018): 16; Plotkin, *Freud in the Pampas: The Emergence and Development of a Psychoanalytic Culture in Argentina* (Redwood, CA: Stanford University Press, 2001).

20. Federico Vaccarezza, "Políticas de desarrollo industrial en la Argentina (1940–2001)" (PhD diss., Universidad Nacional de Tres de Febrero, 2010).

21. Interview with Saul S., Buenos Aires, July 18, 2016.

22. Anat Helman, *A Coat of Many Colors: Dress Culture in the Young State of Israel* (Brookline, MA: Academic Studies Press, 2011).

23. Carlos Zyman, "Letters to Aurora," *Aurora*, July 1, 1966.

24. Guershon Zak, "Wait, We Are to Blame," *Davar*, September 23, 1966; A. Shubatz, "According to the Law," *Davar*, June 8, 1966; "The Yordim from Greece," *Davar*, July 13, 1966.

25. Shlomo Ginozar, "700 Schlihim, Who Are They and What Do They Do?" *Davar*, April 4, 1966.

26. Shlomo Zalman Shragai, "Olim, Yordim, and Returnees," *Hatsofe*, August 23, 1963, CZA, S62/316; Shragai, "Consciousness about Aliyah and Absorption Programs," *Hatsofe*, September 6, 1963; Shragai, "Jewish Minyan for *Aliyah*?" *Hatsofe*, August 30, 1963.

27. David Ben-Gurion, "The First 4 Years," *Davar*, March 10, 1966.

28. Moshe Kitron, "The Ejected Aliyah," *Davar*, September 28, 1966.

29. Shlomo Ginozar, "I Believe We Took the Right Path," *Davar*, September 30 1966.

30. Yoram Ben Porath, "Self-Employed and Wage Earners in Israel: Findings from the Population Census 1972" (research paper, Institute for Economic Research, Jerusalem, 1981), 248.

31. *Immigrant Arrivals in 1969-70*, special series (Jerusalem: Central Bureau of Statistics/ Ministry of Immigrant Absorption, 1974), 15; *Immigrant Arrivals 1969-70/1971-72* (Jerusalem: Central Bureau of Statistics, 1976), 12.

32. Interview with José C., April 23, 2016.

33. Moshe Brawer, "The Image of Israel's Geographical Transformation," *Israel Studies* 13, no. 1 (Spring 2008): 152–59; Jacob Dash, "Israel: Urban Development Achievements and Future Plans," *Official Architecture and Planning* 28, no. 11 (November 1965): 1607–10.

34. Aziza Khazzoom, "Did the Israeli State Engineer Segregation? On the Placement of Jewish Immigrants in Development Towns in the 1950s," *Social Forces* 84, no. 1 (September 2005): 115–34.

35. Klor, *Between Exile and Exodus*, 140 (see intro, n. 29).

36. Robert Sarly, "Failure of the New Towns," *Built Environment* 3, no. 12 (December 1974): 612–16.

37. Sarly, "Failure of the New Towns.

38. Sarly.

39. Y. Karmon, "Ashdod: A New Mediterranean Port in Israel," *Geography* 51, no. 3 (July 1966): 254–58.

40. Haim Yacobi and Erez Tzfadia, "Multiculturalism, Nationalism, and the Politics of the Israeli City," *International Journal of Middle East Studies* 41, no. 2 (May 2009): 289–307.

41. On ethnic differentiation within Israeli society, see Sammy Smooha, *Israel: Pluralism and Conflict* (Oakland: University of California Press, 1978); Smooha, "Pluralism: A Study of Intergroup Relations in Israel" (PhD diss., University of California, 1973); Smooha, "The Mass Immigrations to Israel: A Comparison of the Failure of the Mizrahi Immigrants of the 1950s with the Success of the Russian Immigrants of the 1990s," *Journal of Israeli History* 27, no. 1 (March 2008): 1–27.

42. John Warren, "The Five Schools Project," *Built Environment* 3, no. 12 (December 1974): 623–24.

43. "*Olim* dejan el país," *Aurora*, March 25, 1965.

44. Anna Goren, "Argentine Immigrants (*olim*) Emigrate (*yordim*)," *Haaretz*, September 20, 1965, CZA, S62/316.

45. Goren, "Argentine Immigrants"; on prices and immigration, see Saul Lach, "Immigration and Prices," *Journal of Political Economy* 115, no. 4 (August 2007): 548–87.

46. "Comprender al Olé de América Latina," *Aurora*, July 8, 1966.

47. "Protesta pública de Latino Americanos en Ashdod," *Aurora*, December 9, 1965; Teodoro Ducach, "¿Porqué se van? En el puerto de Ashdod," *Aurora*, December 23, 1965; "Representantes de la Agencia Judía en Ashdod," *Aurora*, December 30, 1965.

48. Teodoro Ducach, "La agencia cometió serios desatinos," *Aurora*, December 30, 1965.

49. Interview with *Aurora* director Aryeh Avidor, Tel Aviv, July 18, 2017.

50. Teodoro Ducach, "¿Porqué vuelven los Sudamericanos?" *La Luz*, March 4, 1966.

51. S. Z. Shragai to A. Cygel, September 11, 1966, CZA, S62/316.

52. A. Cygel to S. Z. Shragai, November 2, 1966, CZA, S62/316.

53. "Posible cierre del Puerto de Ashdod," *Aurora*, February 1, 1966.

54. "Disturbios en Ashdod y Dimona, el 1 de mayo por desocupación," *Aurora*, May 6, 1966; "Pan y Trabajo," *Aurora*, May 6, 1966.

55. "Obreros despedidos de Layland impiden vuelta al trabajo," *Aurora*, May 6, 1966.

56. Aviva Sten, "Exodus 1966," *Hayom*, June 14, 1966, CZA, S62/351.

57. The moshav was founded in 1950 by Iraqi immigrants and abandoned during the economic crisis of 1952.

58. Henry Near, "Paths to Utopia," in *Where Community Happens: The Kibbutz and the Philosophy of Communalism* (Bern: Peter Lang, 2011), 197–218; Raymond Russell, Robert Hanneman, and Shlomo Getz, "The Transformation of the Kibbutzim," *Israel Studies* 16, no. 2 (Summer 2011): 109–26; Levia Applebaum and Michael Sofer, "The Moshav in Israel: Agricultural Communities in a Process of Change—A Current View," *Horizons in Geography* 79/80 (2012): 194–209; Michael Sofer, "The Future of Family Farming in Israel: The Second Generation in the Moshav," *Geographical Journal* 171, no. 4 (December 2005): 357–68.

59. "514 *Olim* Arrived Yesterday from Latin American Countries," *Hatzofe*, August 19, 1963.

60. Interview with Dov Feldman, Israel, May 26, 2018.

61. Sarly, "Failure of the New Towns."

62. "Elecciones al estilo Kojav," *Aurora*, February 25, 1965.

63. Amos Jadad, "Yordim from Moshav Kochav in Lakish," *Haaretz*, June 1, 1966, CZA, S39/2379.

64. C. Levanon to M. Kramer, June 9, 1966, CZA, S39/2379.

65. M. Kramer to C. Levanon, June 23, 1966, CZA, S39/2379.

66. Exodus 16:3: "If only we had died by the LORD's hand in the land of Egypt! . . . There we sat by pots of meat and ate our fill of bread, but you have brought us into this desert to starve this whole assembly to death!" *Holy Bible* (Pittsburgh, PA: Bible Hub). The expression was incorporated into Zionism by Herzl, who used it in his foundational text. He wrote: "If we leave *Mitzraim* (Egypt) again, we will not forget the pots." Herzl, *Jewish State*, 81 (see ch. 1, n. 2).

67. "Cuatro familias de Kojav retornan a la Argentina," *Aurora*, June 3, 1966; "Retornan cuatro familias del Moshav Kochav," *La Luz*, July 8, 1966.

68. Ora Yanov, "The Yerida Also Affected Moshav Kochav Where Almost All Residents Are South Americans," *Maariv*, March 19, 1967, Tsrifin Logistic Center (henceforth, TLC), 216327.

69. Interview with Dov Feldman, Israel, May 26, 2018.

70. "Tres argentinos huyeron del país y fueron detenidos en Barcelona," *Aurora*, August 18, 1967.

71. "Kojav Michaell Sobell: Ejemplo de alia exitosa," *Aurora*, March 12, 1970.

72. Another twenty-five families joined the moshav by mid-1971. "25 Families from Argentina to Moshav Kochav," *Maariv*, July 19, 1971.

73. Arie Shoshani, "1963–1970 Presente y futuro del Moshav Kojav Mijael Sobell," *Aurora*, June 4, 1970.

74. "Reception of Olim from the US and South America in Moshavim and Attraction of Olim from the USSR," *Davar*, December 12, 1971.

75. Ariel Elnecavé, "La familia Elnecavé y la revista La Luz," Radio Sefarad, 2009.

76. Elnecavé, *Crisol de vivencias judías* (see intro, n. 16).

77. Nissim Elnecavé, "De regreso de eretz Israel," *La Luz*, June 10, 1938.

78. On Sephardic Jews and Zionism in Argentina, see Susana Brauner Rodgers, "La comunidad judía alepina en Buenos Aires: De la ortodoxia religiosa a la apertura y de la apertura a la ortodoxia religiosa (1930-1953)," in *Estudios Interdisciplinarios de América Latina y el Caribe* 11, no. 1 (2014): 45–64; Adriana M. Brodsky, "'Belonging to Many Homes': Argentine Sephardi Youth in Buenos Aires and Israel, 1956–76," in *Transnational Histories of Youth in the Twentieth Century*, ed. Richard Ivan Jobs and David M. Pomfret (London: Palgrave Macmillan, 2015), 213–35.

79. "Con 600 olim zarpara el 4 de marzo para Israel el buque Flaminia," *La Luz*, February 14, 1963.

80. "Inepcia para atender la alia de la clase media: El caso del 'Flaminia,'" *La Luz*, January 31, 1963.

81. "El Dr Goldenberg opina sobre los judíos de la Argentina y la 'alia,'" *La Luz*, March 15, 1963.

82. "A la 'alia' de la clase media asesora Y. Kurland," *La Luz*, March 29, 1963.

83. Idan Dor, "721 inmigrantes y un recién nacido," *La Luz*, April 26, 1963.

84. "En el diferendo entre la OSA y *La Luz* interviene Sharett," *La Luz*, May 10, 1963.

85. "La alia a la luz del exodo de la Argentina," *La Luz*, June 21, 1963.

86. "El fenomeno del 'shelijismo' causa honda preocupacion," *La Luz*, October 2, 1964.

87. "Alia de la Argentina," *La Luz*, November 12, 1965.

88. "Argentine Immigrants Return in Their Thousands," *Jewish Chronicle*, November 5, 1965.

89. S. Shragai to S. Levenberg, November 17, 1965, CZA, S62/351.

90. S. Shragai to Z. Lurie, November 22, 1965, CZA, S62/351.

91. Dor, "721 inmigrantes."

92. "Argentine Jewry," *Jewish Chronicle*, December 17, 1965.

93. Joni Benda, "La alia de la Argentina en la prensa judeo-británica," *La Luz*, January 7, 1966.

94. Teodoro Ducach, "Latinoamericanos abandonan Israel," *La Luz*, January 7, 1966.

95. R. Yaglom to S. Shragai, February 17, 1966, CZA, S62/351.

96. D. Stein to A. Cygel and A. Dulczin, February 21, 1966, CZA, S62/351.

97. Teodoro Ducach, "*La Luz* entrevista a Nicolas Goldberg," *La Luz*, July 8, 1966; Ducach, "Agravase la tendencia de la 'yerida,'" *La Luz*, September 2, 1966.

98. Nissim Elnecavé, "La aliya, la clase media y los que regresan," *La Luz*, March 4, 1966.

99. Teodoro Ducach, "Preocupa la crisis de 'alia' en Israel," *La Luz*, July 8, 1966.

100. Nissim Elnecavé, "Controversia en torno a la alia," *La Luz*, January 6, 1967.

101. "Alia: ¿para qué y cómo?," *La Luz*, November 1967; Teodoro Ducach, "Ocio e inacción en la Agencia Judía," *La Luz*, October 20, 1967.

102. N. Elnecavé to S. Z. Shragai, October 23, 1967, CZA, S62/351.

103. Nissim Elnecavé, "Latin American Jewry," *Jewish Chronicle*, August 10, 1973.

## Chapter 3

1. Marta caught a plane to Marseille to catch up with the ship. "Retúvose viaje de joven argentina," *Aurora*, December 9, 1965; Teodoro Ducach, "Latinoamericanos abandonan Israel," *La Luz*, January 7, 1966. According to a message sent from Brazil to R. Stein at the JA immigration department, this episode was also reported in the Jewish Brazilian magazine *Aonde Vamos?* on January 13, 1966, under the title "Embittered *Olim* in Israel," S62/351, CZA.

2. "Proceedings of the Meeting Held by the Commission to Stop the Yerida of Latin American *Olim*," January 28, 1964, CZA, S39/2379.

3. "Proceedings of the Meeting Held by the Commission to Stop the Yerida."

4. The protracted and unresolved exchange of letters regarding new appointments to the commission, discussions, and conclusions suggest that the commission was active for a longer period than expected and would appear again with different people and goals in the years to come. Y. Giladi to A. Pincus, November 26, 1965; B. Duvdevany to S. Z. Shragai, November 29, 1965, CZA, S39/2379.

5. The creation of a second commission, focusing only on economic aspects, was suggested, but A. Dulczin decided that only one commission should deal with all the immigrants' difficulties. A. Dulczin to A. Cygel, January 23, 1966, CZA, S39/2379.

6. A. Cygel to Members of the Commission to Stop the Yerida of South American Olim, January 1, 1966, CZA, S39/2379; A. Akhbas to Y. Kurland, February 10, 1966; A. Akhbas to Y. Kurland, February 18, 1966, CZA, S39/2379; M. Mizrahi to A. Dulczin, February 18, 1966, CZA, S39/2379.

7. M. Kitron to A. Pincus, December 12, 1965, CZA, 62/351.

8. The new commission included Yehoshua Wolberg from the immigration department and Haim Arenberg from the economics department. A. Duvdevany to A. Pincus, November 29, 1965; Y. Gilady to A. Pincus, November 26, 1965, CZA, 62/351.

9. Tom Segev, *1967: Israel, the War, and the Year That Transformed the Middle East* (New York: Metropolitan Books, 2007), 132.

10. S. Z. Shragai to B. Shitrit, August 20, 1965, CZA, S62/316.

11. B. Shitrit to S. Z. Shragai, October 10, 1965, CZA, S62/316.

12. "Olim se escapan por Ashdod," *Aurora*, August 26, 1965.

13. Aviva Sten, "Exodus 1966," *Hayom*, June 14, 1966, CZA, S62/351.

14. "The Agency Denies Rumors of a Large Yerida of South American Immigrants," *Al Hamishmar*, June 22, 1966.

15. "'I Saw, I Heard': Immigrants Escape," *Haaretz*, August 10, 1966, CZA, S62/316.

16. "Dos argentinos de Ashdod se fugaron al extranjero," *Aurora*, July 15, 1966.

17. "La ley por su cuenta," *Aurora*, July 15, 1966.

18. Teodoro Ducach, "Fuerte custodia de barco argentino en Ashdod," *La Luz*, August 19, 1966.

19. "Two Young People Hiding on Ship Returned," *Davar*, July 31, 1963; "Two Passengers Hidden on the *Flaminia*," *Davar*, July 8, 1963; "Two Young Israelis," *Davar*, August 1, 1963.

20. Interview with Mario L., Jerusalem, August 30, 2017.

21. José Zarco, "La OLEI amenaza con juicios," *Aurora*, March 10, 1966.

22. J. S., "Carta de lectores," *Aurora*, July 1, 1966.

23. J. Arenberg to R. Stein, April 23, 1967, CZA S62/351.

24. N. Davidovich and E. Cwik to JA Economics Department in Montevideo, March 31, 1966, CZA S1/10214. See also related letters: Economics Department in Montevideo to Collection Department in Jerusalem, April 28, 1966, CZA S1/10214; Economic Department in Montevideo to Collection Department in Jerusalem, June 30, 1966, CZA S1/10214; Economic Department in Montevideo to Collection Department, Jerusalem, November 15, 1966, CZA S1/10214; Collection Department in Jerusalem to Economic Department in Montevideo, March 3, 1967, CZA S1/10214.

25. In Chile and Peru, it is called *perro muerto* (death dog), a name derived from the fact that in small villages the neighbors would care for the dog of a dead person. Nowadays, Spaniards speak of *sinpa*, contracting the two words *sin* and *pagar* (without paying).

26. *Hayom* was published between 1965 and 1969 and was linked to the Gahal party (Herut-Liberal block) led by Menahem Begin. Aryeh Naor, "Rightist Political Dailies in Israel: Ideology, Politics and the Failure of Privatization," *Kesher* 25 (1999): 71–79.

27. Sten, "Exodus 1966." In 2016 a series of articles published in *Yedioth Ahronoth* included Sten in a list of KGB informants active in Israel during the Cold War. See Ronen Bergman, "At the Service of Mother Russia," *Yedioth Ahronoth*, October 26, 2016.

28. Y. Dominitz to S. Z. Shragai, August 31, 1966, CZA, S62/351.

29. Shraga Erguil, "The Yordim Set Sail in the Ship *Jerusalem*," *Maariv*, August 31, 1966.

30. A. Lebanony to E. Akbas, September 2, 1966, CZA, S39/2379.

31. A. Lebanony to E. Akbas.

32. "50 Yordim among 350 Travelers to South America," *Davar*, September 2, 1966.

33. "Partió el Jerusalem en viaje a Sud America," *Aurora*, September 3, 1966.

34. For similar encounters of newcomers and frustrated immigrants in the port of Haifa during the early twentieth century, see Alroey, *Unpromising Land*.

35. For more information on the Jews of Uruguay, see Rafael Porcezansky, *El Uruguay judío: Demografía e identidad* (Montevideo: Ediciones Trilce, 2006).

36. A. Gozik to P. Shamir and S. Mizrahi, September 22, 1966, CZA, S39/2379.

37. "Carta abierta de los *yordim* que viajan en el barco *Jerusalem* al pueblo de Israel," September 20, 1966, CZA, S39/2379.

38. Teodoro Ducach, "200 'Yordim' en el Jerusalem," *La Luz*, September 30, 1966.

39. "Proceedings of Emissaries' Meeting," September 23, 1966, S62/351, CZA.

40. A. Bar-Kahan to B. Duvdevany, September 26, 1966, S62/351, CZA.

41. A. Bar-Kahan to B. Duvdevany.

42. A. Bar-Kahan to B. Duvdevany.

43. A. Cygel to Absorption and Immigration Committee, September 27, 1966, CZA, S62/316.

44. Interview with José C., Buenos Aires, April 5, 2016.

45. A. Koblovitz, *Facts about Yerida*. Jerusalem, 1968, CZA, S61/10200.

46. Koblovitz, *Facts about Yerida*.

47. Koblovitz.

48. "200 Emigrated Yesterday," *Haaretz*, May 17, 1966, CZA, S62/316.

49. "Partió el Jerusalem en viaje a Sud America," *Aurora*, September 3, 1966.

50. "Llegan numerosos 'yordim' en el Teodoro Herzl," *La Luz*, February 24, 1967.

51. A. Pincus and A. Dulczin to S. Z. Shragai and A. Cygel, November 22, 1967, CZA, S62/351.

52. Guillermo O'Donnell, "Reflections on the Patterns of Change in the Bureaucratic-Authoritarian State," *Latin American Research Review* 13, no. 1 (January–April 1978): 3–38; Peter T. Johnson, "Academic Press Censorship under Military and Civilian Regimes: The Argentine and Brazilian Cases, 1964–1975," *Luso-Brazilian Review* 15, no. 1 (Summer 1978): 3–25; Paul G. Buchanan, "State Corporatism in Argentina: Labor Administration under Peron and Ongania," *Latin American Research Review* 20, no. 1 (January–April 1985): 61–95.

53. James P. Brennan and Mónica B. Gordillo, "Working Class Protest, Popular Revolt, and Urban Insurrection in Argentina: The 1969 'Cordobazo,'" *Journal of Social History* 27, no. 3 (Spring 1994): 477–98.

54. "633 Applications for Relative's Aliyah Submitted to Sochnut," *Al HaMishmar*, 1956, 3.

55. On Jewish agriculture in Argentina, see Haim Avni and Sibila Seibert, "La agricultura judía en la Argentina ¿éxito o fracaso?" *Desarrollo Económico* 22, no. 88 (January–March 1983): 535–48; Morton D. Winsberg, "Jewish Agricultural Colonization in Argentina," *Geographical Review* 54, no. 4 (October 1964): 487–501; Yehuda Levin, "Labor and Land at the Start of Jewish Settlement in Argentina," *Jewish History* 21, nos. 3–4 (July–December 2007): 341–59.

56. "El rumor no afecta a la continua inmigración desde América Latina," *Aurora*, January 13, 1967, 3.

57. "Emissaries Meeting," July 28, 1966, CZA, S62/351. Despite criticism of *Aurora*'s coverage of return migration, its circulation of eighty-five hundred offered the opportunity to communicate with immigrants and potential immigrants; hence, the JA used it to publish a series of eight articles on the meaning, reasons, and challenges of aliyah for "ideological reinforcement," as well as other information. A. Cygel to A. Pincus, November 17, 1966, CZA, S62/351.

58. Moreno, *La noche de los bastones largos* (see intro, n. 52); Johnson, "Academic Press Censorship."

59. Histadrut Unit for Immigration in Buenos [no signature] to Y. Koren, August 31, 1966, CZA S62/351.

60. Histadrut Unit for Immigration in Buenos [no signature] to Y. Koren.

61. Michael Goebel, "A Movement from Right to Left in Argentine Nationalism? The

Alianza Libertadora Nacionalista and Tacuara as Stages of Militancy," *Bulletin of Latin American Research* 26, no. 3 (July 2007): 356–77.

62. The crisis affected Jewish schools for several years. See Elnecavé, "Latin America," 435 (see intro, n. 61).

63. A. Bar-Khan to S. Z Shragai, August 1, 1966, CZA S62/351.

64. S. Z. Shragai to A. Pincus, August 18, 1966, CZA, S62/351

65. "Clasismo, disociación y otros problemas," *Raíces*, May 1970, 73.

66. On unpopular economic measures as part of the Krieger Vasena program, see Robert A. Potash, *The Army and Politics in Argentina* (Stanford, CA: Stanford University Press, 1969), 219; "The New Look of the Onganía Administration," Central Intelligence Agency, Washington, DC, 1967; Guillermo A. O'Donnell, *Bureaucratic Authoritarianism: Argentina, 1966–1973, in Comparative Perspective* (Berkeley: University of California Press, 1988), 103.

67. "Informe sobre pobreza," *Raíces*, June 1970, 63–64.

68. Y. Harel to Y. Wolberg, January 20, 1970, TLC, 220172.

69. Y. Harel to S. Schmit, June 8, 1970, TLC, 220172.

70. Y. Wolberg to M. Yakir, September 3, 1970, TLC, 220172; Y. Ward to U. Narkis, July 27, 1969, TLC, 220172.

71. K. Grossman to U. Narkis, March 19, 1974, TLC, 220232.

72. N. Bar-Giora to Y. Harel, October 29, 1970, TLC, 220172.

73. Nevo to Y. Dominitz, Y. Wolberg, November 22, 1970, TLC, 220172; Yanai to Y. Harel, November 19, 1970, TLC, 220172; Nevo to Y. Wolberg, November 22, 1970, TLC, 220172.

## Chapter 4

1. In fact, there was an increase of 30 percent over 1972 in monies received from AMIA membership dues and funerals, an indicator of the general economic recovery. See Elnecavé, "Latin America," 361 (see intro, n. 61).

2. Marcelo N. Rougier Voilláz and Juan Carlos Odisio, "Del dicho al hecho. El 'modelo integrado y abierto' de Aldo Ferrer y la política económica en la Argentina de la segunda posguerra," *América Latina en la Historia Económica* (2012): 101–30; Gonzalo de Amézola, "El cambio del modelo económico de la segunda etapa de la revolución Argentina (1970–1971)," *Signos Históricos* (2001): 115–45.

3. Romero, *History of Argentina*, 198-99.

4. K. Grossman to U. Narkis, March 19, 1974, TLC, 220756; Sebastian Klor, "Database 10,487" (unpublished, provided to author by Sebastian Klor).

5. Nissim Elnecavé, "Situation Good in Argentina," *Jewish Chronicle*, March 3, 1972.

6. Elnecavé, "Juan Perón's Return," *Jewish Chronicle*, July 20, 1973.

7. Elnecavé, "Latin American Jewry," *Jewish Chronicle*, August 10, 1973.

8. Y. Harel to U. Narkis, November 27, 1972, TLC, 220754.

9. Y. Harel to U. Narkis, March 1, 1972, TLC, 220754.

10. Y. Harel to U. Narkis, May 8, 1972, TLC, 220754.

11. "En una reunión de DAIA se evaluó el proceso eleccionario del país," *Informativo DAIA* (April 1973).

12. During his first government, 1946 to 1955, Perón failed to gain DAIA's support. As a result, he promoted the creation of the Organización Israelita Argentina (Israelite Argentine Organization) to compete with DAIA. See Rein, *Argentina, Israel, and the Jews* (see intro, n. 40).

13. "Informe del secretario general sobre la reunión del ejecutivo del CJM, en la sesión especial del Consejo Directivo de DAIA" *Informativo DAIA* (July 1973).

14. On the challenges of accommodating national and ethnic identities, see Beatrice D. Gurwitz, "Zionism, Third Worldism, and Argentine Youth at the Crossroads," *Journal of Jewish Identities* 8 no. 2 (July 2015): 13–32.

15. Raanan Rein, "El reverso de una imagen: El retorno de Perón al poder en la prensa hebrea," in *El retorno de Perón y el peronismo en la visión de la prensa nacional y extranjera*, ed. Raanan Rein and Claudio Panella (La Plata: EDULP, 2009), 364.

16. "Conozcanos Major" (Buenos Aires: Movimiento de Alia Juvenil, 1973), TLC, 220754.

17. K. Grossman to U. Narkis, September 14, 1973, TLC, 220754.

18. K. Grossman to U. Narkis, October 4, 1973, TLC, 220754.

19. For a comprehensive study of Argentine guerrilla groups, see María Jose Moyano, *Argentina's Lost Patrol: Armed Struggle, 1969–1979* (New Haven: Yale University Press, 2012). On the related general strike and massive demonstration of August 31, 1973, see Norberto Galasso, *Perón: Exilio, resistencia, retorno y muerte, 1955–1974* (Buenos Aires: Ediciones Colihue, 2005), 1231.

20. This is clearly demonstrated, for example, in Viktor Karády, *The Jews of Europe in the Modern Era: A Socio-Historical Outline* (Budapest: Central European University Press, 2004).

21. Aritz Recalde, "La Universidad de Buenos Aires en la década de 1970: Análisis del comunicado de prensa en solidaridad con Rodolfo Puiggrós," *Salud Colectiva* 8, no. 3 (2012): 316.

22. Laura Graciela Rodríguez, "La universidad durante el tercer gobierno peronista (1973–1976)," *Conflicto Social* 7, no. 12 (2014): 115.

23. Sergio Friedemann, *La Universidad Nacional y Popular de Buenos Aires (1973–1974): Una reforma universitaria inconclusa* (Buenos Aires: Universidad de Buenos Aires, 2015), 688.

24. For a thorough explanation of the two scenarios, see the methodological appendix to chapter 4.

25. See appendix to chapter 4.

26. K. Grossman to U. Narkis, March 3, 1974, TLC, 220232.

27. For different approaches to Israeli stratification, see Tally Katz-Gerro and Yossi Shavit, "The Stratification of Leisure and Taste: Classes and Lifestyles in Israel," *European Sociological Review* 14, no. 4 (December 1998): 369–86; Meir Yaish, "The Consequences of Immigration for Social Mobility: The Experience of Israel," *European Sociological Review* 18, no. 4 (December 2002): 449–71; Erez Tzfadia, "The Ethno-Class Trajectory of New Neighborhoods in Israel," *GeoJournal* 64, no. 2 (January–June 2005): 141–51.

28. C. Oscar to U. Narkis, January 24, 1971, CZA, S5/12615.

29. Rachel Klein, *The Aliyah from South America and Its Absorption* (Jerusalem, 1978), Israel State Archives (hencehorth, ISA), 10907/5. Data collection took place during 1974-75.

30. K. Grossman to U. Narkis, October 4, 1973, TLC, 220754.

31. *Proteksia*, a term of Eastern European origin, is used in Israel to mean "favoritism" or "good connections" in relation to taking on employees, dealing with bureaucrats, and obtaining benefits. Smooha, *Israel: Pluralism and Conflict* (see ch. 2, n. 41).

32. K. Abraham to A. Argov, March 12, 1973, TLC, 220754.

33. "Información para el *ole*," *Tnuat Aliah* (Buenos Aires, June 1969), 8, TLC, 220760.

34. Noah Lewin-Epstein and Moshe Semyonov, "Migration, Ethnicity, and Inequality: Homeownership in Israel," *Social Problems* 47, no. 3 (August 2000): 425–44.

35. "Como puede adquirir su vivienda en condiciones ventajosas," *Aurora*, October 8, 1964.

36. Historian Anita Shapira used the term "euphoria" to depict the Israeli climate in the aftermath of the war. See Shapira, *Israel: A History*, 319 (see ch. 1, n. 3). For a broader perspective, see Eli Lederhendler, *The Six-Day War and World Jewry* (Bethesda: University Press of Maryland, 2000).

37. K. Abraham to A. Argov, May 5, 1973, TLC, 220754.

38. K. Abraham to A. Argov, May 8, 1973, TLC, 220754.

39. Beutel to Clauda, March 26, 1974, TLC, 220756.

40. "Members of *Tnuat Aliyah* in Argentina Ask to Be Settled in Development Cities," *Al HaMishmar*, August 21, 1974, and "*Aliyah* Activists in Argentina Will Settle in Development Cities," *Maariv*, August 21, 1974, TLC, 220757; C. Snaider and J. Esrubilsky to J. Baran, August 29, 1974, TLC, 220757.

41. "Inquietante amargura también entre los olim latinoamericanos," *Aurora*, July 10, 1973, 8.

42. "Son reconocidos los serios problemas en la alia latinoamericana," *Aurora*, August 2, 1973, 8.

43. Horowitz, "Immigrants in Transition" (see intro, n. 56).

44. Horowitz, "Immigrants in Transition," 296-97.

45. "Cuarenta familias de olim latinoamericanos en Natania amenazan irse de Israel," *Aurora*, August 2, 1973.

46. "Hablan los olim del ulpan de Natania: 'Continua nuestra precaria situación,'" *Aurora*, August 9, 1973.

47. José Krasilovsky, "Respuesta a los *olim* del ulpan de Natania," *Aurora*, August 23, 1973.

48. "Fue condenado un funcionario de Amidar," *Aurora*, August 9, 1973.

49. Oved Cohen, *Immigrant Absorption in 1975: Summary and Conclusions* (Jerusalem, 1976), 3, CZA, S85/163.

50. Cohen, *Immigrant Absorption in 1975*.

51. B. Krivitzky to D. Horowitz, December 7, 1963; document included in David Horowitz, "The Jewish Community in Argentina and Aliyah from There, 1962-1973" (Ph.D. diss., Tel Aviv University, 2003), appendix 7.

52. B. Krivitzky to D. Horowitz, December 7, 1963.

53. Klein, *Aliyah from South America*.

54. Moshe V. to A. Argov, March 12, 1973, TLC, 220754.

55. Graciela Spector, "La identidad alquilada," in *Emigracion, salud mental y cultura*, ed. Silvio Gutkowski and Maria Isabel Pasos de Winograd (Buenos Aires: Ediciones del Candil, 2003), 125–38.

56. In 1963 JA absorption department director A. Cygel publicly defended the use of force against immigrant unrest at ports. "We Will Use Force Also in the Future," *Maariv*, December 11, 1963.

57. On the Agranat Commission, see Pnina Lahav, *Judgment in Jerusalem: Chief Justice Simon Agranat and the Zionist Century* (Berkeley: University of California Press, 1997), ch. 13.

58. On the impact of the Yom Kippur War on world Jewry, see Moshe Davis, ed., *The Yom Kippur War: Israel and the Jewish People* (New York: Arno Press, 1974).

59. Cohen, *Immigrant Absorption in 1975*, 3.

60. On anti-Semitism during that period, see Senkman, "El antisemitismo bajo dos experiencias democráticas" (see intro, n. 24).

61. K. Grossman to U. Narkis, December 6, 1973, TLC, 220756.

62. Y. Arzi to U. Narkis, December 21, 1973, TLC, 220756.

63. K. Grossman to U. Narkis, January 3, 1974, TLC, 220756.

64. In 1962 Yaacov Israeli, director of the JA immigration department in Buenos Aires, reported that the Jews' reaction did not reflect the political situation. Two rival military factions had deployed troops and tanks in the streets and Israelis wrote of the Jewish Argentines that "they continue about their lives as though nothing had happened." Klor, *Between Exile and Exodus*, 53 (see intro, n. 29).

65. K. Grossman to U. Narkis, January 3, 1974, TLC, 220756.

66. Naomi F. Meyer, "Latin America Argentina Domestic Affairs," *American Jewish Year Book*, 263.

67. Samuel Kaplan, "La *ierida* no desciende (I)," *Aurora*, February 13, 1974. In this interview, the vice director said that the main returnees were single people from the United States, who accounted for 45 percent. They usually returned after completing their Hebrew study program in a kibbutz when finding an apartment became difficult. See also "Carmiel: Nuevos casos de olim que abandonan el país," *Aurora*, February 19, 1974.

68. "La ierida no desciende. Gueula Javkin: No acepto la ierida en el primer o segundo año en Israel," *Aurora*, March 13, 1974, 3.

69. "La ierida no desciende. Gueula Javkin."

70. "La ierida no desciende: Atravesamos una época difícil pero escapar no es una solución," *Aurora*, March 13, 1974.

71. Interview with José C., Buenos Aires, April 5, 2016.

72. Interview with Saúl S., Buenos Aires, July 17, 2016.

73. Interview with Daniel F., Buenos Aires, November 24, 2016.

74. "Continua la '*ierida*' de inmigrantes sudamericanos," *Aurora*, April 12, 1974.

75. K. Grossman to U. Narkis, March 19, 1974, TLC, 220756.

76. "Cartas de olim," *Tnuat Aliá Informa* (Buenos Aires: November 1973), TLC, 311597.

77. "Cartas de olim."

78. "Nos escribe una buena amiga," *Tnuat Aliá Informa* (Buenos Aires: December 1973), TLC, 311597.

79. K. Grossman to U. Narkis, March 19, 1974, TLC, 220756.

80. K. Grossman to U. Narkis.

81. This number does not include tourists and volunteers who subsequently changed their visa status in Israel.

82. K. Grossman to U. Narkis, March 3, 1974, TLC, 220232.

83. Y. Arazi to U. Narkis, January 31, 1974, TLC, 220756; K. Grossman to U. Narkis, March 7, 1974, TLC, 220756.

84. Valeria Manzano, "Argentina tercer mundo: Nueva izquierda, emociones y política revolucionaria en las décadas de 1960 y 1970," *Desarrollo Económico* 54, no. 212 (May–August 2014): 79–104; Rodríguez, "La universidad durante"; Friedemann, *La Universidad Nacional*; Recalde, "La Universidad de Buenos Aires."

## Chapter 5

1. Y. Arazi to U. Narkis, January 31, 1974, TLC, 220756.

2. On the *Navarrazo*, see Munck, "Crisis of Late Peronism " (see intro, n. 58); Ronaldo Munck, "Movimiento obrero, economía y política en Argentina: 1955-1985," *Estudios Sociológicos* 5, no. 13 (January–April 1987): 87–109; Daniela Slipak, "De lealtades y tradiciones: El enfrentamiento de la JP lealtad von montoneros a través de sus revistas," *Estudios Sociológicos* 31, no. 92 (May–August 2013): 345–67.

3. Y. Arazi to U. Narkis, March 1, 1974, TLC, 220756.

4. Y. Arazi to U. Narkis, March 31, 1974, TLC, 220756.

5. On internal Peronist fighting and armed struggles, see Moyano, *Argentina's Lost Patrol* (see ch. 4, n. 19); Marcelo Larraquy, *Marcados a fuego II (1945-1973): De Perón a Montoneros* (Buenos Aires: Aguilar, 2010); Richard Gillespie, *Soldiers of Peron: Argentina's Montoneros* (Oxford: Clarendon, 1982). Dozens of businessmen were kidnapped for ransom during this period. The most notorious case was the kidnapping of Jorge and Juan Born for whom a ransom of $60 million was paid to the Peronist guerrilla Montoneros. See María O'Donnell, *El secuestro de los Born* (Buenos Aires: Debate, 2016); Fiszbein, "La economía del stop and go" (see intro, n. 59).

6. K. Grossman to U. Narkis, April 5, 1974, TLC, 220756.

7. K. Grossman to Y. Wolverg, March 7, 1974, TLC, 220232.

8. Y. Arazi to U. Narkis, April 30, 1974, TLC, 220756.

9. "La espeluznante plaga del 'shelijismo,'" *La Luz*, April 17, 1974.

10. "Normas de conducta para los enviados de la Agencia Judía," *Aurora*, April 24, 1975.

11. K. Grossman to U. Narkis, May 16, 1974, TLC, 220756. Among the anti-Semitic incidents Grossman listed were the following two: An invitation to celebrate a Sunday mass in memory of Hitler was published in Buenos Aires, causing shock not only in Argentina but also in Uruguay; and a bomb was planted in the building of the Jewish community of Santa Fe and deactivated at the last moment.

12. K. Grossman to U. Narkis.

13. Bar-Giora to K. Grossman, July 2, 1974, TLC, 220171. By mid-May discussions were being held about conducting an inquiry into Latin America's Tnuat Aliyah, but it is not clear whether it took place.

14. T. Tzvik to K. Grossman, July 25, 1974, TLC, 220171.

15. Y. Rivkin to U. Narkis, November 10, 1974, TLC, 220757.

16. K. Grossman to U. Narkis, November 25, 1974, TLC, 220757. Although it was called a "census," it combined aspects of a survey, a demographic study, and an outreach initiative. The initiative was conducted by an alliance between central Jewish organizations in various areas of the country.

17. Y. Rivkin to U. Narkis, December 5, 1974, TLC, 220757

18. María Cecilia Míguez, "El regreso del peronismo al poder en 1973 y las relaciones internacionales: La repercusión regional y mundial de la asunción de Héctor Cámpora," *Postdata: Revista de Reflexión y Análisis Político* 23, no. 1 (April–September 2018): 11–47.

19. K. Grossman to U. Narkis, December 6, 1974, TLC, 220757.

20. Manzano, "Argentina tercer mundo" (see ch. 4, n. 84); Gurwitz, *Argentine Jews in the Age of Revolt* (see intro, n. 23).

21. "La solidaridad con Israel expresada con un enfoque de juventud progresista y pacífica," *La Opinión*, October 9, 1973.

22. K. Grossman to U. Narkis, January 10, 1974, TLC, 220757.

23. Y. Rivkin to U. Narkis, January 16, 1975, TLC, 220757.

24. Y Rivkin to U. Narkis, Februay 4, 1975, TLC, 220757.

25. "Klita, klita y no hay klita," *Aurora*, May 3, 1975.

26. Meyer, "Argentina Domestic Affairs," 262 (see ch. 4, n. 66).

27. Meyer, "Argentina Domestic Affairs," 360, 362.

28. Carlota Jackisch, "Peronismo y dictadura militar (1973-1983): Un ciclo anómico en la reciente historia Argentina," *Ibero-Amerikanisches Archiv* 23, nos. 3-4 (July–December 1997): 439–62; Marcelo Larraquy, *Lopez Rega* (Buenos Aires: Punto de Lectura, 2007). On the Peronist right wing, see Juan Luis Besoky, "La derecha peronista en perspectiva," *Nuevo Mundo, Mundos Nuevos*, 2013, online; Besoky, "The Administration of Minister Ivanissevich and the Peronist Right Wing: The 100 Days of Ottalagano," *Folia Histórica del Nordeste* (2017): 145–74; Besoky, "La era de los culatas: La derecha peronista y el patoterismo sindical," *Prohistoria* 19 (2013): 146–48).

29. This was a new group, using the same name of a previously created group in 1969 but no connections between the two are known. Amos was a biblical prophet known for his harsh criticism of social injustice and his name was used in Argentina in various periods by youth groups seeking to participate in Argentine politics while affirming their Jewish identity. Adrián Krupnik, "Cuando camino al Kibbutz vieron pasar al Che. Radicalización política y juventud judía: Argentina, 1966–1976," in *Marginados y consagrados: Nuevos estudios sobre la vida judía en Argentina*, ed. Emmanuel Kahan et al. (Buenos Aires: Lumiere, 2011), 311–27; Adriana Mariel Brodsky, "Argentine Sephardi Youth: Between Aliyah and Activism, 1960–1970," *Journal of Jewish Identities* 8, no. 2 (July 2015): 113–35.

30. Y. Rivkin to U. Narkis, March 6, 1975, TLC, 220757.

31. Y. Rivkin to U. Narkis.

32. "Es grave la yerida," *La Luz*, January 7, 1975.

33. U. Narkis to Emissaries in South America, June 8, 1975, TLC, 220960.

34. Restivo Néstor and Raúl Dellatorre, El Rodrigazo, 30 años después: un ajuste que cambió al país (Buenos Aires: Capital Intelectual, 2005); Federico Marongiu, "Políticas de shock en la agonía del estado peronista: El rodrigazo y el Mondelliazo," *Anales de las V Jornadas Nacionales de Historia Moderna y Contemporánea*, 2006, online.

35. Interview with Saúl S., Buenos Aires, July 17, 2016.

36. "¿Se terminó el problema," *Nueva Sion*, September 3, 1973.

37. Meyer, "Argentina Domestic Affairs," 346.

38. On the historical devaluation known as the *Rodrigazo*, see Edward Epstein, "Recent Stabilization Programs in Argentina, 1973–1986," *World Development* 15, no. 8 (August 1987): 991–1005; Marongiu, "Políticas de shock."

39. Jerry W. Knudson, "Veil of Silence: The Argentine Press and the Dirty War, 1976–1983," *Latin American Perspectives* 24, no. 6 (November 1997): 93–112.

40. Joel Barromi, "Israel frente a la dictadura militar argentina: El episodio de Córdoba y el caso Timerman," in *El legado del autoritarismo*, ed. Leonardo Senkman and Mario Sznajder (Buenos Aires: Grupo Editor Latinoamericano, 1995), 325–51; Barromi, "Israeli Policies towards Argentina and Argentine Jewry during the Military Junta, 1977–83," *Israel Affairs* 5, no. 1 (April 1998): 27–44.

41. "La pauperización de la clase media y su influencia en la comunidad judía," *Nueva Sion*, March 19, 1976.

42. On humanism and Judaism in Argentina and other syntheses, see Gurwitz, "Zionism."

43. N. Resnizky to J. Almogy, September 9, 1976, ISA, 6476/25.

44. N. Resnizky to S. Edenburg, September 9, 1976, ISA, 6476/25; S. Edenburg to N. Resnizky, n.d., ISA, 6476/25.

45. Journalist Herman Schiller, editor of *Nueva Presencia* during the time of military rule, is a clear example of the previously mentioned view. See, for example, Herman Schiller, "El judaísmo oficial y la dictadura," *Equipo Nizkor* (2007) (online).

46. Daniel Rosenfeld, dir., 2018, *Los años del Tiburón* (Argentina: Daniel Rosenfeld Films, 2018).

47. H. Inbar to Israeli Foreign Ministry—Unit for Latin America and the Caribbean, September 27, 1976, ISA, 6476/25.

48. "Censo muestra: Jefes de familia inscriptos en instituciones judías de Buenos Aires," n.d., ISA, 6476/25.

49. "Report on the Situation in Argentina" [no details], January 12, 1977, TLC, 471090.

50. R. Nirgad to Y. Anug, February 17, 1977, ISA, 6476/25.

51. R. Nirgad to [?] Anug, February 17, 1977, ISA, 6476/25.

52. Marcel Zohar, *Let My People Go to Hell* (Tel Aviv: Tzitrin, 1998) [in Hebrew].

53. Mario Wainstein, "Ram Nirgad fue una gloria para Israel," *Aurora*, August 8, 1991; "Daniel Recanati rompe el silencio: Lo de Zohar es ridículo," *Aurora*, August 8, 1991.

54. R. Nirgad to [?] Anug, February 17, 1977, ISA, 6476/25. The author of the report (the ambassador) talked about "Nazis," but he was using the term generically for any far-Right racist organization; they were not literally Germans affiliated with the National Socialist German Workers' ("Nazi") Party before, during or after World War II.

55. R. Nirgad to [?] Anug.

56. A. Argov to Y. Pundak, April 22, 1977, TLC, 471090.

57. A Yaffe et al., "Protocols of the Meeting to Discuss the Argentine Situation," April 26, 1977 (Jerusalem, 1977), TLC, 471090.

58. DAIA to J. Almogy, July 6, 1977, ISA, 6476/25. There is no further information about Pundak's declarations.

59. "Dirigentes judeoargentinos piden la remoción del Cnel Pundak," *Aurora*, August 23, 1977.

60. Graciela Mochkofsky, *Timerman: El periodista que quiso ser parte del poder (1923-1999)*, 3rd ed. (Buenos Aires: Editorial Sudamericana, 2004); Mauricio Schoijet, "The Timerman Affair, Argentina, and the United States," *Crime and Social Justice* 20 (1983): 16–36.

61. Fernando J. Ruíz, *Las palabras son acciones: Historia politica y profesional de la opinión de Jacobo Timerman, 1971-1977* (Buenos Aires: Perfil Libros, 2001); Juan Gasparini, *David Graiver: El banquero de los montoneros* (Buenos Aires: Grupo Editorial Norma, 2007).

62. Abraham Bargil, *Ni silencio, ni olvido* (Buenos Aires: Acervo Cultural, 2015), 45.

63. Some examples of anti-Semitic attempts combined with other crimes included the following: In Cordoba, a bomb destroyed a cinema that had shown the film *Raid on Entebbe* for three weeks; at the same time, an armed group robbed the local branch of the Banco Israelita; in Buenos Aires, a Jewish school was bombed. "Argentine Theatre That Showed 'Entebbe' Film Is Destroyed by Bomb," *Sentinel*, February 3, 1977.

64. "AJC Leaves Argentina after Threats against Representative's Family," *Sentinel*, July 21, 1977.

65. "AJC Leaves Argentina."

66. "Threats Cause AJC Office in Argentina to Close," *B'nai B'rith Messenger*, July 15, 1977.

67. "Signs of the Times," *B'nai B'rith Messenger*, August 26, 1977.

68. Bargil, *Ni Silencio*.

69. "Israel, Argentina Plan to Expand Exchanges between the Two Countries," *Sentinel*, August 18, 1977.

70. Hernan Dobry and Daniel Goldman, *Ser judío en los años setent: Testimonios del horror y la resistencia durante la última dictadura* (Buenos Aires: Siglo Veintiuno Editores, 2014), 109.

71. Kahan, *Memories That Lie a Little* (see intro, n. 23)

72. Dobry and Goldman, *Ser judío en los años setent*, 114.

73. For details about the case of Alejandra Jaimovich, see H.I.J.O.S Córdoba, "Alejandra Jaimovich," *Diario del Juicio*, online, accessed May 2, 2019.

74. For a detailed explanation of the division of the territory by military rule and characteristics of the repressive forces, see Larraquy, *Marcados a fuego*.

75. Quique Peinado, *Futbolistas de izquierda* (Madrid: Leeme Editories, 2013).

76. Michael A. Meyer, "Liability of Prisoners of War for Offences Committed Prior to Capture: The Astiz Affair," *International and Comparative Law Quarterly* 32, no. 4 (October 1983): 948–80.

77. "Argentine Jews Upset by Article in Magazine," *Sentinel*, September 1, 1977.

78. *New York Times* article quoted in "Argentine Jewish Community Alarmed by Punishment Imposed on Publisher," *Sentinel*, December 1, 1977.

79. On CONADEP, see *Nunca más: Informe de la comisión nacional sobre la desaparición de personas* (Buenos Aires: EUDEBA, 1984). The actual number is likely higher because not all cases were reported officially. Many people who feared the return of military rule or were threatened by the repressors chose to remain silent.

80. Marisa Braylan, *Informe sobre la situación de los detenidos-desaparecidos judíos durante el genocidio perpetrado en Argentina* (Buenos Aires: CES-DAIA, 2007); Edy Kaufman, "Jewish Victims of Repression in Argentina under Military Rule (1976–1983)," *Holocaust and Genocide Studies* 4, no. 4 (April 1989): 479–99.

81. "Argentine Jewish Community Alarmed by Punishment Imposed on Publisher."

82. "Meetings with the Commission of Argentina Jewish Community Leaders, August 22 and 28," September 7, 1977, TLC, 471090.

83. "Briefing of Two Meetings between the Argentine Committee and the Prime Minister" [no details], TLC, 471090.

84. While recognizing that it was unrealistic for Jewish Argentine leaders to curb intermarriage rates in Argentina, efforts to present immigration to Israel as the solution for this "problem" might have worked in individual cases, from the perspective of the parents, if they convinced their children to go to Israel. Nevertheless, even if that idea existed within circles active in Jewish Argentine organizations, it was irrelevant to the vast majority of Jews in Argentina, who were never affiliated with them. On the efforts of the leaders of Jewish Argentine organizations to make immigration the solution to assimilation, see Gurwitz, *Argentine Jews in the Age of Revolt*.

85. Bar-Mor to Office of the Foreign Ministry, August 23, 1977, ISA, 10907/5. According to the schedule, Argentine leaders also toured an absorption center on August 23.

86. Yosef Waksman, "Jewish Argentine Leaders Say That an Increase in Aliyah Is the Solution for Their Community," *Maariv*, August 19, 1977, TLC, 471090.

87. Alon Guidon, “A Petition to Return All the JA Emissaries in Latin America to Israel,” *Haaretz*, February 23, 1977, TLC, 471090.

88. Adolfo Canitrot, “La disciplina como objetivo de la politica económica: Un ensayo sobre el programa económico del gobierno argentino desde 1976,” *Desarrollo Económico* 19, no. 76 (January–March 1980): 453–75.

89. Daniel Fridman, “A New Mentality for a New Economy: Performing the Homo Economicus in Argentina (1976–83),” *Economy and Society* 39, no. 2 (April 2010): 271–302.

90. Fridman, “New Mentality for a New Economy.”

91. Y. Koifman to U. Narkis, October 30, 1977, TLC, 471090.

92. Y. Koifman to U. Narkis.

93. Y. Koifman to U. Narkis.

94. On state terrorism and genocidal practices in Argentina, see Daniel Feierstein, *Genocide as Social Practice: Reorganizing Society under the Nazis and Argentina's Military Juntas* (New Brunswick, NJ: Rutgers University Press, 2014).

95. “Project Latin America: Meeting Protocols,” January 19, 1978, ISA, 10907/5.

96. “Aliyah from Argentina: Meeting Protocols,” April 12, 1978, ISA, 10907/5. Members included Haim Aron (OLEI), Yoram Hirshberg (economic unit of the Absorption Ministry), Shmuel Adler (economic adviser, Absorption Ministry), Moshe Haimovsky (Investments Authority), and Moshe Yagar (Prime Minister's Office).

97. Moshe Yagar, “Subcommittee for Argentine Judaism: Protocols,” April 17, 1978, ISA, 10907/5.

98. Moshe Yagar, “Subcommittee for Argentine Judaism: Second Meeting Protocols,” May 2, 1978, May 7, 1978, ISA, 10907/5.

99. Klein, *Aliyah from South America* (see ch. 4, n. 38).

100. Klein, *Aliyah from South America*.

101. At the time, a study conducted by the Hebrew University of Jerusalem estimated that some three hundred thousand Jews were living in Argentina. Meyer, “Latin America Argentina Domestic Affairs,” 210.

102. Agar Nadav, “Committee for the Immigration of Argentine Jews,” June 1, 1978, 1, ISA, 10907/5.

103. Ben Eliezer to Avni, May 19, 1978, ISA, 10907/5; Ben Eliezer to A. Dulczin, May 18, 1978, ISA, 10907/5; A. Dulczin to Ben Aliezer, May 4, 1978, ISA, 10907/5.

104. “Subcommittee of Latin American Immigration from Argentina,” May 25, 1978, ISA, 10907/5.

105. Immigrants at Netanya Ulpan to Minister of Absorption David Levi, September 19, 1978, TLC, 471078.

106. Immigrants at Netanya Ulpan Minister of Absorption David Levi.

107. L. Melamed to A. Argov, January 22, 1979, TLC, 471078.

108. Between 350 and 400 people obtained special assistance from Israel to leave Argentina and move to the Jewish state because they had been incarcerated or were endangered due to their political activities. Mario Sznajder and Luis Roniger, “From Argentina to Israel: Escape, Evacuation and Exile,” *Journal of Latin American Studies* 37, no. 2 (May 2015): 351–77; Roniger et al., *Exile, Diaspora, and Return* (see intro, n. 19).

109. Interview with José Itzigsohn, December 31, 2014.

110. José Itzigsohn, “Conflictos de identidad judía en América Latina,” *Dispersión y Unidad* 1 (1979): 38–56.

111. Interview with Silvia R., January 3, 2018; interview with Ricardo A., November 7, 2018.

112. Interview with Adrián Merajver, Buenos Aires, January 22, 2018.

## Epilogue

1. William C. Smith, "Democracy, Distributional Conflicts and Macroeconomic Policymaking in Argentina, 1983-89," *Journal of Interamerican Studies and World Affairs* 32, no. 2 (Summer 1990): 1–42.

2. There are no figures for later years. See Riki Mandelzweig, "Klita and Yerida One Year after Arrival in Israel," 1985, TLC 225341.

3. "Acciones para recuperar el diario La Opinión," *Aurora*, January 12, 1984; Mochkofsky, *Timerman* (see ch. 5, n. 60).

4. Paul Beckerman, "Central Bank 'Distress' and Hyperinflation in Argentina, 1989-90," *Journal of Latin American Studies* 27, no. 3 (October 1995): 663–82; Javier Corrales, "Do Economic Crises Contribute to Economic Reform? Argentina and Venezuela in the 1990s," *Political Science Quarterly* 112, no. 4 (Winter 1997–1998): 617–44.

5. Smith, "Democracy." Many people resorted to looting after becoming impoverished. Sergio Serulnikov, "When Looting Becomes a Right: Urban Poverty and Food Riots in Argentina," *Latin American Perspectives* 21, no. 3 (Summer1994): 69–89; Serulnikov, "Pobreza y revuelta de la subsistencia: Los saqueos de 1989 en Argentina," *Historia Social* (May–August 2017): 63–85.

6. A. Argov to T. Wisevand, January 26, 1989, TLC, 476701; A. Grunberg and H. Ostrower to A. Dinitz, January 3, 1989, TLC, 476701.

7. D. S. to A. Dinitz, April 2, 1989, TLC, 476701.

8. K. Grossman to A. Ben Abo, July 6, 1989, ISA, 41715/8.

9. Roberto Frenkel, "Argentina: A Decade of the Convertibility Regime," *Challenge* 45, no. 4 (July–August 2002): 41–59.

10. R. Frenkel and L. Simpson, "The Two Waves of Financial Liberalization in Latin America," in *Development Economics and Structuralist Macroeconomics: Essays in Honor of Lance Taylor*, ed. Amitava Krishna Dutt and Jaime Ros (Northampton, MA: Edward Elgar, 2003), 206–26.

11. Daniel Treisman, "Stabilization Tactics in Latin America: Menem, Cardoso, and the Politics of Low Inflation," *Comparative Politics* 36, no. 4 (July 2004): 399–419; Frenkel, "Argentina: A Decade of the Convertibility."

12. No one had been convicted of the attacks at the time of writing. In the case of the embassy, the investigation did not even reach the trial stage. In that of AMIA, there has been more than one trial and many people, including Rubén Beraja, were accused of obstruction of justice.

13. A. Arieli to U. Gordon, July 24, 1995, TLC, 227887.

14. Gabriel Kessler and María Mercedes di Virgilio, "Impoverishment of the Middle Class in Argentina: The 'New Poor,' in 'Latin America,'" *Laboratorium: Russian Review of Social Research* 2, no. 2 (September 2010): 200–220.

15. Francesco Bortot, "Frozen Savings and Depressed Development in Argentina," *Savings and Development* 27, no. 2 (April–June 2003): 161–202.

16. Those who blocked roads were called *piqueteros*. Fynn Kaese and Jonas Wolff, "Piqueteros after the Hype: Unemployed Movements in Argentina, 2008-2015," *European Review*

*of Latin American and Caribbean Studies/Revista Europea de Estudios Latinoamericanos y del Caribe* 102 (October 2016): 47–68; Edward C. Epstein, "The Piquetero Movement of Greater Buenos Aires: Working Class Protest during the Current Argentine Crisis," *Canadian Journal of Latin American and Caribbean Studies/Revue Canadienne Des Études Latino-Américaines et Caraïbes* 28, nos. 55–56 (2003): 11–36. The act of protest of banging pans was called *cacerolazo*. See Federico Matías Rossi, "Aparición, auge y declinacón de un movimiento social: Las asambleas vecinales y populares de Buenos Aires, 2001-2003," *European Review of Latin American and Caribbean Studies/Revista Europea de Estudios Latinoamericanos y del Caribe* 78 (April 2005): 67–88; Chase Madar, "The Unemployed in the Popular Uprising of December, 2001: Report from Greater Buenos Aires," *International Journal of Political Economy* 31, no. 1 (2001): 11–23.

17. Ana C. Dinerstein, "¡Que se vayan todos! Popular Insurrection and the Asambleas Barriales in Argentina," *Bulletin of Latin American Research* 22, no. 2 (April 2003): 187–200; Ronaldo Munck, "Argentina, or the Political Economy of Collapse," *International Journal of Political Economy* 31, no. 3 (Fall 2001): 67–88.

18. Pamina Firchow, "Power and Resistance in the Shaping of Argentine Domestic Policy," *Latin American Perspectives* 42, no. 1 (January 2015): 74–83.

19. "Jews from Troubled Argentina Seeking a Better Life in Israel," Israe121c, March 4, 2002 (online).

20. Cohen, "From Overt Rejection to Enthusiastic Embracement" (see intro, n. 25).

21. "Action Plan for Promoting and Absorbing Aliyah from Argentina in 2003," Jewish Agency for Israel, Department of Immigration and Absorption, TLC, 343488.

22. J. Schwartz to Members of the Jewish Agency Executive, "Background on Argentine Aliyah," December 23, 2002, TLC, 343488.

23. The Second Intifada began in 2000 and effectively ended the period of hope inaugurated by the Oslo Accords. A clear symbol of the end of the period of hope was the construction of a security fence. Dov Waxman, "Living with Terror, Not Living in Terror," *Perspectives on Terrorism* 5, nos. 5–6 (December 2011): 4–26; Ravi Bhavnani, Dan Miodownik, and Hyun Jin Choi, "Three Two Tango: Territorial Control and Selective Violence in Israel, the West Bank, and Gaza," *Journal of Conflict Resolution* 55, no. 1 (February 2011): 133–58; Ophir Falk, "Measuring the Effectiveness of Israel's 'Targeted Killing' Campaign," *Perspectives on Terrorism* 9, no. 1 (February 2015): 2–26.

24. "Sudamericanos victimas del terrorismo palestino," *Aurora*, November 14, 2002. "Un Atentado, un héroe y el dolor de todos los que lo recuerdan," *Aurora*, November 14, 2002.

25. Jean Grugel and Maria Pia Riggirozzi, "The Return of the State in Argentina," *International Affairs* 83, no. 1 (January 2007): 87–107.

26. Ariel Rubinsky, "La falta de trabajo y la incertidumbre carcome a la alia de Argentina," *Aurora*, December 25, 2003.

27. M. Haram to A. Pincus, November 25, 1965, CZA S62/351.

28. "OLEI's Eighth Territorial Congress in Tel Aviv," Conference Proceedings, June 29, 1966.

29. Koblovitz, *Facts about Yerida* (see ch. 3, n. 45).

30. Riki Mandelzweig, "Klita and Yerida One Year after Arrival in Israel," 1985, TLC 225341.

31. Schmuel Adler, "Yerida among Olim from Argentina Who Immigrated within the Period 1/1/1989 to 31/12/2002," Ministry of Absorption, Israel, March 2004, 6. The report

considered the total number of immigrants who arrived in Israel during the period from 1989 to 2002, including those from the highest peak in history. However, it did not include their return rates beyond 2003. It is easy to see how this fact completely changes the estimated leaving rate. Taking into account the 20,261 Argentines who arrived in Israel between 1989 and the last day of 2002—and based on the fact that 2,334 of them were not in Israel by the last day of 2003—the report calculated the leaving rate at 11.5 percent. However, disregarding the immigrants who arrived after 1997, the last year for which the report made the three different measurements—three years later, five years later, and the last day of 2003—the picture changes. Then, out of a total of 9,722 immigrants, we see that 1,832 (18.84 percent) had left.

32. Tzvetan Todorov, "The Coexistence of Cultures," *Policy Futures in Education* 8, no. 3–4 (January 2010): 419–26.

33. Roberto M. Goldstein, "Migración, identidad, lenguaje y resentimiento," in *Emigracion, salud mental y cultura*, ed. Silvio Gutkowski and Maria Isabel Pazos de Winograd (Buenos Aires: Ediciones del Candil, 2003), 43–45.

34. Interview with Susana M., Buenos Aires, November 30, 2018.

35. Latin American women in Israel are less represented than their male counterparts in the labor force. One of the factors causing this gap is the absence of social networks that usually assist native-born Israelis in the daily care of children and the elderly. Thus, some immigrant women are likely to restrict or give up their job search. Moreover, more than half of economically active Latin American women are concentrated in the social services sector. While Latin American women in Israel might get a job in certain areas of the Israeli job market faster than their male counterparts, in the long term the latter will tend to obtain better positions. Raijman and Ophir, "Economic Integration."

36. Interview with Silvi B., Ramat Gan, April 5, 2016.

37. Interview with Miriam K., Buenos Aires, April 3, 2018.

38. Interview with Mariano M., Tel Aviv, April 8, 2016.

39. Carlos Gardel, "To Return," 1935. Translated by Walter Kane. Lyrics available on the Planet-Tango website.

# BIBLIOGRAPHY


Adamovsky, Ezequiel. *Historia de la clase media argentina*. Buenos Aires: Planeta, 2009.

Aldrighi, Clara, ed. *Antisemitismo en Uruguay: Raíces, discursos, imágenes (1870–1940)*. Montevideo: Ediciones Trilce, 2000.

Alroey, Gur. "The Jewish Emigration from Palestine in the Early Twentieth Century." *Journal of Modern Jewish Studies* 2, no. 2 (August 2003): 111–31.

———. *An Unpromising Land: Jewish Migration to Palestine in the Early Twentieth Century*. Redwood, CA: Stanford University Press, 2014.

Amézola, Gonzalo de. "El cambio del modelo económico de la segunda etapa de la revolución Argentina (1970–1971)." *Signos Históricos* (2001): 115–45.

Applebaum, Levia, and Michael Sofer. "The Moshav in Israel: Agricultural Communities in a Process of Change—A Current View." *Horizons in Geography* 79/80 (2012): 194–209.

Avni, Haim. *Argentina and the Jews: A History of Jewish Immigration*. Tuscaloosa: University of Alabama Press, 1991.

———. "The Impact of the Six-Day War on a Zionist Community: The Case of Argentina." In Lederhendler, *Six-Day War and World Jewry*, 137–65.

Avni, Haim, and Sibila Seibert. "La agricultura judía en la Argentina ¿éxito o fracaso?" *Desarrollo Económico* 22, no. 88 (January–March 1983): 535–48.

Ayres, Robert L. "The 'Social Pact' as Anti-Inflationary Policy: The Argentine Experience since 1973." *World Politics* 28, no. 4 (July 1976): 473–501.

Bar Adon, Aaron. "The Contribution of the Second Aliyah to the Revival of Hebrew—Perceptions and Reality." In *Proceedings of the World Congress of Jewish Studies: Hebrew and Jewish Languages*, 63–70. Jerusalem: World Union of Jewish Studies, 1985.

Bargil, Abraham. *Ni silencio, ni olvido*. Buenos Aires: Acervo Cultural, 2015.

Bar-Gil, Shlomo. *We Started with a Dream*. Beer Sheva: Ben-Gurion University, 2005.

Barromi, Joel. "Israel frente a la dictadura militar argentina: El episodio de Córdoba y el caso Timerman." In *El legado del autoritarismo*, edited by Senkman Leonardo and Sznajder Mario, 325–51. Buenos Aires: Grupo Editor Latinoamericano, 1995.

Barromi, Joel. "Israeli Policies towards Argentina and Argentine Jewry during the Military Junta, 1977–83." *Israel Affairs* 5, no. 1 (April 1998): 27–44.

Beckerman, Paul. "Central-Bank 'Distress' and Hyperinflation in Argentina, 1989–90." *Journal of Latin American Studies* 27, no. 3 (October 1995): 663–82.

Beenstock, Michael. "Failure to Absorb: Remigration by Immigrants into Israel." *International Migration Review* 30, no. 4 (Winter 1996): 950–78.

Ben-Gurion, David. "The First 4 Years." *Davar*, March 10, 1966.

Ben Israel, David. *De América Latina a Israel, Al Kibutz*. Merhavia: Merhavia Press, 1978.

Ben-Porat, A. "Class Consciousness before Class: The Emergence of a Jewish Working Class in Palestine." *Theory and Society* 16, no. 5 (September 1987): 741–69.

Ben Porath, Yoram. "Self-Employed and Wage Earners in Israel: Findings from the Census of Population 1972." Research paper, Institute for Economic Research, Jerusalem, 1981.

Berry, John W. "Psychology of Acculturation: Understanding Individuals Moving between Cultures." In *Applied Cross-Cultural Psychology*, edited by Richard W. Brislin, 232–53. Newbury Park, CA: Sage, 1990.

Besoky, Juan Luis. "The Administration of Minister Ivanissevich and the Peronist Right Wing: The 100 Days of Ottalagano." *Folia Histórica del Nordeste* 29 (2017): 145–74.

———. "La derecha peronista en perspectiva." *Nuevo Mundo, Mundos Nuevos* (2013). Online.

———. "La era de los culatas: La derecha peronista y el patoterismo sindical." *Prohistoria* 19, (2013): 146–48.

Bhavnani, Ravi, Dan Miodownik, and Hyun Jin Choi. "Three Two Tango: Territorial Control and Selective Violence in Israel, the West Bank, and Gaza." *Journal of Conflict Resolution* 55, no. 1 (February 2011): 133–58.

Birmajer, Marcelo. *Tres mosqueteros*. Buenos Aires: Debate, 2001.

Blejer, Mario, and Yitzhak Goldberg. "Return Migration—Expectations versus Reality: A Case Study of Western Immigrants to Israel." *Research in Population Economics* 2 (1980): 433–49.

Bortot, Francesco. "Frozen Savings and Depressed Development in Argentina." *Savings and Development* 27, no. 2 (April–June 2003): 161–202.

Brauner Rodgers, Susana. "La comunidad judía alepina en Buenos Aires: De la ortodoxia religiosa a la apertura y de la apertura a la ortodoxia religiosa (1930–1953)." *Estudios Interdisciplinarios de América Latina y el Caribe* 11, no. 1 (2000): 41–64.

Brawer, Moshe. "The Image of Israel's Geographical Transformation." *Israel Studies* 13, no. 1 (Spring 2008): 152–59.

Braylan, Marisa. *Informe sobre la situación de los detenidos-desaparecidos judíos durante el genocidio perpetrado en Argentina*. Buenos Aires: CES-DAIA, 2007.

Brennan, James P., and Mónica B. Gordillo. "Working Class Protest, Popular Revolt, and Urban Insurrection in Argentina: The 1969 'Cordobazo.'" *Journal of Social History* 27, no. 3 (Spring 1994): 477–98.

Brodsky, Adriana M. "'Belonging to Many Homes': Argentine Sephardi Youth in Buenos Aires and Israel, 1956–76." In *Transnational Histories of Youth in the Twentieth Century*, edited by Richard Ivan Jobs and David M. Pomfret, 213–35. London: Palgrave Macmillan, 2015.

Brodsky, Adriana Mariel. "Argentine Sephardi Youth: Between Aliyah and Activism, 1960–1970." *Journal of Jewish Identities* 8, no. 2 (July 2015): 113–35.

Buchanan, Paul G. "State Corporatism in Argentina: Labor Administration under Peron and Ongania." *Latin American Research Review* 20, no. 1 (January–April 1985): 61–95.

Burman, Daniel, dir. *El abrazo Partido*. 2003; Buenos Aires: Bd Cine, 2003.

Canitrot, Adolfo. "La disciplina como objetivo de la politica económica: Un ensayo sobre el programa económico del gobierno argentino desde 1976." *Desarrollo económico* 19, no. 76 (January–March 1980): 453–75.

Cassain, Laura. "Migration Trajectories and Return Processes: An Exploration of Multi-Generational Family Experiences between Spain and Argentina." *Transnational Social Review* 6, nos. 1–2 (June 2016): 41–59.

Cassarino, Jean-Pierre. "Theorising Return Migration: The Conceptual Approach to Return

Migrants Revisited." *International Journal on Multicultural Societies* 6, no. 2 (December 2004): 253–79.

Castellani, Ana. "Privileged Accumulation Spaces and Restrictions on Development of State-Business Relations in Argentina (1966–1989)." *American Journal of Economics and Sociology* 72, no. 1 (January 2013): 90–121.

*Censo nacional de población 1960*. Buenos Aires: Dirección Nacional de Estadísticas y Censos, 1960.

Cohen, Michael J. "Appeasement in the Middle East: The British White Paper on Palestine, May 1939." *Historical Journal* 16, no. 3 (September 1973): 571–96.

Cohen, Nir. "Come Home, Be Professional: Ethno-Nationalism and Economic Rationalism in Israel's Return Migration Strategy." *Immigrants and Minorities* 27, no. 1 (December 2009): 1–28.

———. "From Nation to Profession: Israeli State Strategy toward Highly-Skilled Return Migration, 1949–2012." *Journal of Historical Geography* 42 (October 2013): 1–11.

———. "From Overt Rejection to Enthusiastic Embracement: Changing State Discourses on Israeli Emigration." *GeoJournal* 68, nos. 2–3 (June 2007): 267–78.

———. "Rights beyond Borders: Everyday Politics of Citizenship in the Israeli Diaspora." *Journal of Ethnic and Migration Studies* 37, no. 7 (May 2011): 1137–53.

———. "State, Migrants, and the Negotiation of Second-Generation Citizenship in the Israeli Diaspora." *Diaspora: A Journal of Transnational Studies* 16, nos. 1–2 (Spring–Fall 2007): 133–58.

Cohen, Yinon. "Economic Assimilation in the United States of Arab and Jewish Immigrants from Israel and the Territories." *Israel Studies* 1, no. 2 (Fall 1996): 75–97.

———. "Israeli-Born Emigrants: Size, Destinations and Selectivity." *International Journal of Comparative Sociology* 52, nos. 1–2 (February 2011): 45–62.

———. "Migration Patterns to and from Israel." *Contemporary Jewry* 29, no. 2 (August 2009): 115–25.

Cohen, Yinon, and Yitchak Haberfeld. "The Number of Israeli Immigrants in the United States in 1990." *Demography* 34, no. 2 (May 1997): 199–212.

———. "Self-Selection and Return Migration: Israeli-Born Jews Returning Home from the United States during the 1980s." *Population Studies* 55, no.1 (August 2001): 79–91.

Cohen, Yinon, and Andrea Tyree. "Palestinian and Jewish Israeli-Born Immigrants in the United States." *International Migration Review* 28, no. 2 (Summer 1994): 243–55.

Cook-Martín, David, and Anahí Viladrich. "The Problem with Similarity: Ethnic-Affinity Migrants in Spain." *Journal of Ethnic and Migration Studies* 35, no. 1 (2009): 151–70.

Corrales, Javier. "Do Economic Crises Contribute to Economic Reform? Argentina and Venezuela in the 1990s." *Political Science Quarterly* 112, no. 4 (Winter 1997–1998): 617–44.

Cosse, Isabella. "Ese monstruito: Mafalda, generaciones y género en una construcción mítica." *Revista latinoamericana de ciencias sociales, niñez y juventud*, 14.2 (2016): 1549- 61.

Cyrus, Stephen Cousins. "General Onganía and the Argentine Military Revolution of the Right: Anti-Communism and Morality, 1966-1970." *Historia Actual Online* (Fall 2009): 65–79.

Dadak, Casmir. "National Heritage and Economic Policies in Free and Sovereign Poland after 1918." *Contemporary European History* 21, no. 2 (May 2012): 193–214.

Dash, Jacob. "Israel: Urban Development Achievements and Future Plans." *Official Architecture and Planning* 28, no. 11 (November 1965): 1607–10.

Davis, Moshe. *The Yom Kippur War: Israel and the Jewish People.* New York: Arno Press, 1974.

DellaPergola, Sergio. *Jewish Demographic Policies: Population Trends and Options in Israel and in the Diaspora.* Jerusalem: Jewish People Policy Institute, 2011.

———. "National Uniqueness and Transnational Parallelism: Reflections on the Comparative Study of Jewish Communities in Latin America." In *Judaica Latinoamericana—Estudios históricos, sociales y literarios,* vol. 7, edited by M. Bejarno, F. Goldberg, and E. Zadoff, 73–100. Jerusalem: AMILAT-Magnes, 2013.

———. *Population Change and Political Transitions Demography in Israel/Palestine: Trends, Prospects, Policy Implications.* Jerusalem: Hebrew University of Jerusalem, 2001.

———. "World Jewish Population, 2019." In *American Jewish Year Book, 2019,* vol. 119, edited by Arnold Dashefsky and Ira M. Sheskin, 263–353. Dordrecht: Springer, 2020.

Diamand, Marcelo. "La estructura productiva desequilibrada Argentina y el tipo de cambio." *Desarrollo Económico* 12, no. 45 (April/June 1972): 25–47.

Dinerstein, Ana C. "¡Que se vayan todos! Popular Insurrection and the Asambleas Barriales in Argentina." *Bulletin of Latin American Research* 22, no. 2 (April 2003): 187–200.

Dobry, Hernan, and Daniel Goldman, *Ser judío en los años setent: Testimonios del horror y la resistencia durante la última dictadura.* Buenos Aires: Siglo Veintiuno Editores, 2014.

Elnecavé, Bruria. *Crisol de vivencias judias.* Buenos Aires: Ediciones La Luz, 1994.

Elnecavé, Nissim. "Latin America." In *American Jewish Year Book* 73 (1972): 428–40.

Engel, Gerald. "Comparison between Americans Living in Israel and Those Who Returned to America: Part I, American Background." *Journal of Psychology* 74, no. 2 (January 1970): 195–204.

———. "Comparison between Americans Living in Israel and Those Who Returned to America: Part II, Israeli Background." *Journal of Psychology* 75, no. 2 (May 1970): 243–51.

———. "Comparison Between Americans Living in Israel and Those Who Returned to America: Part III, Predictions about America and Israel." *Journal of Psychology* 76, no. 1 (July 1970): 117–23.

Epstein, Edward C. "The Piquetero Movement of Greater Buenos Aires: Working Class Protest during the Current Argentine Crisis." *Canadian Journal of Latin American and Caribbean Studies* 28, nos. 55–56 (2003): 11–36.

———. "Recent Stabilization Programs in Argentina, 1973–1986." *World Development* 15, no. 8 (August 1987): 991–1005.

Erez, Yehuda. *The Third Aliyah.* Jerusalem: Zionist Organization, Youth Department, 1948.

Esherick, Joseph W., Hasan Kayali, and Eric Van Young, eds. *Empire to Nation: Historical Perspectives on the Making of the Modern World.* Lanham, MD: Rowman and Littlefield, 2006.

Eshkoli-Wagman, Hava. "Yishuv Zionism: Its Attitude to Nazism and the Third Reich Reconsidered." *Modern Judaism* 19, no. 1 (February 1999): 21–40.

Faingold, Eduardo. *Exile from Argentina: A Jewish Family and the Military Dictatorship (1976-1983).* Charlotte, NC: Information Age, 2008.

Falk, Ophir. "Measuring the Effectiveness of Israel's 'Targeted Killing' Campaign." *Perspectives on Terrorism* 9, no. 1 (February 2015): 2–26.

Feierstein, Daniel. *Genocide as Social Practice: Reorganizing Society under the Nazis and Argentina's Military Juntas.* New Brunswick, NJ: Rutgers University Press, 2014.

Feierstein, Ricardo. *El caramelo descompuesto.* Buenos Aires: Ediciones Nueva Presencia, 1979.

Firchow, Pamina. "Power and Resistance in the Shaping of Argentine Domestic Policy." *Latin American Perspectives* 42, no. 1 (January 2015): 74–83.

Fiszbein, Martín. "La economía del stop and go: Las ideas estructuralistas en la Argentina, 1945–1976." *Desarrollo Económico* 55, no. 216 (September–December 2015): 187–210.

Frenkel, R., and L. Simpson. "The Two Waves of Financial Liberalization in Latin America." In *Development Economics and Structuralist Macroeconomics: Essays in Honor of Lance Taylor*, edited by Amitava Krishna Dutt and Jaime Ros, 206–26. Northampton, MA: Edward Elgar, 2003.

Frenkel, Roberto. "Argentina: A Decade of the Convertibility Regime." *Challenge* 45, no. 4 (July–August 2002): 41–59.

Fridman, Daniel. "A New Mentality for a New Economy: Performing the Homo Economicus in Argentina (1976–83)." *Economy and Society* 39, no. 2 (April 2010): 271–302.

Friedemann, Sergio. *La Universidad Nacional y Popular de Buenos Aires (1973–1974): Una reforma universitaria inconclusa*. Buenos Aires: Universidad de Buenos Aires, 2015.

Galasso, Norberto. *Perón: Exilio, resistencia, retorno y muerte, 1955–1974*. Buenos Aires: Ediciones Colihue, 2005.

Gasparini, Juan. *David Graiver: El banquero de los Montoneros*. Buenos Aires: Grupo Editorial Norma, 2007.

Gillespie, Richard. *Soldiers of Peron: Argentina's Montoneros*. Oxford: Clarendon, 1982.

Gitelman, Zvi, and David Naveh. "Elite Accommodation and Organizational Effectiveness: The Case of Immigrant Absorption in Israel." *Journal of Politics* 38, no. 4 (November 1976): 963–86.

Goebel, Michael. "A Movement from Right to Left in Argentine Nationalism? The Alianza Libertadora Nacionalista and Tacuara as Stages of Militancy." *Bulletin of Latin American Research* 26, no. 3 (July 2007): 356–77.

Gold, Steven J. "From Nationality to Peoplehood: Adaptation and Identity Formation in the Israeli Diaspora." *Diaspora: A Journal of Transnational Studies* 13, nos. 2–3 (Fall–Winter 2004): 3316–58.

Gold, Steven, and Rona Hart. "Transnational Ties during a Time of Crisis: Israeli Emigration, 2000 to 2004." *International Migration* 51, no. 3 (June 2013): 194–216.

Goldberg, Florinda, and Iosef Rozen, eds. *Los Latinoamericanos en Israel: Antología de una aliá*. Buenos Aires: Editorial Contexto, 1988.

Goldberg, Mauricio. *Donde sopla la nostalgia*. Buenos Aires: Grupo Editor Latinoamericano, 1985.

Goldstein, Roberto M. "Migración, identidad, lenguaje y resentimiento." In *Emigracion, salud mental y cultura*, edited by Silvio Gutkowski and Maria Isabel Pazos de Winograd, 43–45. Buenos Aires: Ediciones del Candil, 2003.

Gorny, Yoseph. "Changes in the Social and Political Structure of the Second Aliyah between 1904 and 1940." In *Essential Papers on Zionism*, edited by Jehuda Reinharz and Anita Shapira, 371–421. New York: New York University Press, 1996.

Grugel, Jean, and Maria Pia Riggirozzi. "The Return of the State in Argentina." *International Affairs* 83, no. 1 (January 2007): 87–107.

Gurvich, Jorge, and Shlomo Slutzky, dirs. *El año que viene . . . en Argentina*. 2005; Buenos Aires: National Center for Jewish Films, 2005.

Gurwitz, Beatrice D. *Argentine Jews in the Age of Revolt: Between the New World and the Third World*. Leiden: Brill, 2016.

———. "Zionism, Third Worldism, and Argentine Youth at the Crossroads." *Journal of Jewish Identities* 8, no. 2 (July 2015): 13–32.

Haim, Yehoyada. "Zionist Policies and Attitudes towards the Arabs on the Eve of the Arab Revolt, 1936." *Middle Eastern Studies* 14, no. 2 (May 1978): 211–31.

Halpern, Ben, and Jehuda Reinharz. "The Cultural and Social Background of the Second Aliyah." *Middle Eastern Studies* 27, no. 3 (July 1991): 487–517.

Harpaz, Yossi. "Ancestry into Opportunity: How Global Inequality Drives Demand for Long-Distance European Union Citizenship." *Journal of Ethnic and Migration Studies* 41, no. 13 (May 2015): 2081–104.

Helman, Anat. *A Coat of Many Colors: Dress Culture in the Young State of Israel*. Brookline, MA: Academic Studies Press, 2011.

Hertzberg, Arthur. *The Zionist Idea: A Historical Analysis and Reader*. New York: Jewish Publication Society, 2014.

Herzl, Theodor. *The Jewish State*. New York: Dover, 1988.

Honig, Frederick. "The Reparations Agreement between Israel and the Federal Republic of Germany." *American Journal of International Law* 48, no. 4 (October 1954): 564–78.

Horowitz, Ruth Tamar. "Immigrants in Transition: The Israeli Absorption Center." *International Migration* 15, no. 4 (October 1977): 288–99.

*Immigrants Arrived 1969-70/1971-72*. Jerusalem: Central Bureau of Statistics/Ministry of Immigrant Absorption/Jewish Agency, 1976.

*Immigrants Arrived in 1969-70*. Special Series. Jerusalem: Central Bureau of Statistics/Ministry of Immigrant Absorption, 1974.

*Immigrants from Latin America One Year and Three Years after Immigration, Arrived between 1969 and 1974*. Special Series no. 652, Jerusalem: Central Bureau of Statistics, 1981.

Itzigsohn, José. "Conflictos de identidad judía en América Latina." *Dispersión y Unidad* 1 (1979): 38–56.

———. *Una experiencia judía contemporánea: Memorias y reflexiones*. Buenos Aires: Editorial Paidós, 1969.

Jackisch, Carlota. "Peronismo y dictadura militar (1973–1983): Un ciclo anómico en la reciente historia argentina." *Ibero-Amerikanisches Archiv* 23, nos. 3–4 (July–December 1997): 439–62.

Jmelnizky, Adrián, and Ezequiel Erdei. *La población judía de Buenos Aires: Estudio sociodemográfico*. Buenos Aires: Centro de Documentación e Información sobre Judaísmo Argentino Marc Turkow, JDC-Meida, 2005.

Johnson, Peter T. "Academic Press Censorship under Military and Civilian Regimes: The Argentine and Brazilian Cases, 1964–1975." *Luso-Brazilian Review* 15, no. 1 (Summer 1978): 3–25.

Kaese, Fynn, and Jonas Wolff. "Piqueteros after the Hype: Unemployed Movements in Argentina, 2008–2015." *European Review of Latin American and Caribbean Studies/Revista Europea de Estudios Latinoamericanos y del Caribe* 102 (October 2016): 47–68.

Kahan, Emmanuel. *Memories That Lie a Little: Jewish Experiences during the Argentine Dictatorship*. Leiden: Brill, 2018.

Kaniel, Yehoshua. *Continuity and Change: Old Yishuv and New Yishuv during the First and Second Aliyah*. Jerusalem: Yad Ben-Zvi, 1981.

———. "Emigration from Palestine during the Period of the First and Second Aliyot." *Cathedra* 73 (September 1994): 115–38.

Karády, Viktor. *The Jews of Europe in the Modern Era: A Socio-Historical Outline*. Budapest: Central European University Press, 2004.

Karmon, Y. "Ashdod: A New Mediterranean Port in Israel." *Geography* 51, no. 3 (July 1966): 254–58.

Katz, Maya Balakirsky. "The De-Politicization of Israeli Political Cartoons." *Israel Studies* 18, no. 1 (Spring 2013): 1–30.

Katz-Gerro, Tally, and Yossi Shavit. "The Stratification of Leisure and Taste: Classes and Lifestyles in Israel." *European Sociological Review* 14, no. 4 (December 1998): 369–86.

Kaufman, Edy. "Jewish Victims of Repression in Argentina under Military Rule (1976–1983)." *Holocaust and Genocide Studies* 4, no. 4 (April 1989): 479–99.

Kessler, Gabriel, and María Mercedes di Virgilio. "Impoverishment of the Middle Class in Argentina: The 'New Poor' in Latin America." *Laboratorium: Russian Review of Social Research* 2, no. 2 (September 2012): 200–220.

Khazzoom, Aziza. "Did the Israeli State Engineer Segregation? On the Placement of Jewish Immigrants in Development Towns in the 1950s." *Social Forces* 84, no. 1 (September 2005): 115–34.

Klor, Sebastian. "Aliyah from Argentina in the Years 1962-1963 in the Shadow of the Eichmann Affair." *Studies on the Creation of the State of Israel* 25 (2015): 1–30.

———. *Between Exile and Exodus*. Detroit: Wayne State University Press, 2017.

Knudson, Jerry W. "Veil of Silence: The Argentine Press and the Dirty War, 1976–1983." *Latin American Perspectives* 24, no. 6 (November 1997): 93–112.

Krupnik, Adrián. "Cuando camino al Kibbutz vieron pasar al Che. Radicalización política y juventud judía: Argentina, 1966–1976." In *Marginados y consagrados: Nuevos estudios sobre la vida judía en Argentina*, edited by Emmanuel Kahan, Laura Schenquer, Damián Setton, and Alejandro Dujovne, 311–27. Buenos Aires: Lumiere, 2011.

Lach, Saul. "Immigration and Prices." *Journal of Political Economy* 115, no. 4 (August 207): 548–87.

Lahav, Pnina. *Judgment in Jerusalem: Chief Justice Simon Agranat and the Zionist Century*. Berkeley: University of California Press, 1997.

Lamdani, Ruben. "Emigration from Israel." *Economic Quarterly* 30, no. 116 (1983): 462–78.

Landi, Óscar. "La tercera presidencia de Perón: Gobierno de emergencia y crisis política." *Revista Mexicana de Sociología* 40, no. 4 (October–December 1978): 1353–410.

Larraquy, Marcelo. *Lopez Rega*. Buenos Aires: Punto de Lectura, 2007.

———. *Marcados a fuego II (1945–1973): De Perón a Montoneros*. Buenos Aires: Aguilar, 2010.

Lederhendler, Eli, ed. *The Six-Day War and World Jewry*. Bethesda: University Press of Maryland, 2000.

Lerner, Natán. "Las raíces ideológicas del antisemitismo en la Argentina y el nacionalismo." In Senkman, *El antisemitismo en la Argentina*, 195–208.

Lesser, Jeffrey, and Raanan Rein, eds. *Rethinking Jewish-Latin Americans*. Albuquerque: University of New Mexico Press, 2008.

Levin, Yehuda. "Labor and Land at the Start of Jewish Settlement in Argentina." *Jewish History* 21, nos. 3–4 (July–December 2007): 341–59.

Lewan, Kenneth M. "How West Germany Helped to Build Israel." *Journal of Palestine Studies* 4, no. 4 (Summer 1975): 41–64.

Lewin, Boleslao. *Cómo fue la inmigración judía en la Argentina*. Buenos Aires: Plus Ultra, 1983.

Lewin-Epstein, Noah, and Moshe Semyonov. "Migration, Ethnicity, and Inequality: Homeownership in Israel." *Social Problems* 47, no. 3 (August 2000): 425–44.

Lewis, Herbert S. *After the Eagles Landed: The Yemenites of Israel.* Boulder, CO: Westview Press, 1989.

Lockman, Zachary. "The Left in Israel: Zionism vs. Socialism." *MERIP Reports* 49 (July 1976): 3–18.

Luchilo, Lucas. *Migración de retorno: El caso argentino*. Buenos Aires: Centroredes, 2007.

Madar, Chase. "The Unemployed in the Popular Uprising of December, 2001: Report from Greater Buenos Aires." *International Journal of Political Economy* 31, no. 1 (Spring 2001): 11–23.

Manzano, Valeria. "Argentina tercer mundo: Nueva izquierda, emociones y política revolucionaria en las décadas de 1960 y 1970." *Desarrollo Económico* 54, no. 212 (May–August 2014): 79–104.

Marongiu, Federico. "Políticas de shock en la agonía del estado peronista: El rodrigazo y el Mondelliazo." *Anales de las V Jornadas Nacionales de Historia Moderna y Contemporánea* (2006). Online.

Martegani, Fiammetta. *The Israeli Defence Forces' Representation in Israeli Cinema: Did David Betray His Soldiers?* Newcastle-upon-Tyne: Cambridge Scholars, 2017.

Meyer, Michael A. "Liability of Prisoners of War for Offences Committed Prior to Capture: The Astiz Affair." *International and Comparative Law Quarterly* 32, no. 4 (October 1983): 948–80.

Míguez, María Cecilia. "El regreso del peronismo al poder en 1973 y las relaciones internacionales: La repercusión regional y mundial de la asunción de Héctor Cámpora." *Postdata* 23, no. 1 (April–September 2018): 1–19.

Millington, Thomas M. "President Arturo Illia and the Argentine Military." *Journal of Inter-American Studies* 6, no. 3 (July 1964): 405–24.

Mills, C. Wright. *The Sociological Imagination*. Oxford: Oxford University Press, 2000.

Mirelman, Victor A. "The Semana Trágica of 1919 and the Jews in Argentina." *Jewish Social Studies* 37, no. 1 (Winter 1975): 61–73.

Mochkofsky, Graciela. *Timerman: El periodista que quiso ser parte del poder (1923–1999).* Buenos Aires: Editorial Sudamericana, 2004.

Montes Garcés, Elizabeth. "Sentido de lugar y género en Condorito y Mafalda." *Revista Canadiense de Estudios Hispánicos* 43, no. 1 (2018): 17–41.

Moreno, Sergio. *La noche de los bastones largos*. Buenos Aires: EUDEBA, 2016.

Moyano, María José. *Argentina's Lost Patrol: Armed Struggle, 1969–1979.* New Haven: Yale University Press, 1995.

Munck, Ronaldo. "Argentina, or the Political Economy of Collapse." *International Journal of Political Economy* 31, no. 3 (Fall 2001): 67–88.

———. "The Crisis of Late Peronism and the Working Class 1973–1976." *Bulletin of the Society for Latin American Studies* 30 (April 1979): 5–34.

———. "Movimiento obrero, economía y política en Argentina: 1955–1985." *Estudios Sociológicos* 5, no. 13 (January–April 1987): 87–109.

Naor, Aryeh. "Rightist Political Dailies in Israel: Ideology, Politics and the Failure of Privatization." *Kesher* no. 25 (1999): 71–79.

Near, Henry. "Paths to Utopia: The Kibbutz and the Philosophy of Communalism." In

*Where Community Happens: The Kibbutz and the Philosophy of Communalism*, 197–218. Bern: Peter Lang, 2011.

"The New Look of the Onganía Administration." Washington, DC: Central Intelligence Agency, 1967.

Nillni, David Horacio. *Guerrillero y soldado: Una vida entre La Plata y Beersheva*. Buenos Aires: AMIA, 2015.

*Nunca más: Informe de la comisión nacional sobre la desaparición de personas*. Buenos Aires: EUDEBA, 1984.

O'Donnell, Guillermo. *Bureaucratic Authoritarianism: Argentina, 1966–1973, in Comparative Perspective*. Berkeley: University of California Press, 1988.

———. *Modernization and Bureaucratic-Authoritarianism: Studies in South American Politics*. Berkeley: University of California Press, 1973.

———. "Reflections on the Patterns of Change in the Bureaucratic-Authoritarian State." *Latin American Research Review* 13, no. 1 (January–April 1978): 3–38.

O'Donnell, María. *El secuestro de los Born*. Buenos Aires: Debate, 2016.

Peinado, Quique. *Futbolistas de Izquierda*. Madrid: Leeme Editories, 2013.

Plotkin, Mariano Ben. *Freud in the Pampas: The Emergence and Development of a Psychoanalytic Culture in Argentina*. Redwood, CA: Stanford University Press, 2001.

———. "Freudian Slips: On the Complicated—and Lingering—Legacy of Psychoanalysis in Argentina." *World Policy Journal* 35, no. 1 (Spring 2018): 16–22.

Porcezansky, Rafael. *El Uruguay judío: Demografía e identidad*. Montevideo: Ediciones Trilce, 2006.

Portelli, Alessandro. *The Death of Luigi Trastulli, and Other Stories: Form and Meaning in Oral History*. Albany: State University of New York Press, 1991.

Potash, Robert A. *The Army and Politics in Argentina*. Stanford, CA: Stanford University Press, 1969.

Raijman, Rebeca, and Ariane Ophir. "The Economic Integration of Latin Americans in Israel." *Canadian Ethnic Studies* 46, no. 3 (December 2014): 77–102.

Recalde, Aritz. "La Universidad de Buenos Aires en la década de 1970: Análisis del Comunicado de prensa en solidaridad con Rodolfo Puiggrós." *Salud Colectiva* 8, no. 3 (2012): 315–22.

Reich, Bernard. *A Brief History of Israel*. 2nd ed. New York: Checkmark Books, 2008.

Rein, Raanan. *Argentina, Israel, and the Jews: Peron, the Eichmann Capture and After*. Bethesda: University Press of Maryland, 2003.

———. *Argentine Jews or Jewish Argentines? Essays on Ethnicity, Identity, and Diaspora*. Leiden: Brill, 2010.

———. "The Eichmann Kidnapping: Its Effects on Argentine-Israeli Relations and the Local Jewish Community." *Jewish Social Studies* 7, no. 3 (Spring–Summer 2001): 101–30.

———. *Los muchachos peronistas judíos: Los argentinos judíos y el apoyo al justicialismo*. Buenos Aires: Sudamericana, 2015.

———. "El reverso de una imagen: El retorno de Perón al poder en la prensa hebrea." In *El retorno de Perón y el peronismo en la visión de la prensa nacional y extranjera*, edited by Raanan Rein and Claudio Panella, 339–380. La Plata: EDULP, 2009.

Rein, Raanan, and Claudio Panella, eds. *La segunda línea: Liderazgo peronista, 1945–1955*. Buenos Aires: Editorial de la Universidad Nacional de Tres de Febrero, 2013.

Rein, Raanan, and Jeffrey Lesser. "Challenging Particularity: Jews as a Lens on Latin American Ethnicity." *Latin American and Caribbean Ethnic Studies* 1, no. 2 (November 2006): 249–63.

Remennick, Larissa. "Transnational Lifestyles among Russian Israelis: A Follow-Up Study." *Global Networks* 13, no. 4 (October 2013): 478–97.

"The Reparations Agreement with Germany—General Debate and Decision: Knesset Sessions 38-40, 7-9.1.1952." In *The Reparations Controversy: The Jewish State and German Money in the Shadow of the Holocaust 1951-1952*, edited by Yaakov Sharett, 161–272. Berlin: De Gruyter, 2011.

Restivo, Néstor, and Raúl Dellatorre. *El Rodrigazo, 30 años después: Un ajuste que cambió al país*. Buenos Aires: Capital Intelectual, 2005.

Rivlin, Paul. *The Israeli Economy from the Foundation of the State through the 21st Century*. New York: Cambridge University Press, 2010.

Rodríguez, Laura Graciela. "La universidad durante el tercer gobierno peronista (1973–1976)." *Conflicto Social* 7, no. 12 (2014): 114–45.

Romero, Luis Alberto. *A History of Argentina in the Twentieth Century*. University Park: Pennsylvania State University Press, 2002.

Roniger, Luis, and Deby Babis. "Latin American Israelis: The Collective Identity of an Invisible Community." In *Identities in an Era of Globalization and Multiculturalism*, edited by Judit Bokser Liwerant, Eliezer Ben-Rafael, Yosef Gorny, and Raanan Rein, 297–320. Boston: Brill, 2008.

Roniger, Luis, Leonardo Senkman, Saúl Sosnowski, and Mario Sznajder. *Exile, Diaspora, and Return: Changing Cultural Landscapes in Argentina, Chile, Paraguay, and Uruguay*. New York: Oxford University Press, 2018.

Rosenfeld, Daniel, dir. *Los años del Tiburón*. 2018. Buenos Aires: Daniel Rosenfeld Films, 2018.

Rossi, Federico Matías. "Aparición, auge y declinación de un movimiento social: Las asambleas vecinales y populares de Buenos Aires, 2001–2003." *European Review of Latin American and Caribbean studies/Revista Europea de Estudios Latinoamericanos y del Caribe*, no. 78 (April 2005): 67–88.

Rougier Voilláz, Marcelo N., and Juan Carlos Odisio. "Del dicho al hecho: El modelo integrado y abierto de Aldo Ferrer y la política económica en la Argentina de la segunda posguerra." *América Latina en la historia econômica* 19, no.1 (2012): 99–130.

Rouquié, Alain. *Poder militar y sociedad política en la Argentina: Práctica y mecanismos del poder militar. Anatomía del poder militar, ensayo de interpretación*. Buenos Aires: Hyspamérica, 1986.

Ruíz, Fernando J. *Las palabras son acciones: Historia politica y profesional de la Opinion de Jacobo Timerman, 1971–1977*. Buenos Aires: Perfil Libros, 2001.

Russell, Raymond, Robert Hanneman, and Shlomo Getz. "The Transformation of the Kibbutzim." *Israel Studies* 16, no. 2 (Summer 2011): 109–26.

Sarly, Robert. "Failure of the New Towns." *Built Environment* 3, no. 12 (December 1974): 612–16.

Sarna, Jonathan D. "The Myth of No Return: Jewish Return Migration to Eastern Europe, 1881–1914." *American Jewish History* 71, no. 2 (December 1981): 256–68.

Schiller, Herman. "El judaísmo oficial y la dictadura." *Equipo Nizkor*, 2007. Online.

Schoijet, Mauricio. "The Timerman Affair, Argentina, and the United States." *Social Justice* 20 (1983): 16–36.

Segev, Tom. *1967: Israel, the War, and the Year That Transformed the Middle East*. New York: Metropolitan Books, 2007.

Senkman, Leonardo. "El antisemitismo bajo dos experiencias democráticas: Argentina 1959/1966 y 1973/1977." In Senkman, *El antisemitismo en la Argentina*, 117–90.

———. "Populismo y empresarios judíos: Actuación pública de Horacio Lafer y José B. Gelbard durante Vargas y Perón." *Araucaria* 8, no. 15 (January–June 2006): 46–76.

Senkman, Leonardo, ed. *El antisemitismo en la Argentina*, edited by Leonardo Senkman. Buenos Aires: CEAL, 1989.

Seoane, María. *El burgués maldito: Los secretos de Gelbard, el último líder del capitalismo nacional*. Buenos Aires: Editorial Sudamericana, 2002.

Serulnikov, Sergio. "Pobreza y revuelta de subsistencia: Los saqueos de 1989 en Argentina." *Historia social* 88 (May–August 2017): 63–85.

———. "When Looting Becomes a Right: Urban Poverty and Food Riots in Argentina." *Latin American Perspectives* 21, no. 3 (Summer 1994): 69–89.

Shapira, Anita. *Israel: A History*. Waltham, MA: Brandeis University Press, 2012.

Silber, Marcos. "Immigrants from Poland Want to Go Back: The Politics of Return Migration and Nation Building in 1950s' Israel." *Journal of Israeli History* 27, no. 2 (September 2008): 201–19.

Silbereisen, Rainer K., Peter F. Titzmann, and Yossi Shavit, eds. *The Challenges of Diaspora Migration. Interdisciplinary Perspectives on Israel and Germany*. New York: Routledge, 2016.

Slipak, Daniela. "De lealtades y tradiciones: El enfrentamiento de la JP Lealtad con Montoneros a través de sus revistas." *Estudios sociológicos* 31, no. 92 (May–August 2013): 345–67.

Smith, William C. "Democracy, Distributional Conflicts and Macroeconomic Policymaking in Argentina, 1983–89." *Journal of Inter-American Studies and World Affairs* 32, no. 2 (Summer 1990): 1–42.

Smooha, Sammy. *Israel: Pluralism and Conflict*. Oakland: University of California Press, 1978.

———. "The Mass Immigrations to Israel: A Comparison of the Failure of the Mizrahi Immigrants of the 1950s with the Success of the Russian Immigrants of the 1990s." *Journal of Israeli History* 27, no. 1 (March 2008): 1–27.

———. "Pluralism: A Study of Intergroup Relations in Israel." PhD diss., University of California, 1973.

Sofer, Michael. "The Future of Family Farming in Israel: The Second Generation in the Moshav." *Geographical Journal* 171, no. 4 (December 2005): 357–68.

Spector, Graciela. "La identidad alquilada." In *Emigracion, salud mental y cultura*, edited by Silvio Gutkowski and Maria Isabel Pasos de Winograd, 125–38. Buenos Aires: Ediciones del Candil, 2003, 125–38.

Sznajder, Mario, and Luis Roniger. "From Argentina to Israel: Escape, Evacuation and Exile." *Journal of Latin American Studies* 37, no. 2 (May 2005): 351–77.

Tcach Abad, César, and Celso Rodríguez. *Arturo Illia: Un sueño breve: El rol del peronismo y de los Estados Unidos en el golpe militar de 1966*. Buenos Aires: Edhasa, 2006.

Tella, Guido di. *Argentina under Peron, 1973–76: The Nation's Experience with a Labour-Based Government*. New York: St. Martin's, 1983.

Todorov, Tzvetan. "The Coexistence of Cultures." *Policy Futures in Education* 8, nos. 3–4 (January 2010): 419–26.

Treisman, Daniel. "Stabilization Tactics in Latin America: Menem, Cardoso, and the Politics of Low Inflation." *Comparative Politics* 36, no. 4 (July 2004): 399–419.

Triana, Alfredo A. "Argentina: La política como cultura o los años del GAN. La primacía de la política. Lanusse, Perón y la Nueva Izquierda en tiempos del GAN." *Sociohistórica* 7, no. 7 (January–June 2000): 337–45.

Troen, Ilan. "Calculating the 'Economic Absorptive Capacity' of Palestine: A Study of the Political Uses of Scientific Research." *Contemporary Jewry* 10, no. 2 (September 1989): 19–38.

Tsuda Gaku, Takeyuki. "Ethnic Return Migration and the Nation-State: Encouraging the Diaspora to Return 'Home.'" *Nations and Nationalism* 16, no. 4 (October 2010): 616–36.

Tzfadia, Erez. "The Ethno-Class Trajectory of New Neighborhoods in Israel." *GeoJournal* 64, no. 2 (January–June 2005): 141–51.

Vaccarezza, Federico. "Políticas de desarrollo industrial en la Argentina (1940–2001)." PhD diss., Universidad Nacional de Tres de Febrero, 2010.

Vitto, Cecilia. "Plan económico del tercer gobierno peronista: Gestión de Gelbard (1973–1974)." *Problemas del desarrollo* 43, no. 171 (2012): 111–34.

Warren, John. "The Five Schools Project." *Built Environment* 3, no. 12 (December 1974): 623–24.

Waxman, Chaim I. "Critical Sociology and the End of Ideology in Israel." *Israel Studies* 2, no. 1 (Spring 1997): 194–210.

Waxman, Chaim, and Michael Appel. *To Israel and Back: American Aliyah and Return Migration*. New York: American Jewish Committee, 1986.

Waxman, Dov. "Living with Terror, Not Living in Terror: The Impact of Chronic Terrorism on Israeli Society." *Perspectives on Terrorism* 5, nos. 5–6 (December 2011): 4–26.

Weissbrod, Lily. "Economic Factors and Political Strategies: The Defeat of the Revisionists in Mandatory Palestine." *Middle Eastern Studies* 19, no. 3 (July 1983): 326–44.

Winsberg, Morton D. "Jewish Agricultural Colonization in Argentina." *Geographical Review* 54, no. 4 (October 1964): 487–501.

Wolf-Monzon, Tamar. "Uri Zvi Greenberg and the Pioneers of the Third Aliyah: A Case of Reception." *Prooftexts* 29, no. 1 (Winter 2009): 31–62.

Yacobi, Haim, and Erez Tzfadia. "Multiculturalism, Nationalism, and the Politics of the Israeli City." *International Journal of Middle East Studies* 41, no. 2 (May 2009): 289–307.

Yaish, Meir. "The Consequences of Immigration for Social Mobility: The Experience of Israel." *European Sociological Review* 18, no. 4 (December 2002): 449–71.

Yehudai, Ori. "Displaced in the National Home: Jewish Repatriation from Palestine to Europe, 1945–48." *Jewish Social Studies* 20, no. 2 (Winter 2014): 69–110.

———. "Forth from Zion: Jewish Emigration from Palestine and Israel, 1945–1960." PhD diss., University of Chicago, 2013.

Yisraeli, David. "The Third Reich and the Transfer Agreement." *Journal of Contemporary History* 6, no. 2 (April 1971): 129–48.

Zohar, Marcel. *Let My People Go to Hell*. Tel Aviv: Tzitrin, 1998. [in Hebrew].

# INDEX

*Page numbers in italics refer to figures and tables.*


Abramovich, Guidon, 44
absorption, immigrant, 38, 39, 43, 44, 47, 51, 52, 54, 56, 59, 63, 65, 66–69, 94–101, 104, 106, 108, 133–40, 149, 151; absorption centers, 15, 94–98, 101, 123, 135, 181n85; absorption capacity, 167n73, 176n56; Absorption and Immigration Committee, 71, *72*; Absorption Ministry, 99, 100, 101, 135, 139, *147*, 151, 184n31; absorption policies, 5, 14, 78, 133, 152; Department for Immigrant Absorption, 15, 38, 52, 63, 73, 134, 138, *150*, *176n56*
ACPIA, Asociación de Comedores Populares Israelitas en Argnetina (association of popular Israelite cafeterías in Argentina), 79
Agranat Commission, 102
agriculture, 11, 20, 21, 25, 26, 41, 42, 45, 49–50, 53–54, 80, *112*, *115*, *116–17*, 124, 134, 173n55. *See also* kibbutz; moshavim, Moshav Kochav Michael Sobell (Kochav)
AJC, (American Jewish Committee), 130
*Al HaMishmar*, 25
*Aliyah Beth*, 21, 164n15
Almogy, Josef, 126, 136
Alroey, Gur, 8, 172n34
*American Jewish Year Book*, 103, 123
AMIA (Asociación Mutual Israelita de la Argentina), 67, 78, 133, 146, 174n1, 183n12
Amidar (organization for immigrant homebuilding), 95, 98
Amos (social justice group named after prophet), 123, 125, 179n29
anti-Jewish, 11, 108. *See also* anti-Semitism; Holocaust; Nazi; pogrom
anti-Semitism, 7–8, 12, 14, 16, 19, 20, 33–35, 40, 50, 51, 78, 81, 84, 85, 86, 121, 122, 129–33, 136, 177n60, 178n11, 180n54, 180n63; attacks on Jewish Argentine students, 12, 34, 112, 162n41. *See also* anti-Jewish; Holocaust; Nazi; pogrom
Anug, Yeshayahu, 138
Arab League, 85, 86, 102
Arab Revolt, 21
Arad, Israel, 139
Arazi, Yosef, 103, 119, 120
Arenberg, Haim, 171n8
Argentine Revolution, 14
Argov, Abraham, 94, 95
Arieli, Aliza, 146
Aron, Haim, 137
Ashdod, Israel, 4, 14, 41, 46, 49–52, 55, 59, 65, 66
Astiz, Alfredo, 131
*Atzmaut* (ship), 51
*Aurora* (weekly Spanish-language paper), 37, 39, 47, 50, 51, 54, 65–66, 70, 74, 77, 95–98, 104, 106, 123, 173n57, 177n67
Avni, Haim, 8

Babis, Deby, 6
Bahía Blanca, Argentina, 103
Balfour Declaration, 20
Barilko, Jaime, 133

Bar-Kahan, Abraham, 71
Bar-Yehuda, Yisrael, 30
Bat Yam, Israel, 37
Bauhaus (architectural style), 21
Beersheba, Israel, 37, 50, 53, 99, 133, 138
Begin, Menachem, 16, 134, 172n26
Ben-Gurion, David, 22, 47
Ben Hamu, Schlomo, 126, 133
Ben-Elieser, Eliyahu, 139
Berry, John, 11, 154
Bible: Exodus, 170n66; Genesis, 56
Birmajer, Marcelo, 155
Bitan, Uzi, 69
Blejer, Mario, 154
B'nai B'rith, 130
Brazil, 31, 33, 52, 63, 71, 75, 130, 166n46, 171n1
Brieger, Pedro, 155
British Mandate, 20, 21
Brodsky, Sara, 131
Buenos Aires, Argentina, 1, 3, 4, 7, 12, 14, 16, 26, 32, 43, 45, 46, 48, 53, 54, 56, 57, 62, 66, 68, 71, 74, 77, 78, 80, 83–85, 99, 102, 118, 120, 121, 124, 126, 130, 131, 134, 145, 146, 148, 154, 155

Cámpora, Héctor José, 15, 83, 85, 122
Carmiel, Israel, 133, 138, 139
Catholicism, 11, 25, 75, 128
*chalutzim* (pioneers), 20, 51, 55
Chile, 51, 172n25
Club Atlético Sefaradí Argentino, 133
Club Náutico Hacoaj, 133
Cohen, Yinon, 8
Cold War, 125, 172n27
*Colombo* (ship), 121
Commission to Stop the Yerida of Latin American Olim, 63, 171nn4–5
CONADEP, (National Commission for the Investigacion of Disappeared People), 132, 181n79
Concordia, Argentina, 103
Córdoba, Argentina, 103, 118–20, 122, 123, 125, 127, 131, 134, 137
Cordobazo (civil uprising), 15, 62, 75, 78, 81
Cosse, Isabella, 42
Cygel, Abraham, 38, 52, 65, 71, 72

DAIA (Delegación de Asociaciones Israelitas de la Argentina), 14, 85, 86, 126–31, 133, 174n12
*Davar*, 25, 33, 38, 44, 70
Dayan, Moshe, 129
de la Rúa, Fernando, 148
debt, 14, 61–68, 136, 146
Declaration of Independence, Israel's, 21, 22
Defense Ministry, 37
Deganya (kibbutz), 20
DellaPergola, Sergio, 8, 19
demonstrations, 52, 97, 175n19
Despersión y Unidad, 141
development town, 49, 134
Di Marzzo (Captain), 34
diaspora (*golah*), 2, 5, 7, 9, 19, 25, 31, 41, 51, 57, 60, 71, 84, 94, 96, 101, 133, 134, 152, 153, 158
Dinitz, Simcha, 145
Dirty War, 125
disappeared, 128, 131, 132, 144, 181n79
displaced persons, 21, 31, 158, 166n46
Dominitz, Yehuda, 31, 52, 68
Ducach, Teodoro, 51, 52, 71
Duvdevany, Baruch, 30, 45, 60

Echeverria, Esteban, 45
Eco, Umberto, 42
Eichmann, Adolf, 12, 33, 34
Eilat, Israel, 133
Elnecavé, David, 56
Elnecavé, Nissim, 56–60, 84, 85
ERP (People's Revolutionary Army), 126
ethnicity, 5, 7, 9–10, 50, 71, 119, 158, 169n41, 175n14
Exodus (book of the Bible). *See* Bible: Exodus
*Exodus* (movie), 1
Ezra Ubitzaron (neighborhood in Tel Aviv), 66

Fainguersch, Gregorio, 78
Feldman, Dov, 53, 55

Felenbok, Simon, 133
Fernández de Kirchner, Cristina, 150
Fisherman, Abraham, 126
Fixler, Ben Zion, 33, 34, 52
*Flaminia* (ship), 32–34, 37, 40, 56, 57
*fraier* (sucker), 98
Frankel, William, 58
Frondizi, Arturo, 12

Gardel, Carlos, 45, 156
Gardosh, Kariel "Dosh", 41
*garinim* (youth groups, literally "kernels"), 119
Gelbard, José Ber, 15–16, 120, 163n58
Gerchunoff, Pablo, 83
Golan, Reuven, 51
Gold, Ernest, 1
Goldberg Nicolas, 59
Goldin, Y., 30
Gorenstein, Mario, 130, 133
Gozik, Abraham, 70
Graiver, David, 130
Grondona, Mariano, 132
Grossman, Kalman, 83, 87–91, 102, 103, 106, 108–12, 114–16, 120–22, 178n11
Grynberg, Enrique, 87
Grynberg, Jenny, 95, 96, 107
guerrillas, 16, 124, 129, 141, 175n19, 178n5
Gurwitz, Beatrice, 7
Gutkin, Emilio, 57, 58

*Haaretz*, 50, 51, 54, 64, 65, 74, 106, 136
Hagelin, Dagmar, 131
Haifa, Israel, 59, 63, 68, 69, 72, 95, 172n34
*Halakha*, 164n18
Harel (kibbutz), 106
Harel, Yitzhak, 80, 85, 104, 123
Hashomer (kibbutz), 20
Hashomer Hatzair (group), 56, 125
*Hatzofe* (newspaper), 33, 34
*Hayom* (newspaper), 65, 68, 172n26
Hebrew University of Jerusalem, 21, 30, 154; study estimating Jewish population of Argentina, 182n101
Helman, Anat, 46
*Herut* (newspaper), 44
Herzcowitz, Moises, 34
Herzl, Theodor (person) 22, 39, 170n66
*Herzl, Theodor* (ship). See *Theodor Herzl* (ship)
Hirsch, Maurice de, 11
Histadrut (General Organization of Workers), 25, 44, 70
Holocaust, 21, 41, 56, 166n46
Holon, Israel, 94–96
Horowitz, David, 99
Hospital Israelita Ezrah, 103
housing, 2, 15, 16, 22, 49, 50, 82, 94–96, 98–102, 104, 106, 123, 138–40

identity, 4, 9–11, 22, 39, 45, 56, 60, 100, 128, 134, 155, 156
ideology, 4, 6, 9, 16, 18, 22, 24, 39, 86, 98, 101, 105, 107, 108,110, 119, 127, 146
Ikar HaOved (peasant worker), 53
immigration assistance (from Israel to leave Argentina and move to Israel), 182n108
import substitution industrialization (ISI), 13, 42, 136
Inbar, Herzl, 126, 127
inflation, 22, 42, 78, 102, 120, 122, 124, 137, 142, 144, 146, 158
Interior Ministry, 30, 50, 127, 131
intermarriage, 129, 181n84, 138, 181n84
INTI (National Institute of Industrial Technology), 124
intifada, 149, 152, 184n23
Israeli, Yaacov, 177n64
Italmar (navigation company), 121
Itzigsohn, José, 141

JA, Jewish Agency for Israel, 2, 5, 12, 14–16, 27, 30–34, 37, 40, 44, 45, 47, 50–60, 62–64, 66–74, 77, 78, 80, 81, 83–85, 87, 93, 95–97, 99, 100, 102, 103, 106, 110, 118–23, 125, 127, 128, 129, 133, 134, 137, 138, 142, 146, 149, 150, 151, 153, 165n32, 173n57, 177n64
Jaimovich, Alejandra, 131
Javkin, Geula, 104–5
Jerusalem (city), 2–4, 21, 31, 50, 66, 86, 94, 133, 134, 138–40, 156

*Jerusalem* (ship), 14, 25, 62, 68, 70, 72–74, 81
*Jewish Chronicle*, 56–58, 60, 84
Jewish education, 20, 25, 33, 78–79, 94, 108, 127–29, 133, 134, 174n62

Kahan, Emmanuel, 7
Kaplan, Zeev, 44
Keren Hayesod (United Israel Appeal), 134
Kfar Argentina, 25
KGB, 172n27. *See also* Cold War
kibbutz, 25, 41, 43, 49, *49*, 53, 56, 70, 77, 93, 105, 106, 134, 159n9, 177n67
Kirchner, Néstor, 150
Kiryat Gat, Israel, 52, 53, 133, 138, 139
Kiryat Yam, Israel, 94
Kitron, Moshe, 47, 64
Klor, Sebastian, 8–9, 35, 36, *36*, 83, *87*, *88*, *89*, 90, *90*, 114, *114*, 177n64
Knesset (Israeli parliament), 22
Koifman, Yoav, 137
*Kol Israel (state radio)*, 129
Korin, Moshe, 78
Kovadloff, Jacobo, 130, 132
Krieger Vasena, Adalbert, 14, 174n66
*kupot holim* (health insurance organizations), 48
Kurland, Yitzhak, 57

*La Luz* (Jewish magazine), 14, 40, 41, 54, 56–60, 66, 71, 74, 120, 123
*La Opinión* (newspaper), 106, 129, 130
LAJSA (Latin American Jewish Studies Association), 7
Lamdani, Reuben, 8
Lavado, Joaquin, "Quino," 42
Law of Return, 12, 22, 162n46, 164n18
Lebanon War, 141
Lebanony, A., 69
left, leftist, 16, 84, 85, 103, 104, 120, 122–25, 129, 132–35, 137
Lesser, Jeffrey, 7, 9
Levenberg, Schneier, 58, 84
Leyland (truck assembly plant), 50, 52
lifestyle, 15, 21, 38, 49, 51, 93, 142, 148, 152
literary works, on Jewish Argentine return migration from Israel, 160n16
Llach, Juan José, 83
loans, 14, 22, 50, 63, 64–67, 69
Lopez Rega, José, 16, 123, 124

Maalot, Israel, 139
*Maariv* (newspaper), 41, 54, 64, 69, 96, 136, 150
Maass, Richard, 130
Maccabi, 133
*machon lemadrichim* (leadership school), 66
Mafalda (cartoon character), 14, 41, 42, 48
Manguel, Pablo, 25, 165n23
Mapai Labor Party, 70
Martínez de Hoz, José Alfredo, 136
Martínez de Perón, María Estela, 16, 125
Meir, Golda, 26
Mendoza, Argentina, 45, 103
Merajver, Adrián, 141
*Messenger* (B'nai B'rith publication), 130
Mesilot (kibbutz), 56, 63
mezuzah, 3, 159n6
Meyer, Marshall, 128, 133
middle class, 14, 20, 21, 25, 33, 36–42, 44, 46, 48, 50, 52, 56–58, 60, 78, 79, 84, 85, 121, 126, 140, 146, 148
Migdal HaEmek, 133
migrant numbers, from Argentina to Israel, 4–6, 8, 10, 12, 14–17, 22, 24–26, 32–40, 52, 63–64, 74–81, *80*, 84–113, *91*, 114–43, 144–58; after 2005, 183n2; 1948–1970, *35*; 1948–1964, *38*; 1948–2016, *23*; 1954–1967, *36*; 1963, *87*, *88*, *89*, 90, *90*, *114*; 1963–70, *79*; 1966, *49*; 1967, *49*, *75*, *76*; 1968, *75*, *76*; 1969–74, *92*; 1970–83, *118*; 1973, *87*, *88*, *89*, 90, *90*, *91*, *102*, *108*, *109*, *111*, *112*, *115*, *116–17*, 125; 1974, *102*, *108*, *109*, *111*, *112*; 1975, *102*, 125; 1980–2005, *145*; 1989–2002, *147*; 2002, *150*
migrant numbers, from Israel, *27*, *28*, *32*, *73*, 74, *124*; from Israel to Argentina / elsewhere in Latin America, 7, 14, 17, 26–27, *29*, 30–31, 32, 47–48, 68–74, *80*, 104–6, 118–25, *124*, 140–43, 144, 146–58; 1948–1964, *38*; 1951–66, *72*; 1953–56, *26*; 1965, *73*, *74*; 1966, *49*;

1967, *49*; 1970–79, *141*; 1989–2002, *147*
mixed marriage. *See* intermarriage
Montes Garcés, Elizabeth, 42
Montoneros (Peronist guerrilla group), 124, 130, 178n5
moshavim, Moshav Kochav Michael Sobell (Kochav), 14, 40, 52–56, 53, 94, 133
Mossad, 12, 34

Narkis, Uzi, 15, 138
Navarrazo (a provincial coup d'état in Córdoba), 119
Nazereth Illit, Israel, 133
Nazi, 12, 21, 34, 86, 129, 136; generic use of the word to refer to any far-Right racist organization, 180n54
Netanya, Israel, 96–98, 100, 138, 139
Neuquén, Argentina,103
New Left, 83, 122
*New York Times, The*, 130, 132
Nirgad, Ram, 128, 129
Noche de los Bastones Largos (the night of long batons), 77
*Nueva Sion* (Jewish Argentine newspaper), 56, 130

Ofer, Abraham, 98
OLEI (Organization of Latin American Immigrants), 38, 44, 47, 51, 59, 64–66, 95, 104, 106
Onganía, Juan Carlos, 77, 78
Ophir, Ariane, 6
Organización Israelita Argentina (Israelite Argentine Organization), 174n12

Palestine (pre-state), 8, 19–21, *19*, 23, 33, 39, 56, 59, 60, *73*, 159n11, 167n73
Paraná, Argentina, 103
*patria socialista* (socialist homeland), 89
Perón, Juan Domingo, 12, 15, 16, 42, 82–84, 87, 110, 118, 121, 125, 174n12
Peronism, Peronist, 15, 16, 82–89, 93, 102, 108, 119, 120, 122–24, 129, 130, 150, 178n5
Peru, 172n25
Piazzolla, Astor, 126
Pincus, Aryeh, 47, 64, 84
pogrom, 11, 19, 20, 130, 162n39
policies, 5, 8, 17, 60, 64, 75, 78, 86, 140, 152
Pompas, Jaime, 127
population: of Israel, *19*, *24*,
population dispersal, 49, 99
Portelli, Alessandro, 10
"pot of meat" (biblical expression referring to Jews who preferred to be slaves in Egypt as long as they were given food), 54, 55, 170n66
*Princess Leopoldina* (ship), 52, 53
proteksia (favoritism), 94, 175n31
protests, 15, 51, 75, 77, 78–79, 81, 82, 96–101, 131, 148, 183n16
Puiggrós, Rodolfo, 88
Pundak, Yitzhak, 128, 129, 134, 180n58

Rabin, Yitzhak, 4, 148
Raijman, Rebeca, 6
Ramat HaShofet (kibbutz), 136
Recanati, Daniel, 128
recession, 13, 14, 18, 35, 37–44, 48, 50, 52, 54, 55, 61, 62, 68, 69, 71, 74–77, 81, 83, 91, 101, 102, 104, 123, 140, 144, 150, 152–54, 158, 183n5
Rein, Raanan, 7, 9
remigration, *27*, *28*, *32*, *73*, 74–81, *75*, *76*, *80*, *124*; accuracy of statistics for, 162n47; from Israel to Argentina / elsewhere in Latin America, 7, 14, 17, 26–27, *29*, 30–31, 32, 47–48, 68–74, *80*, 104–6, 118–25, *124*, 140–43, 144, 146–58; 1948–1964, *38*; 1951–66, *72*; 1953–56, *26*; 1965, *73*, *74*; 1966, *49*; 1967, *49*; 1970–79, *141*; 1989–2002, *147*
reparations, 32, 43
repression, 14, 16, 75, 81, 119, 125, 128, 132, 135, 140, 141
Resnizky, Marcos, 130, 131
Resnizky, Nehemias, 85, 86, 126, 130–33
revolution, 75, 84, 86, 89
right/rightist, 44, 68, 78, 81, 89, 120, 122, 123, 142

rights (immigrant rights), 2, 10, 13, 18, 22, 32, 39, 57, 70, 80, 81, 95, 99, 101, 119, 122, 125, 130, 132, 133, 136, 139, 140, 144
*Río Quequen* (ship), 65
Rivkin, Tzvi, 122, 123
Rodrigazo (Argentine financial measures), 124
Rodrigo, Celestino, 124
Romero, Luis Alberto, 42, 83
Ronen, Yaakov, 34
Roniger, Luis, 6
Rosario, Argentina, 45, 87, 103, 134, 156
Ruchama (kibbutz), 63
*SS Ruslan* (ship), 20
Russian Revolution, 20

Sapir, Pinchas, 123
Sar, Yehuda, 31
Sarna, Jonathan, 5
Schiller, Herman, 180n45
Segev, Tom, 64
Senkman, Leonardo, 8
Sephardim, 56, 59
Shamir, Pinchas, 51
Shapira, Anita, 21, 176n36
Sharett, Moshe, 31, 33, 57
Shatz, Leon, 66
Shitrit, Benchor, 64, 65
Shofty, Shimon, 136
Shragai, Shlomo Zalman, 31, 47, 52, 58–60, 64, 65, 68
Six-Day War, 15, 46, 55, 57, 60, 62, 74, 76, 81, 82, 93–95, 101, 108, 154
Sociedad Hebraica Argentina, 133, 149
Sokolowicz, Fernando, 154
Srulik (cartoon character), 14, 41, 42, 47, 48
state terrorism, 16, 113, 119, 121, 123, 125, 127–29, 133, 135, 137, 139, 140, 142, 143, 153
Stein, Raúl, 77
Sten, Aviva, 172n27
stop and go (economic model), 42
stowaway, 55, 59, 62, 64–66
Strauss, Usher, 77
students, 1, 2, 12, 14, 15, 34, 36, 42, 46, 65, 75, 77, 80, 82, 88, *88*, 89, 91, 101, 105, 107, 109, 110, 113, 114, 122, 133, 134, 150, 156
Suez War, 27
Sznaider, Manuel, 79
Szwarc, Jaime, 79

Tacuara (anti-Semitic group), 78
Taglit (Birthright), 106
tango, 45, 98, 126, 156
Tapuz (agricultural program), 134
Tarbut (school), 154
Technion (the Israel Institute of Technology), 46, 155
Tel Aviv, Israel, 20, 21, 38, 45, 46, 50, 53, 63, 66, 67, 69, 99
the "tequila effect" (negative spillover of the 1994 Mexican devaluation), 146
terrorism, 13, 121, 146, 149, 152, 183n12. *See also* state terrorism
*Theodor Herzl* (ship), 1, 38, 63, 74, 77
third-country migration, 30, 159n9
Third Worldism, 83
Timerman, Héctor, 154
Timerman, Jacobo, 129, 130, 144
*Tnuat Aliyah* (immigration movement), 94, 106, 178n13
Todorov, Tzvetan, 155
Toronchik, Marta, 63, 171n1
Transfer Agreement, 21
Tucumán, Argentina, 103
*tzena* (austerity and the rationing of goods), 42
Tzvik, Tzvi, 121

*ulpan* (intensive Hebrew-language study program), 95, 97, 100
"uncovered" emigrants (people leaving Israel under the pretense of tourism), 26, 27, 71
unemployment / unemployed, 13, 18, 22, 43, 44, 47, 51, 52, 59, 65, 66, 79, 83, 87, 99, 106, 145, 146, 148–50, 158
Union of Immigrants from Britain in Israel, 57
University of Buenos Aires, 77, 155

Uruguay, 33, 51, 70, 71, 172n35, 178n11; anti-Semitism in, 166n53
Uzi, Narkis, 15, 138

Videla, Jorge Rafael, 130, 132

Weitz, Raanan, 54, 129, 133
White Paper, 21
Wolberg, Yehoshua, 171n8
Women's International Zionist Organization (WIZO), 59
workers, 13, 15, 18, 20, 21, 25, 32, 35–37, *36*, 39, 40, 42, *43*, 48, 50, 52, 70, 75, 79, 80, 83, 89, *89*, 90, *90*, *91*, 95, 96, 109, *109*, *112*, 114–16, *114*, *115*, *116–17*, 119, 128, 133, 148, *150*; working women, 185n35
World Jewish Congress (WJC), 86
World War II, 33
Wull, Abraham, 77

Yagar, Moshe, 138
Yaglom, Raya, 59
Yom Kippur War, 2, 15, 16, 82, 97, 101–10, *108*, *109*, 113, 118, 119, 122, 124, 125, 134, 140, 142, 152, 176n58

Zadok, Haim, 45
ZIM (Israeli navigation company), 34, 59, 68, 74
Ziman, David, 63, 64
*Zion* (ship), 31
Zionist Congress, 15
Zionist Organization of Argentina (ZOA), 57
Zohar, Marcel, 128